How to Do Everything with

Photoshop® 7

Laurie McCanna

McGraw-Hill/Osborne

New York Chicago San Francisco Lisbon
London Madrid Mexico City Milan New Delhi
San Juan Seoul Singapore Sydney Toronto

McGraw-Hill/Osborne
2600 Tenth Street
Berkeley, California 94710
U.S.A.

To arrange bulk purchase discounts for sales promotions, premiums, or fund-raisers, please contact **McGraw-Hill**/Osborne at the above address. For information on translations or book distributors outside the U.S.A., please see the International Contact Information page immediately following the index of this book.

How to Do Everything with Photoshop® 7

34567890 CUS CUS 0198765432

ISBN 0-07-219554-1

Publisher	Brandon A. Nordin
Vice President	
& Associate Publisher	Scott Rogers
Editorial Director	Roger Stewart
Senior Project Editor	Betsy Manini
Acquisitions Coordinator	Tana Allen
Technical Editor	Mark Monciardini
Production	
and Editorial Services	Anzai! Inc.
Illustration Supervisor	Lyssa Wald
Graphic Illustrator	Michael Mueller
Series Design	Mickey Galicia
Cover Series Design	Dodie Shoemaker
Cover Illustration	Laurie McCanna

This book was composed with Corel VENTURA™ Publisher.

Dedication

This book is dedicated to the guys in my life, without whose support and love this book would not have been possible.

This book is for Tim, my partner and best friend, who is gifted with intense loyalty and perseverance, a heart as big as his words, and a wicked sense of humor. This book is also for Teague, who is blessed with depth, intelligence and strength beyond his years. Lastly, this is for Adrian, a young man with a lion heart and an ancient soul.

About the Author

Laurie McCanna received her BFA from the Academy of Art in San Francisco. Currently, she is the Art Director for Information Engineering at BEA Systems, creating software interface elements. Laurie also designs web sites and web interfaces for software applications. In partnership with her husband, Tim McCanna, she created and ran a highly popular forum on AOL, called the Web Diner, that taught tens of thousands of AOL members how to create their first web sites. Her previous book, Creating Great Web Graphics, was a top-ten best selling title for Amazon.com. She has designed several commercial typefaces, including Nimx Scat, Nimx Jitterbug and Jitterbats, and Nimx Nature Mix.

Contents

Acknowledgments

I would like to thank the following people who helped make this book a reality. I had the good fortune of working with Betsy Manini, Roger Stewart, Tana Diminyatz Allen, Tom Anzai, Mark Monciardini and Jan Howarth, whose professionalism and humor made working on this book a pleasure.

I would also like to thank Steve Ruppenthal and Cheryl Solis, who helped make my work schedule flexible and offered encouragement so that I could complete this book. Genelle Cate's many helpful suggestions also contributed to making this a better book. Thanks also to my agent, Margot Maley Hutchinson.

Introduction

Photoshop is the single most powerful tool for creating, manipulating and editing images. It is the standard image manipulation program used around the world by graphic designers, photographic retouchers, and web designers. Photoshop and the companion program, ImageReady, is used for everything from retouching damaged photographs to creating stunning animation for the Web.

I've worked as a graphic designer and art director for a number of years, using Photoshop to do everything from creating images for print to retouching video animation to creating web pages. I've taught many beginners how to use Photoshop, and I've kept those users most in mind while writing this book. I feel strongly that lack of knowledge about software should not be a barrier to expressing your creativity or getting your work done, so this book was written to get you up and running as quickly and painlessly as possible.

Although Photoshop offers a vast array of tools, commands and filters, its powerfulness and depth can be extremely intimidating for a beginner. Starting with Photoshop is akin to being placed in the pilot's seat of a 747, getting a pat on the shoulder, and hearing "You have fun now!" What do you do first? Next? What's the best tool for the task? What are some of these tools used for?

The aim of this book is to guide beginners through the most common uses of Photoshop in a clear and direct manner. I've asked coworkers, friends and family about how they use Photoshop. With their help, I've addressed the most common tasks, effects, and frustrations Photoshop users encounter. I hope you find this book helpful in your Photoshop work.

The Structure of This Book

This book is aimed at beginning to intermediate users, and covers the most commonly used tools and tasks. This book does not cover more advanced topics such as channels or masks.

If you want to get up and running quickly with Photoshop, you'll want to read the first four chapters of the book, which guide you through understanding how Photoshop is organized. You'll also learn the most important concepts for working in Photoshop, layers and selections.

From there, you can jump ahead to chapters that cover the specific tasks or effects you're interested in. If you're working on a project that includes creating web pages with Photoshop, you'll want to read Chapter 5 to understand how to scan and retouch photographs, and Chapter 10 to understand how to save images for the Web and create buttons for web pages.

If, however, you're working on a project of creating beveled text in an image to be used as part of a business presentation, you'll want to jump to Chapters 7 and 8, which cover text and layer effects, then move to Chapter 13, which addresses the best format for saving images for Microsoft PowerPoint.

Part I   Under the Hood

This part of the book will familiarize you with the way Photoshop works, so that you can tap into the most powerful tools quickly. You'll learn the Photoshop interface and how to work with layers. You'll also find out how to configure Photoshop to suit your needs and get the best print results.

Part II   Learn Photoshop Basics

This portion of the book covers the tools and commands you'll use most frequently in Photoshop. You'll learn how to select parts of an image, clean up a scan, and use the paint tools in Photoshop. You'll also learn how to rotate and crop, and add gradients and patterns to your image. Best of all, you'll find out why you'll never worry about making a mistake again, thanks to the History palette.

Part III   Fantastic Effects in Photoshop

Once you've learned the nuts and bolts of Photoshop, you'll be ready to move onto the creative part of Photoshop. In this portion of the book, you'll explore filters, special effects, and layer effects. You'll find out how to create a seamless collage and how to add eye-popping effects with a mouse click.

Part IV   Productivity Techniques

There are an infinite number of things that you can do with Photoshop, but only a finite number of hours in a day. You'll learn how to create images for the Web.

You'll also discover how to create rollover buttons for web pages and animations. You'll also learn how to create time-saving actions, and how to optimize your work for moving between other applications, including Illustrator, After Effects, PowerPoint, and Flash.

Part V   Resources for Photoshop

Photoshop is such a popular program, there are plenty of resources on the Web where you can find tutorials, download brushes and actions, and chat with other Photoshop users. This section of the book also includes a guide for troubleshooting problems in Photoshop, and includes tips for tweaking your computer to get the best performance from Photoshop.

The Conventions of This Book

Because Photoshop is created for both the PC and the Mac, keystrokes are given for both operating systems. The Windows version is listed first, followed by the Mac version, with a slash separating the two. For instance, the keyboard shortcut for copying would be presented as CTRL-C/COMMAND-C.

You will also encounter little nuggets of information sprinked throughout the book.

NOTE   *These are titled and are set apart from the text of the chapter. Notes give you important background information about issues you should understand.*

TIP   *These are quick pointers that will help you understand Photoshop tasks.*

Chapter 1

Understanding the Photoshop Interface

How to...

- Work with the Photoshop interface
- Work with the toolbox
- Work with the options bar
- Use palettes
- Work with the file browser
- Change your view

The Photoshop interface is organized into several areas that contain tools, options, and menu items. As you learn the interface, you'll begin to understand the power of Photoshop, and how to harness this power to help you create the best looking images in the least amount of time. This will give you more time to spend experimenting with new ideas and methods, so that you can enjoy your work and produce more creative results.

Learning the Photoshop Interface

Many of the tools and commands that you use in Photoshop give context-sensitive cues to aid your work. For instance, the cursor changes from a paintbrush to a pencil depending on which tool you choose. Likewise, the options bar, visible at the top of the Photoshop screen, changes to offer you different options associated with the tool you are currently working with.

The Photoshop interface is made up of seven main sections as shown in Figure 1-1. These are the menu bar, the options bar, the toolbox, the image window, the palette well, palettes, and the status bar. The menu bar contains all the menu commands that you can use in Photoshop.

The Status Bar

In order to view the different aspects of the Photoshop workspace, you'll want to open a new image window. Select File | New, and choose the Photoshop Default Size for the new image from the Preset Sizes menu. Click OK.

As shown in Figure 1-1, the status bar in Windows is at the bottom of the screen. On the Mac, this information is displayed at the bottom of the image window. On the left side of the status bar, the zoom percentage is given. You can change the zoom percentage by typing in a new number. Next to the zoom size are two numbers for file size. The first number is the size of the file, in megabytes, if the file were to be flattened. The second number is the estimated size of the file if it is not flattened. You'll find more information in the following chapter about file sizes and flattening files.

By clicking the arrow in the status bar, as shown here, you can change the information displayed from Document Sizes, which is the default, to Document (color) Profile, Document Dimensions, Scratch (disk) Sizes, Efficiency, Timing, or Current Tool (label).

✓ Document Sizes
Document Profile
Document Dimensions
Scratch Sizes
Efficiency
Timing
Current Tool

| 100% | Doc: 532K/OK |

The right side of the status bar also gives context-sensitive information about the tool you're using. It can give you tips and shortcuts for any tool you select, and can be a helpful reminder of how to use the currently selected tool, as shown in Figure 1-1.

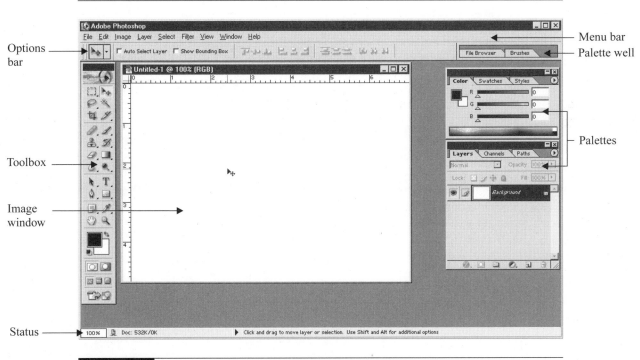

FIGURE 1-1 The Photoshop interface includes menu bar, a context-sensitive options bar, toolbox, palettes, palette well, image window, and status bar.

Cues from Cursors

As you use different tools in Photoshop, you'll see that the cursor changes into different images that provide cues to help you recognize the use of the tool. You can set the cursors to display a different image for each tool by selecting Edit | Preferences | Display & Cursors, and setting the Cursors to use the Standard cursor style.

With some tools, the cursor changes depending on how you're using the tool. As the illustration on the right shows, the pen tool cursor changes when you add, delete, start a new path, or close a path.

Watching for cues from both the cursors and the status bar can help you to understand how to use Photoshop tools more efficiently.

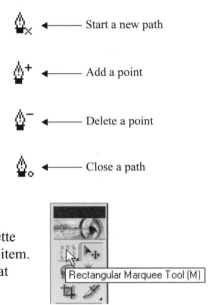

←———— Start a new path

←———— Add a point

←———— Delete a point

←———— Close a path

Tool Tips for Identification

If you let your mouse hover over a menu or palette item, a tool tip pops up, giving the name of that item. This is especially helpful for reminding you what certain tools do, as shown here.

Context-Sensitive Menus

While you're using Photoshop, you can gain access to additional functions and menu items through context-sensitive menus, as shown in Figure 1-2. Right-click/ CTRL-click on the image window to reveal a menu for additional choices. You can access context-sensitive menus by clicking on palettes and image windows.

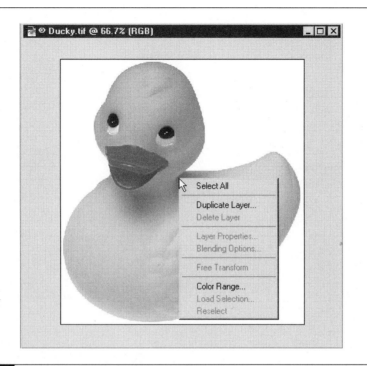

FIGURE 1-2   An example of a context-sensitive menu.

Learning the Toolbox

The Photoshop toolbox contains a large array of tools. This toolbox can be dragged to any position on the screen. Many of the tools, as shown in Figure 1-3, actually contain a set of related tools. A small arrow in the corner of the Tool icon indicates the presence of related tools. Click and hold the icon to reveal them. When you reveal these tools, you'll see a label and the keyboard shortcut for each tool. For instance, if you select the eraser tool and decide to use the paintbrush tool instead, you can simply press the letter B to change to the paintbrush tool.

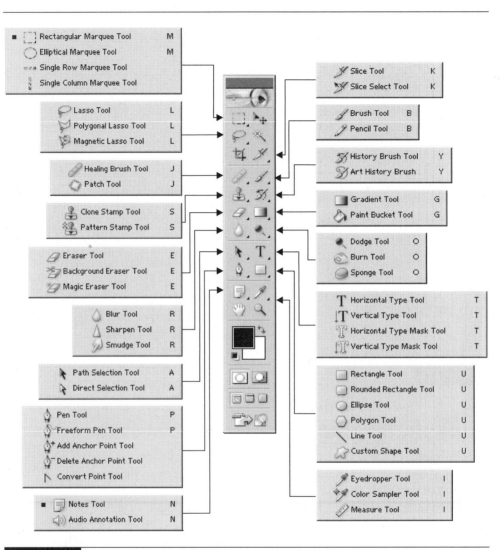

FIGURE 1-3   Many of the Photoshop tools are grouped with a set of related tools, which are revealed when you click and hold the mouse on the tool icon in the Photoshop toolbox.

Choosing Colors

Below the tools on the toolbox are the currently selected foreground and background colors. The foreground color is the color that the paintbrush, type tool, or paint bucket tools use. To change the color, click on the color swatch in the toolbox and the Photoshop Color Picker will open.

The Photoshop Color Picker displays a preview of colors. Change the preview by adjusting the color slider as shown here. Select a color by clicking within the preview.

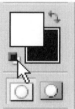

You'll see that color values are represented in a number of different ways, including Hue, Saturation, and Brightness values; RGB (Red, Green, Blue) values; Lab colors; and CMYK (Cyan, Magenta, Yellow, Black) values. You can also choose to restrain your color choices to the web-safe color palette, a limited palette of 216 colors. To constrain your color to the web-safe palette, check the Only Web Colors box. Colors are also shown with their hexcode color values, as shown in Figure 1-4. Hexcode values are used in creating web pages.

By selecting the Custom button in the Color Picker, you'll find a further selection of color systems for choosing colors, including Pantone and Trumatch.

Once you've selected a color, you can change between the foreground and background colors on the toolbox by clicking the arrow above the color swatches in the toolbox. You can also reset the values of the foreground and background colors to black and white by clicking the Black and White icons below the foreground and background color swatches as shown here.

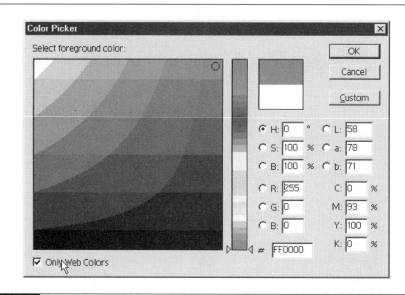

FIGURE 1-4 The Photoshop Color Picker, with the Only Web Colors checkbox selected.

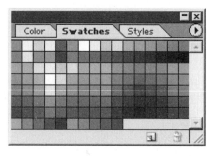

You can also change the foreground color by selecting a color from the Swatches palette or the Color palette, as shown here.

Other Toolbox Options

Below the color swatches, you'll find three other functions of the Photoshop toolbox. The first, as shown in Figure 1-5, toggles between Edit in Standard Mode and Edit in Quick Mask Mode. A quick mask toggles between a selection and a masking function.

Beneath the Quick Mask Mode are three icons for different screen views of your work: from left to right, Standard Screen Mode, Full Screen with Menu Bar, and Full Screen without Menu Bar. When you select screen with menu bar, the screen fills with the image window, temporarily hiding any open images. You can toggle between these different display options by pressing the F key.

At the very bottom of the toolbox, as shown in Figure 1-5, is a link that takes you from Photoshop to ImageReady. ImageReady is a program for creating web graphics that is automatically installed when you install Photoshop. Although you can do many web graphics tasks within Photoshop, some options, such as creating

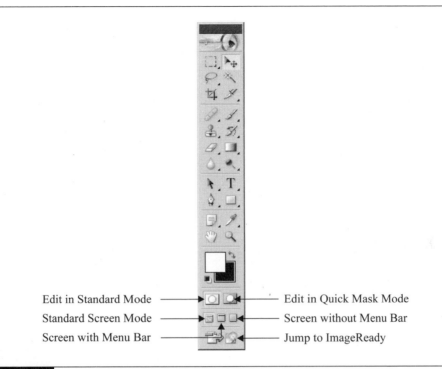

Edit in Standard Mode ———————— Edit in Quick Mask Mode

Standard Screen Mode ———————— Screen without Menu Bar

Screen with Menu Bar ———————— Jump to ImageReady

FIGURE 1-5   Additional toolbox options.

rollovers or animations, can be done only in ImageReady. When you click the Jump
to ImageReady icon, your current Photoshop document automatically opens in
ImageReady. You can return to Photoshop from ImageReady by clicking the
Jump to Photoshop icon located at the bottom of the ImageReady toolbox.

Learning the Options Bar

Below the menu bar is the Photoshop options bar. The options displayed within the
options bar change depending on which tool you have selected, but there are some
options that all tools have in common.

The first option shows the currently selected tool. By clicking the down arrow
next to an option, you can select any tool, or any custom tool preset you have created.
Custom tool presets will be discussed in Chapter 12. Many tools also display an
icon that links to a palette or preset that is related to the tool. This icon is located at

the far right in the options bar. For instance, the Paintbrush Options bar has an icon that links to the Brushes palette, shown here which offers even more options for the currently selected brush.

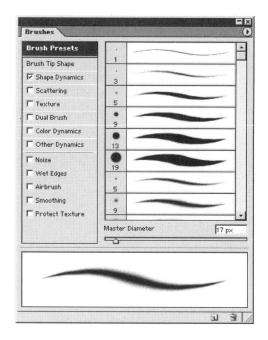

Some tools show a Cancel and Commit icon in the options bar, such as the text tool or the crop tool. The commit icon, represented by a checkmark, applies the changes you've made. The Cancel icon, represented by an ⊘, cancels the changes you've made to your image. Other specific options that appear in the options bar will be discussed in the following chapters.

Drop-Down Menus

You'll often see drop-down menus on the options bar. You can open these by clicking the down arrow. Close an open drop down menu by clicking anywhere outside the menu.

Using Palettes

Palettes offer even more options for your image. You can view or hide palettes through the Window menu. To open palettes, select Window, then select the name of the palette you wish to open. You can also toggle, roll up, dock, and group palettes.

Minimizing and Closing Palettes

At the top of each palette are two icons—one for minimizing the palette and one for closing it. Click the Minimize icon to "roll up" a palette so that it takes up less space on the screen. Click the Close icon to close the palette.

Drop-Down Menus

Most palettes have a drop-down menu that offers more commands, as shown here. To reveal the drop-down menu, click the arrow located at the top of the palette.

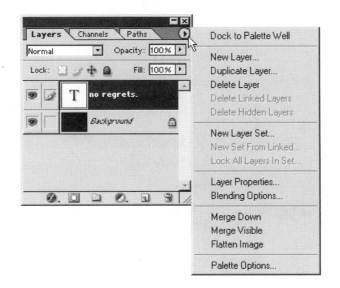

Dragging, Dropping, and Grouping Palettes

You can drag any palette to any position on the screen by clicking the top of the palette and dragging. You can group palettes together by clicking on the name of the palette, as shown in Figure 1-6, and dragging it to another palette until a solid line appears. The solid line indicates the palette is in the correct place. Release the mouse and the palettes are grouped together.

To ungroup palettes, simply click on the tab of the palette you wish to ungroup, and drag the palette away from the group until a dotted line appears. Release the mouse button.

To append one palette to another, so that they appear one above another, drag a palette to the bottom of another palette until a solid line appears, as shown in Figure 1-6. Release the mouse button.

The Palette Well

Because you'll want to devote your screen to viewing your images rather than to displaying a multitude of palettes, you can easily store multiple palettes in a small space by docking them. At the top of the screen, to the right of the options bar is

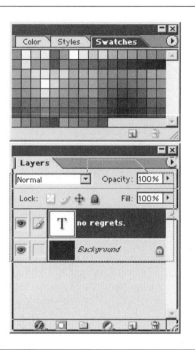

FIGURE 1-6   Palettes grouped together.

the palette well. You can add any palette to this well by either dragging the palette there until a solid line appears, or by selecting Dock to Palette Well from the drop-down menu on the palette as shown in Figure 1-7.

Learning the File Browser

You can open existing files by selecting File | Open from the menu bar in Photoshop, but there is also a more visual way to select files. It's called the file browser, and it is located in the palette well as shown in Figure 1-1. You can also access the file browser by selecting File | Browse from the Photoshop menu bar.

To open the file browser, click the tab labeled File Browser. The file browser opens. On the upper left corner is a "tree" view of your hard drive. Click the folder you wish to view. The images contained in the folder appear in the right pane of the file browser.

When you select an image, a preview, along with specific information about the file, displays in the lower left portion of the file browser. This method of looking for

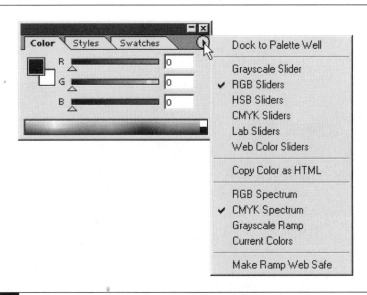

FIGURE 1-7   Selecting Dock to Palette Well from the drop-down menu.

images gives you much more information about the image than you can see using the traditional File | Open method of opening files. Once you've located the file you wish to open, double-click the file. You can also drag files from the file browser into the Photoshop workspace.

The Power of the File Browser

At the bottom of the file browser are several drop-down menus that unleash the real power of this feature. You can move, delete, and batch rename files easily. To select more than one file, CTRL-click/COMMAND-click. To deselect a file, CTRL-click/COMMAND-click again.

If you right-click on a file name in the right pane of the file browser, or click and hold on the Mac, a context-sensitive menu appears as shown here. The file browser menu reveals the options displayed in Figure 1-8.

- ■ **Open**   This option opens the selected file in Photoshop.

- ■ **Select All**   This option selects all images in the selected folder.

- ■ **Deselect All**   This option deselects all images in the selected folder.

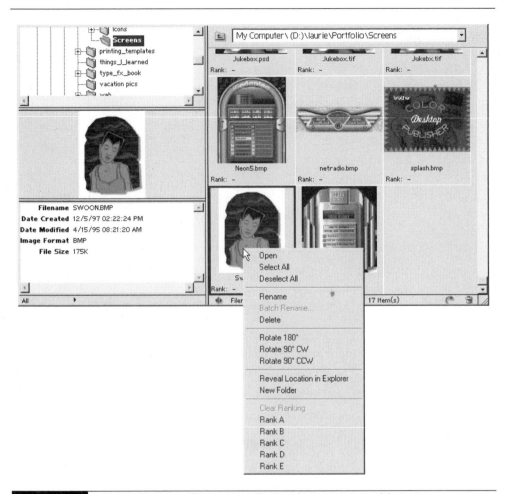

FIGURE 1-8   Right-click on a filename to display the context-sensitive menu.

- ■ **Rename**   This option enables you to rename the selected file.

- ■ **Batch Rename**   This option enables you to rename one or more images. When you select Batch Rename, a new dialog box opens, as shown in Figure 1-9.

    - ■ **Rename in same Folder**   This option enables you to rename the file(s) and leaves them in their current location.

    - ■ **Move to new Folder**   This option enables you to move the selected file(s) to a new folder.

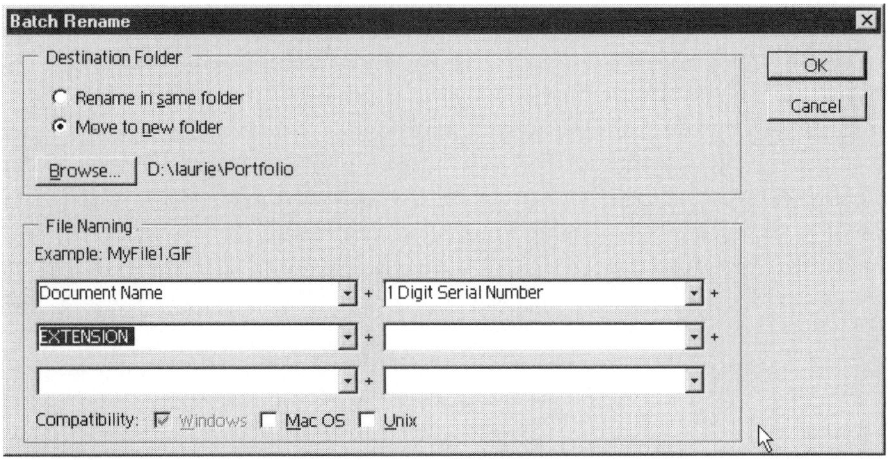

FIGURE 1-9   Batch rename options.

- **File Naming**   Below these options, you can select the way that the files are renamed. A variety of options enables you to rename the file in different ways. For example, to rename a file named splash.gif to splash1.gif, select the following options: Document Name + 1 digit serial number + extension. This would ensure the file would include its original name, plus a single digit number, and the file extension in lower case letters.

- **Delete**   This option deletes the selected file(s).

- **Rotate 180°, Rotate 90° CW, Rotate 90° CCW**   You can choose to rotate all of the files you have selected.

- **Reveal Location**   If you select this option, your operating system's file manager opens, revealing the hard drive location of the file(s) you've selected.

- **New Folder**   This option creates a new folder.

- **Clear Ranking**   If you've ranked files and want to remove the ranking, choose this option.

- **Rank A, B, C, D, E**   This option enables you to rank images by their importance.

You can select the way in which you'd like to see the files ordered in the file browser by clicking the arrow at the bottom of the file browser window, as shown here. You can choose to view the files by Filename, Rank, Width, Height, File Size, Resolution, File Type, Color Profile, Date Created, Date Modified, or Copyright. At the bottom of this drop-down menu, you can choose to view the files in ascending or descending order. If you wished to view files by the date they were modified, with the most recently modified images first, you would choose date modified, and deselect the ascending order selection (see Figure 1-10).

As shown in Figure 1-11, you can also choose how you'd like to view the thumbnails of the files in the file browser. You can select Small, Medium, Large, Large with Rank, or Detail views of the thumbnails.

To close the file browser window, click anywhere outside the file browser.

Changing Your View

You'll be zooming in and out of images frequently as you work on them. You can use the zoom tool, located on the toolbox, to zoom in. To zoom out, hold down CTRL-click/ALT-click while using the zoom tool. To zoom in to a particular area, drag the zoom tool to marquee the area you'd like to focus on, as shown in Figure 1-12.

You can also use the Navigator palette to change the area you're looking at. Drag the red square within the Navigator window to change the area of the image you're looking at. To change the zoom amount, drag the slider located at the bottom of the Navigator palette (see Figure 1-13).

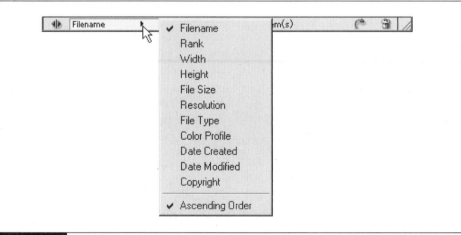

FIGURE 1-10   Click the arrow to view the files by category and order.

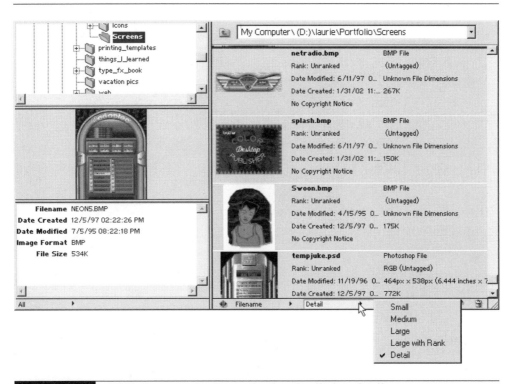

FIGURE 1-11   Click the arrow to choose the thumbnail view detail.

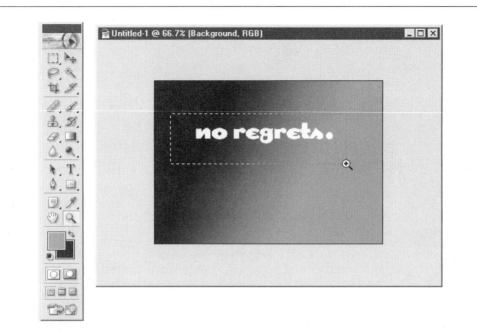

FIGURE 1-13   Drag the zoom tool to marquee the area.

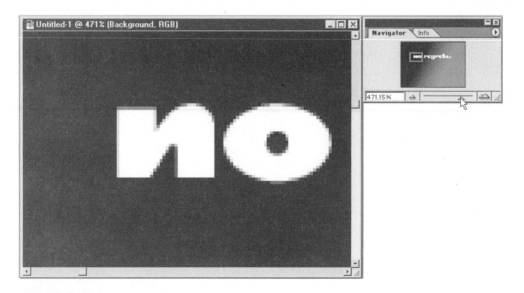

FIGURE 1-12   Drag the Navigator slider to change the level of zoom.

Chapter 2

Creating a Layered Image

How to...

- Create a new file
- Create a new layer
- Work with layers
- Explore blending modes
- Lock transparency of a layer
- Create linked layers
- Merge layers
- Save a file

The key to discovering the power of Photoshop is working with layers. When you work with layers, you can enjoy the freedom to experiment without fear of damaging the image you are working on. Layers can be duplicated, deleted, or moved without affecting other parts of your image. You can easily change the transparency, color, or position of any layer, unleashing a world of creative possibilities for your work in Photoshop. In this chapter, you will create a layered image, move and adjust the layers, and save the finished image.

Learning Layers

The best way to understand layers is to think of each layer as an image on a sheet of glass. Then think of all the sheets of glass stacked together. You can move or erase a layer, or change its transparency, without changing any of the layers above or below it.

To open the Layers palette, if it isn't already open, choose Window | Layers. Until you open an existing file or create a new file, no layers will be displayed in the Layers palette.

The Layers Palette

You will use the Layers palette to organize, delete, and modify layers in your image. In order to experiment with layers, you will want to open a file by selecting File | New.

The Layers palette is composed of several different parts, as shown in Figure 2-1. The sections of the Layers palette include a drop-down menu, accessed by clicking the arrow located at the top right edge of the Layers palette. Listed below the Layers tab are the blending mode settings, which lists Normal as the default. To the right of the blending mode you'll see the Opacity settings. Beneath the blending mode are the Lock settings for layers. From left to right are the following types of lock settings: Lock transparent pixels, Lock image pixels, Lock position, and Lock all. To the right of the lock settings is a setting for the Fill opacity. Fill opacity controls only the opacity for the layer, without affecting the opacity of any layer effects. Located below the layer options are previews of the actual layers. From left to right are icons for layer visibility, layer linking, thumbnail of the layer, and the layer name. Located at the bottom of the Layer palette are icons, from left to right:

- **Add a layer style**   Layer styles are special effects like drop shadows, bevels, and glows that are applied to Layers.

- **Add layer mask**   A layer mask makes part of a layer transparent.

- **Create a new set**   Layer Sets enable you to organize your layers into groups.

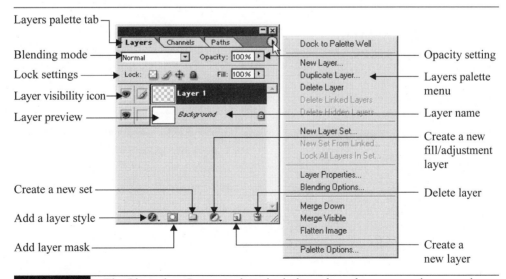

FIGURE 2-1   The Photoshop Layers palette includes a drop-down menu, icons, and commands that enable you to control how you work with layers.

- **Create a new fill or adjustment layer**   Adjustment layers are effects that are applied to a layer to change attributes like contrast, hue, and color balance.

- **Create a new layer**   Add a new, empty layer to your file.

- **Delete layer**   Delete a selected layer from your file.

Changing the Layer Preview

You can customize the size of the previews that are displayed in the Layers palette. Photoshop refers to these previews as thumbnails. If you have a small screen, you may want to stay with the smallest thumbnail size, which is the default. However, if you have a larger screen, it can be helpful to see larger thumbnails of each layer as you work.

NOTE   *The top of the image window also gives you valuable information. Next to the image name, you'll see the zoom amount, color mode, and name of the layer you are currently working on.*

To change the size of the thumbnail, click the arrow within a circle located at the top right corner of the Layers palette to reveal the Layers palette menu. Select Palette Options, and the dialog box appears as shown to the right. You can choose from three different thumbnail sizes.

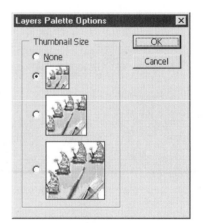

Creating a New File

Create a new file by selecting File | New. Enter a name for the file in the Name entry field as shown in Figure 2-2.

What you use for height and width settings depends on how you intend to use the image. You can select an image size from a number of preset sizes, as shown in Figure 2-3.

As a general guideline, if you are creating a file for print, you will want to use a minimum setting of 300 pixels per inch, and set the width and height of the image in inch measurements.

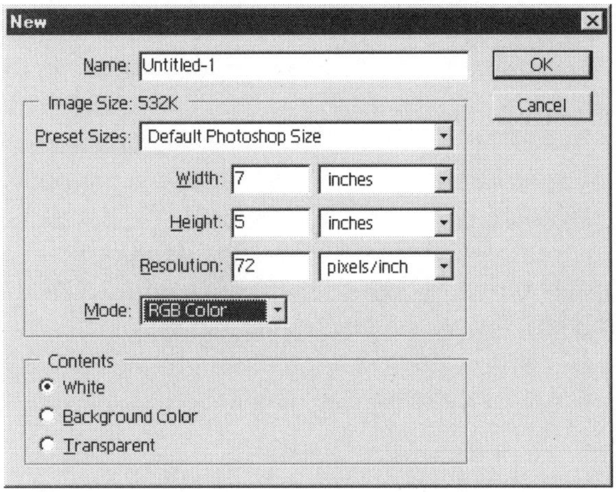

FIGURE 2-2   Naming a new file.

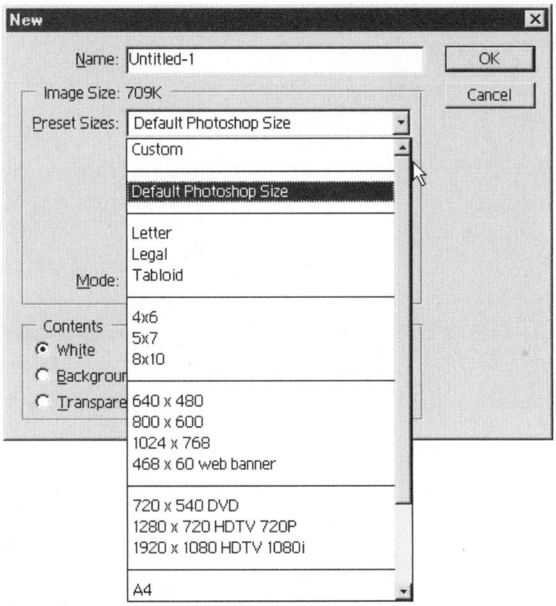

FIGURE 2-3   Preset sizes for a new file.

If you are creating an image for the Web, you'll want to create images that are no larger than a web browser's area, less the size for the title bar and browser window edges. For a monitor set to 640 × 480 pixels—the minimum size monitor display that web designers target—the size of the viewing area is actually 590 pixels wide by 325 pixels high. The number of pixels per inch for web images is not as important as it is for print images, so leave the default setting of 72 pixels per inch. Set the Mode to RGB color.

The Image Mode setting determines what type of color you'll be working with. In most cases, you will want to use the default setting of RGB color. Image size and resolution will be discussed in more depth in Chapter 5.

You can also select whether you want the background of the image filled with white, your currently selected background color, or if you want the background to be transparent.

You'll notice that once you create this new file, the Layers palette displays a single layer named Background.

Creating a New Layer

Because the Background layer is locked, you will generally want to start out by creating or adding new layers. There are several ways to add layers to an image.

Creating a New Empty Layer

To create a new empty layer, click the Create a new layer icon located at the bottom edge of the Layers palette. This creates a new layer, named Layer 1, positioned above the Background layer as shown here.

Creating a New Layer by Copying

You can create a new layer by copying and pasting. You will need to select the contents of a layer before you can copy it. Select everything on a layer by choosing Select | All, or use one of the selection tools as described in Chapter 4 to select only part of the contents of a layer. Next, choose Edit | Copy or use CTRL-C/ COMMAND-C to copy the contents of the layer as shown here.

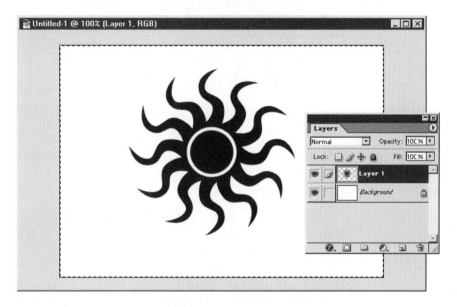

To create a new layer, select Edit | Paste, or use the keystrokes CTRL-V/ COMMAND-V. A new layer appears in the Layers palette, positioned above the layer you have copied, as shown in the following illustration.

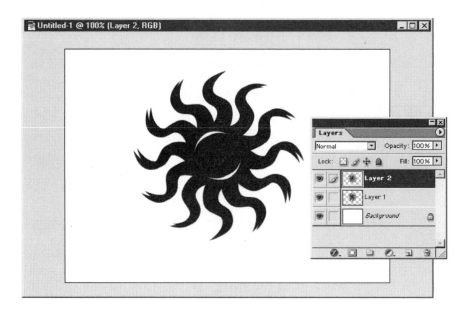

Creating a New Layer by Duplicating

Drag a layer to the New Layer icon at the bottom of the Layers palette as shown in Figure 2-4. This creates a new layer, positioned directly above the original layer.

FIGURE 2-4   Create a duplicate layer by dragging and dropping on the New Layer icon.

The new layer has the same name as the original layer followed by the word Copy. Since it is positioned exactly above the original layer, you'll see only one copy in the image window, but you'll see both copies in the Layers palette thumbnails.

Working with Layers

Once you know how to create layers you're ready to move onto layer basics: naming, filling, and moving layers.

Naming a Layer

Photoshop gives each new layer you create a default name— the word "Layer" followed by a number. Once you begin working with a many-layered file, it can be difficult to remember which number refers to which layer. To avoid this, it's a good idea to name your layers.

The easiest way to rename a layer is to double click on the layer name, and type in a descriptive name, as shown here.

If you'd like to color code your layers to further aid in organizing your layers, click the arrow at the top of the Layers palette to access the Layers palette menu. Select Layer Properties, change the name of the layer if you wish, and select a color for the layer from the menu as shown here.

You can also rename a layer by using right-click/CTRL-click on the name of a layer in the Layers palette, and selecting Layer Properties from the context-sensitive menu that appears.

Filling a Layer

You can fill the entire layer with a solid color, or you can fill part of a layer. By filling part of a layer, you will be able to see layers that are behind the partially filled layer.

Filling the Entire Layer

Make sure you have the layer you wish to fill selected in the Layers palette. A layer is selected when its name is highlighted in the Layers palette and a brush icon appears next to the thumbnail. To fill a layer with a single color, click the paint bucket tool on the toolbox. Then click the paint bucket tool anywhere in the image window, as shown here. Without a selection, the layer is completely filled with the foreground color.

Filling Part of a Layer

Select the rectangular marquee tool from the Photoshop toolbox and click and drag to create a rectangular selection. Click the paint bucket tool icon in the toolbox, and position the paint bucket tool within the rectangle you've created. Click to fill the rectangle with the foreground color, as shown in Figure 2-5.

FIGURE 2-5   An active selection is shown by a dashed line.

You can also use the keyboard shortcut to fill a layer with the foreground color: ALT-BACKSPACE/OPTION-BACKSPACE.

You'll see the selection is active because an animated dashed line surrounds it, as shown in Figure 2-5. To deselect, use CTRL-D/COMMAND-D, or click the marquee tool anywhere outside the rectangle within the image window

Moving Layer Contents

Select the move tool from the toolbox, and click and drag the contents of the layer in the image window so that it overlaps the contents of the layer below it. Notice that when you use the move tool, everything on the layer moves, as shown in Figure 2-6. If you want to move only some of the contents on a layer, use one of the selection tools. These tools are covered in Chapter 4.

You can also nudge the contents of a layer one pixel at a time by using the arrow keys on your keyboard. This is extremely helpful for precise positioning. If you want to move the contents of a selected layer in 10 pixel increments, hold down SHIFT as you use the ARROW keys.

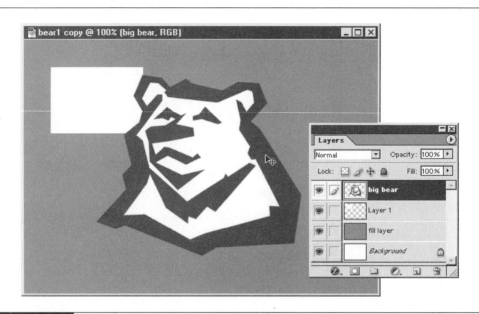

FIGURE 2-6   Using the move tool moves everything on the current layer. To move only portions of a layer, use one of the selection tools.

Changing the Opacity of a Layer

Click the triangle to the right of the Opacity percentage. A slider appears, as shown in Figure 2-7. Move the slider to the left and watch the image window. You'll see that the white rectangle becomes more transparent as you continue to slide the opacity to the left. Adding transparency is a quick and easy way to add subtlety to an image.

Hiding a Layer

While working in Photoshop, it's often easier to concentrate if you view only the layer you're working on. You can isolate layers that you're working on by hiding other layers. To hide a layer, in the Layers palette, click the layer visibility Eye icon to the left of the thumbnails of the layers you want to hide, as shown in Figure 2-8. Click the Eye icon to view the layer again.

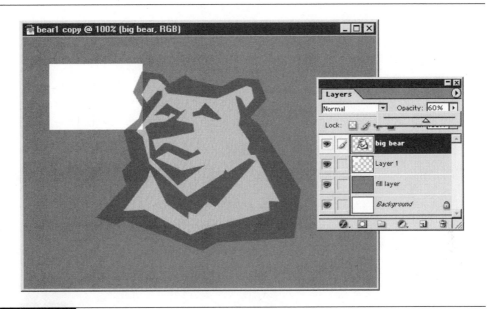

FIGURE 2-7   Use the Opacity slider to change the opacity of a layer.

FIGURE 2-8   Deactivate the layer visibility Eye icon in the Layers palette to hide the layer.

Deleting a Layer

To delete a layer, drag the layer to the Trashcan icon at the bottom of the Layers palette. To undo this, or any operation in Photoshop, press CTRL-Z/COMMAND-Z.

> **NOTE** *You cannot delete a layer if you have selected the Lock All checkbox for that layer.*

Changing the Order of Layers

The layer listed first in the Layers palette appears in front of any layers listed below it. The contents of any layer obscures the view of layers below it. To make one layer appear in front of another layer, change the order of the layers listed in the Layers palette.

To change the order of layers, simply select a layer in the Layers palette and drag it to a new position. A double line appears between the layers as you position the layer, as shown here. Release the mouse to place the layer.

Dragging Layers Between Images

You can easily drag layers between images. With the original image selected, drag a layer to the new image window as shown in Figure 2-9. The layer is copied to the new image, while the layer in the original image remains unchanged. You can also drag linked layers from one image into another. Linking layers is described in a following section.

> **NOTE** *If you seem to be getting unexpected results, check to make sure that you're working on the layer that you think you're working on. Check the Layers palette and make sure the layer you want to work on is highlighted and shows the Brush icon next to it.*

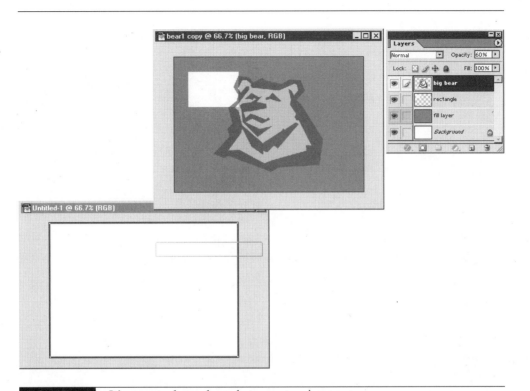

FIGURE 2-9   It's easy to drag a layer between two images.

Exploring Blending Modes

Blending modes control how one layer interacts with the layers positioned below it. You can achieve some exciting effects by experimenting with various blending modes. If you are creating a collage image, blending modes can be an especially effective way to combine disparate elements.

The way a layer is changed by a blending mode is determined by the contents of the layers below it. Blending modes alter the color, opacity, lightness, and darkness of a layer. It's worthwhile to spend a few minutes experimenting with various blending modes to get a feel for the type of effects they can create. In Figure 2-10, you can see how using a multiply mode on the top layer changes the original image.

Select a layer and begin changing the blending mode by clicking the arrow next to the word Normal located at the top of the Layers palette. The default

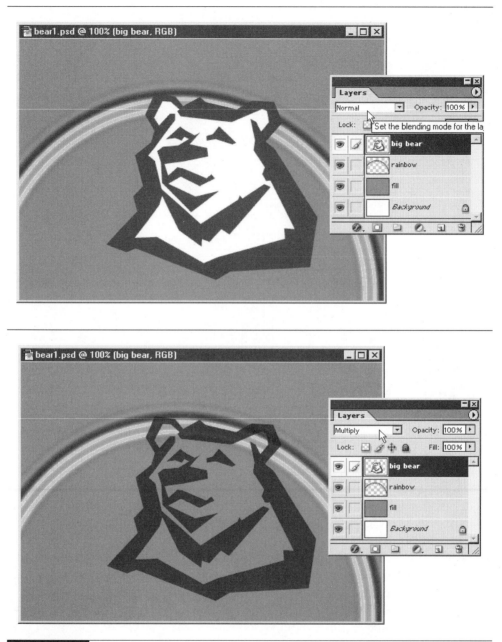

FIGURE 2-10 Compare the original image to the same image with the Blending mode set to Multiply, which changes how the layer interacts with the layers below it.

2

blending mode for all layers is Normal. As you change modes, you'll notice a variety of effects that can be achieved.

Since each layer has its own blending mode, the possibilities are endless for achieving both subtle and striking effects. When you combine blending modes with Opacity changes, the possibilities are infinite.

Blending modes are not always predictable and the results may vary, but, in general, blending modes behave in the following manner:

- **Normal**   If the opacity of the layer is set to 100%, the image is completely opaque and unaffected by the layers below it.

- **Dissolve**   This mode creates a dotted effect on a layer.

- **Darken**   Similar to Multiply.

- **Multiply**   This combines an image with the images below it, creating a dark overlay.

- **Color Burn**   Darkens the layers beneath by combining colors.

- **Linear Burn**   Similar to Color Burn, but more subtle in its effects.

- **Lighten**   Similar to multiply but creates a light overlay.

- **Screen**   Similar to lighten.

- **Color Dodge**   Lightens the layers beneath by combining colors.

- **Linear Dodge**   Similar to Color Dodge, but creates smoother transitions in blending, offering a more subtle effect.

- **Overlay**   Makes the layer semitransparent so that layers beneath show through.

- **Soft Light and Hard Light**   These two blending modes are similar to Overlay. Generally, Soft Light gives a more subtle effect than Hard Light.

- **Vivid Light**   Intensifies the color of a layer by blending it with the layers beneath.

- **Linear Light**   Similar to Vivid Light, this blending mode creates smoother transitions between colors.

- **Pin Light**   Similar to Linear Light.

- **Difference** Affects the colors of the layers and generally darkens images as a result.

- **Exclusion** Similar to Difference, but a subtler change to the layer.

- **Hue** Mixes the colors of the layer with those of the layers below it.

- **Saturation** This mode changes the intensity of colors in the layers below.

- **Color** Creates a color overlay, tinting the layers below.

- **Luminosity** Changes the relative lightness and darkness of the layers below.

Locking the Transparency of a Layer

Once you have created a layer and you're happy with it, you may want to lock the layer to prevent further changes. On the Layers palette, there are four Lock icons that serve to keep you from changing a layer in different ways. The functions of these options are, from left to right, as shown in Figure 2-11.

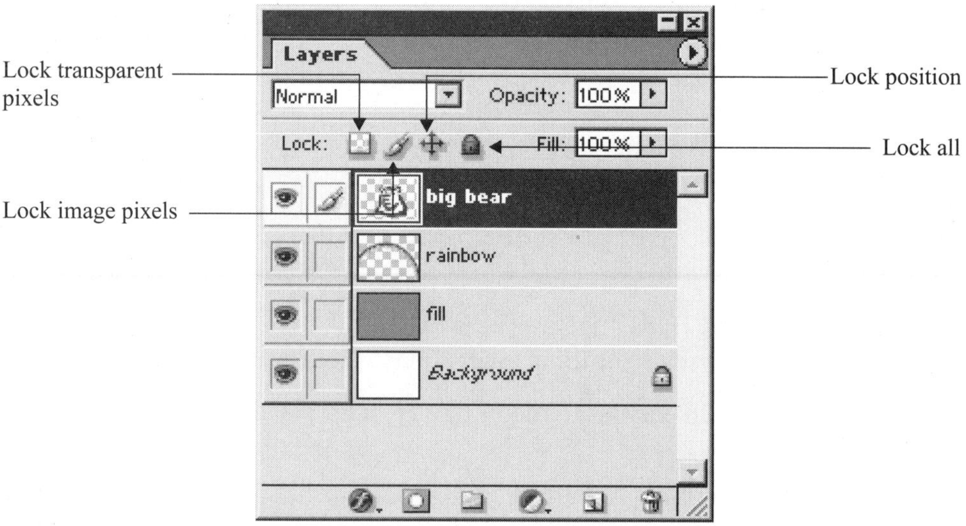

FIGURE 2-11 Use these icons on the Layers palette to lock layers you don't want to change.

- **Lock transparent pixels**   This option protects the transparency of a layer from being changed. You can paint or fill within any area that is already not transparent, but you cannot paint outside the locked transparent area, and you cannot erase within the non-transparent area.

- **Lock image pixels**   This option prevents you from painting or filling on the layer, although you can move and transform the layer.

- **Lock position**   This option prevents you from moving the layer, but you can still erase, paint, and fill the layer.

- **Lock all**   This option locks all of the attributes described above.

> **NOTE**   *The Background layer is always locked. You can unlock the Background layer by renaming it. You can hide the Background layer by clicking the eye icon for the Background layer in the Layers palette. You can delete the Background layer.*

Changing the Color of a Layer by Locking Pixels

If you wish to change the color of something on a layer, click the first icon at the top of the palette, named Lock transparent pixels. A small Lock icon appears to the right of the name for the layer.

Click the foreground color swatch on the toolbox and select a different color than the color you've been working with. Use the paint bucket tool and click anywhere within the image to fill the layer as shown in Figure 2-12. Because you've locked the transparency of the pixels, only the area that was previously filled is now filled with the new color.

The keyboard shortcut for toggling on and off the Lock transparent pixels function is the FORWARD SLASH key (/) on the keyboard, located on the same key as the question mark. The forward slash key toggles on and off the last lock function that you used.

Creating Linked Layers

If you need to reposition or resize more than one layer at a time, you can link the layers. You can link layers so that you can move, transform, align, merge, or create clipping groups from multiple layers at the same time.

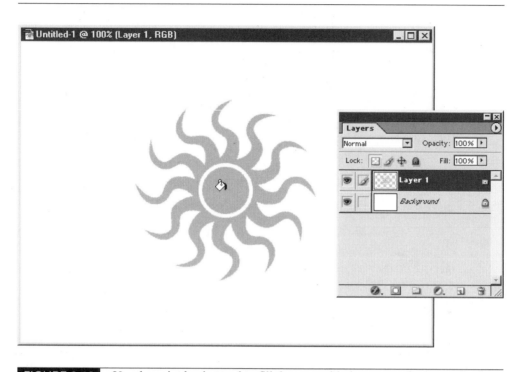

FIGURE 2-12 Use the paint bucket tool to fill the area with the current foreground color.

To link layers, first select a layer and then click the square to the right of the Eye icon for the layer you wish to link. A link icon appears, indicating these two layers are now linked. A set of linked layers is shown here. You can link as many layers as you like. To unlink layers, simply click the Link icon.

Aligning Linked Layer Contents

When you're working on an image with multiple elements, it can be tricky to line up various layers just using your best guess. In order to precisely align the contents of multiple layers, you need to link layers. Once you've linked the layers you want to align, select Layer | Align Linked. You can choose the type of alignment that will be used to align your layers, as shown here.

- Top Edges
- Vertical Centers
- Bottom Edges
- Left Edges
- Horizontal Centers
- Right Edges

You can also align layers that are linked by selecting the move tool from the toolbox, then selecting the appropriate align icon from the options bar.

Organizing with Layer Sets

You can group layers together by creating a layer set. Layer sets can be expanded or collapsed within the Layers palette window, making it easier to organize your layers.

Creating a Layer Set

Select a layer and click the Folder icon at the bottom edge of the Layers palette. A Folder icon appears above the layer. The folder is named Set 1. This is the layer set, and any layers you add to this layer set will be listed below this one. You can also create a new layer set, if you have linked layers, by selecting New Set from Linked in the Layers palette menu, as shown here.

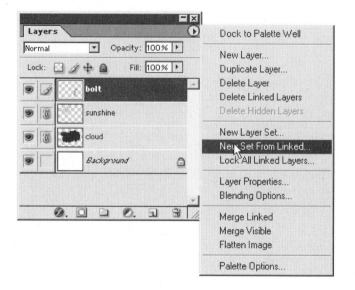

Adding Layers to the Layer Set

Drag layers in the Layers palette to add them to the layer set, as shown here. When you drag the layer, drag it onto the name of the layer. When the set name is highlighted, you can release your mouse button and the layer will be included in the set.

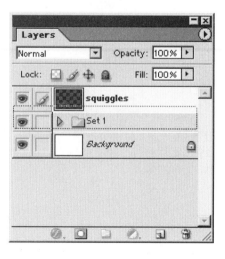

Renaming and Color Coding Layer Sets

You can further organize your layer sets by naming them and selecting a color for each set. These visual cues can help orient you to which set you are working with when a project is complex. From the Menu bar choose Layer | Layer Set Properties, or right-click/CTRL-click on the layer set name. Enter a descriptive name for your layer set, and select a color.

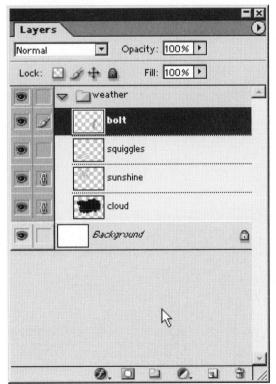

Collapsing and Expanding Layer Sets

Click the arrow to the left of the folder icon to collapse or expand a layer, as shown on the right. This enables you to view more or fewer details about your layers, depending on your needs.

Using Layer Sets

Layer sets are a great way to group related layers together. Because you can expand and collapse layers, you can also save yourself from needing to scroll through a long list of layers to find the layer you are looking for.

You can work with the entire set of layers just as you can with linked layers. Select the Layer set name, and you can move or transform all layers in the set at once.

Working with a Single Layer Within a Layer Set

Click the arrow next to the set to expand the layer set. You can now select any
layer that you wish to work with, and other layers in the set will not be affected.

> **NOTE** *If a Link icon appears next to the layer, you may wish to click it to unlink
> the layer from other layers in the set if you don't want to include those
> layers in any changes you make.*

Merging Layers

Although the ability to work with multiple layers is a benefit, there are times when
you will want to simplify your image and merge layers together. You can merge
some or all of the layers in your image.

> **TIP** *It's a good idea to always keep a copy of your image with all layers intact
> so that, if you need to later edit your image, you will have all information
> available in a flexible format.*

Merging Some, but Not All Layers

There are several ways to merge layers within an image. All of these options are
available by clicking the arrow for the Layers palette menu located at the upper
right edge of the Layers palette as shown here.

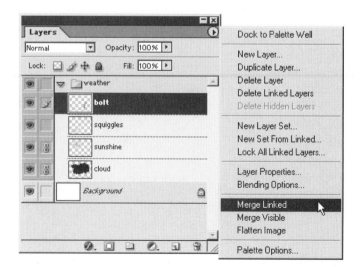

2

Select the top-most layer you want to merge and, from the Layers palette menu on the Layers palette, choose Merge Down. This merges two layers together. Note that you can't merge hidden layers. You can also merge a single layer with the layer beneath it by using CTRL-E/COMMAND-E.

Another method is to hide the layers you don't want to merge by clicking the eye icon next to those layers. Then, from the Layers palette menu, select Merge Visible.

If you have linked layers, you can merge them together by selecting Merge Linked from the Layers palette menu.

NOTE *Type layers need to be rasterized before they can be merged. See Chapter 7 for more information on type layers.*

Merging All Layers

The most common reason to merge all layers within an image is to enable you to save to a file format that requires a file with a single layer. In Photoshop this is called flattening a file. To flatten a file, select Flatten Image from the Layers palette menu.

Saving a File

There are different file formats for different graphic requirements. To keep an editable file with all layers intact, save your files in the Photoshop native file format, .psd. In this format, type and vector shapes remain editable. Some other programs, including Adobe Illustrator, Adobe After Effects, Painter, Corel PhotoPaint, and JASC PaintShop Pro, will open a layered file in PSD format. You can save a file in Photoshop PSD format by following these steps as shown here:

1. Select File | Save.

2. Enter a filename.

3. In the Format drop-down menu, select a file format, in this case Photoshop PSD

4. If you want to create a copy of your image, select the Save As a Copy checkbox.

5. If you have used multiple layers, alpha channels, annotations, or spot colors, you can choose whether or not to keep these intact in the saved file. For maximum editability, be sure to check the Layers checkbox.

6. If you wish to save the color profile for the image, select the checkbox for the color profile.

7. Select the Thumbnail checkbox if you'd like to embed a thumbnail in your image so that you can preview the image before opening it. If you're saving a file for the Web, leave this checkbox unchecked as it can add significantly to the file size of an image.

8. Select the Use Lower Case Extension checkbox if you want to maintain consistency in the way your files are named.

9. Click the Save button and you've finished saving your file.

2

There are other file formats you can save to. Most are used for specific purposes, such as viewing in a web page or for printing. Each file format has benefits and drawbacks. For instance, while a GIF file significantly reduces the file size of an image, it also reduces the quality of the image.

Saving a File for the Web

You'll find out much more detailed information on creating and saving web graphics in Chapter 10. If you want to save a file for the Web, select File | Save for Web. This opens a dialog box that enables you to select from several file types, as shown in Figure 2-13. You'll view a preview of your image as well as a number of drop-down selections. Beneath the Settings drop-down is a place to select a file format for your web graphic.

Preview window   File type

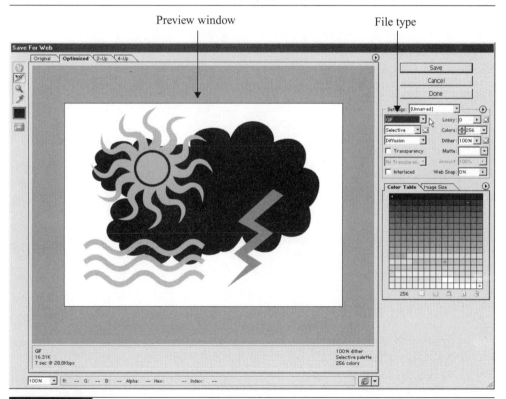

FIGURE 2-13 Using the Save for Web command opens a large dialog box that allows you to preview your image as you select various file settings.

1. GIF files are limited to 256 colors or fewer and can contain transparency information. Select GIF if you need transparency in an image or have a simple image with few colors.

2. JPG files yield the best results for images with many colors, such as photographs.

3. PNG files can contain both full color information and transparency; however, older web browsers do not support them.

Once you've made your file type selection, click OK on the upper right edge of the preview pane.

Saving a File for Print

If you are saving a file for print, save in a format that your page-layout or illustration program can best use. Select EPS or TIF for most print purposes. To save a file to EPS or TIF format, first flatten the file as described in the preceding section.

Saving an EPS File

There are several options to choose from when you save an EPS file. EPS stands for Encapsulated PostScript, and is commonly used for artwork that will be printed.

1. Select File | Save As.

2. Enter a filename.

3. Choose EPS DCS 1.0 from the File Format drop-down menu.

4. Click Save.

5. A second dialog box appears, titled DCS 1.0 Format, as shown here. For Preview, select TIF, (8 bits/pixel). The TIF format is the best format for sharing EPS files between Mac and Windows. Using the 8 bits setting yields the best quality preview for the EPS file.

6. Chose an encoding method. For greatest flexibility, and for sharing files between Mac and Windows platforms, choose ASCII.

7. For low-resolution images, click the Image Interpolation checkbox for the best quality output.

8. Click OK.

Saving a TIFF File

Another very common file format used for print is TIFF. TIFF stands for Tagged Image File Format.

1. Select File | Save As.

2. Enter a filename.

3. Choose TIFF from the File Format drop-down menu.

4. In the TIFF Options dialog box, under Image Compression, select None for greatest flexibility. Many programs can't open TIFF files saved with a compression scheme.

5. Select IBM PC for Byte Order for maximum flexibility between platforms.

6. Click Save.

7. Click OK.

Chapter 3

Setting Your Preferences

How to...

- ■ Set up general preferences in Photoshop
- ■ Set preferences for file handling
- ■ Set preferences for display and cursors
- ■ Set preferences for transparency and gamut
- ■ Set preferences for units and rulers
- ■ Set preferences for guides and grids
- ■ Set preferences for plug-ins and scratch disks
- ■ Set preferences for memory and image cache
- ■ Establish a working color space in Photoshop
- ■ Save your workspace

When you set up your preferences in Photoshop, you take control of your workspace and your work habits. Customizing your preferences can increase your productivity in Photoshop. You'll learn how to set up how you view, save, and measure your Photoshop images.

One of the most important areas of Photoshop, especially if you create files for print, is setting up your color space. The aim of setting up a color space is to enable your work on screen to match your print output as closely as possible. This chapter will introduce you to Photoshop's color settings and help you select the best choices for your specific needs.

Setting Up General Preferences in Photoshop

In Photoshop there are eight dialog boxes that enable you to select your preferences. The first of these is the General Preferences dialog, as seen in Figure 3-1. The general preferences settings are all related to how you work in Photoshop. One of the most useful features is the ability to customize how many history states, or levels of undo, you have.

- ■ **Color Picker** You can choose to use your operating system's Color Picker or Adobe's Color Picker, which has many more options. Figure 3-2 shows

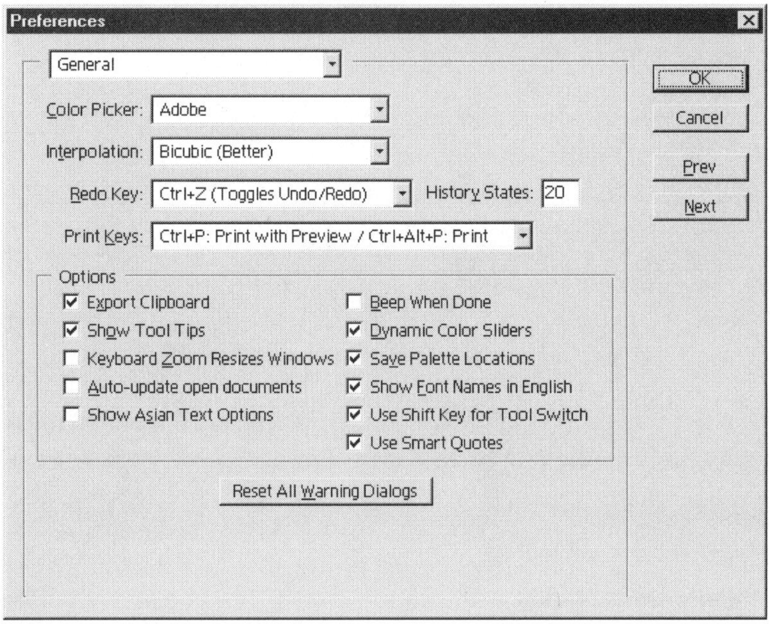

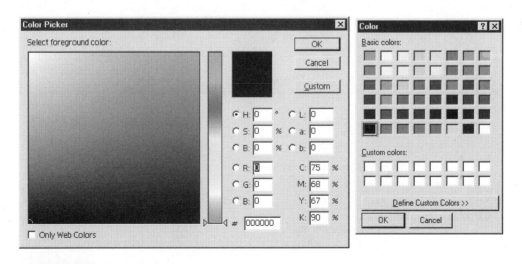

FIGURE 3-1   The General Preferences dialog box.

FIGURE 3-2   The Adobe Color Picker is on the left; the Windows Color Picker, on the right.

the Adobe Color Picker and the Windows Color Picker. You can see that Adobe's Color Picker has many more options, including the option to set colors by RGB, CMYK, or hexcode color values.

■ **Interpolation** This setting determines the method Photoshop uses when an image is resized. The default, Bicubic, yields the best results.

■ **Redo Key** The default is CTRL-Z/COMMAND-Z, but you can change it to another keystroke combination if you wish.

■ **History States** History States are a record of what you've done in Photoshop, and can also be thought of as levels of undo, or how many steps back you can take in your work. Depending on how much memory, or RAM, your computer has, you can set the number of History States to as many as 99. This is a memory intense operation, so you may want to stay with the default, or decrease it if you don't have much RAM to spare.

■ **Export Clipboard** This option enables you to copy from Photoshop to another open application.

■ **Short Pantone Names** Pantone is a system of named colors. If you're working with Pantone colors and may be exporting to older applications, this ensures compatibility.

■ **Show Tool Tips** By all means, show tool tips! Tool tips are those helpful labels that pop up when you place your mouse over an icon, as shown at the right.

■ **Keyboard Zoom Resizes Windows** This option forces Photoshop to change the size of the image window depending on how far you are zoomed in or out. You'll see a smaller image window when you're zoomed out than when you are zoomed in.

■ **Show Asian Text Options** Check this checkbox if you'll be working with Chinese, Korean, or Japanese typefaces.

■ **Beep When Done**   If you want an audio cue when Photoshop's finished working on something, you can check this checkbox.

■ **Dynamic Color Sliders**   Photoshop automatically updates the color sliders in the color palette if you check this checkbox.

■ **Save Palette Locations**   The next time you open Photoshop, you will want to see the same palettes open and in the same position as the last time you worked in Photoshop, so check this checkbox.

■ **Show Font Names in English**   Foreign fonts are labeled with English names in the Options bar and Character palette if you select this checkbox.

■ **Use Shift Key for Tool Switch**   When cycling through "hidden" tools, as described in Chapter 1, using keyboard shortcuts, you can turn off the need to use the SHIFT key in combination with the letter key for the tool.

■ **Reset All Warning Dialogs**   You can turn off a warning dialog by checking Don't show me this warning again. Check this option to reset these warning dialogs.

■ **Reset All Tools**   This resets all tools to their default settings.

Setting Preferences for File Handling

All of these preference settings relate to how Photoshop saves files, so they are important options to understand.

■ **Image Previews**   Image previews are tiny versions of a file that you can see while opening a file in Photoshop's File | Open menu selection. Although this is a helpful feature, if you are working with files for the Web, it's best to turn this option off by selecting Never Save. Image previews can significantly increase the size of the file. If you're not creating files for the Web, you will probably want to turn this feature on by selecting Always Save. If you work both in print and for the Web, select Ask When Saving, and Photoshop will ask you each time you save a file.

■ **File Extension (Use Lower Case)**   For the sake of continuity, it's best to use lower case file extension names. When you save your image, it will be named, for example, picture.psd instead of picture.PSD.

■ **Enable Workgroup Functionality**   Check this box only if you are sharing files on a network.

■ **Recent File List**   The number of files that are listed under File | Open Recent is controlled by this setting, as shown here. The default is four, but feel free to raise the number of recent files you've worked on, as it doesn't hog memory in the same way that, say, the History States mentioned previously do.

Setting Preferences for Display and Cursors

You'll be working with the cursors often in Photoshop, and Photoshop gives you the option to select how you'd like to see your tools displayed as you use them, as shown in Figure 3-3.

■ **Color Channels in Color**   If you'll be working with channels and think it would be helpful to see channels in color rather than grayscale, you can select this option.

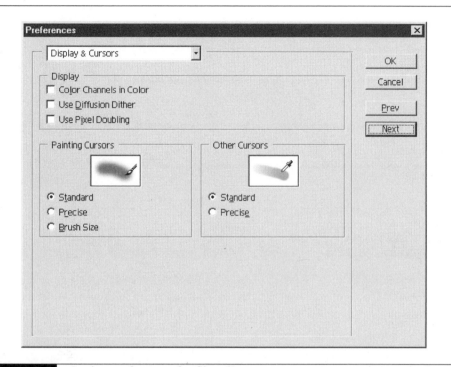

FIGURE 3-3   Setting preferences for files allows you to manage your images in the way that best suits your workflow.

- **Use Diffusion Dither**   This setting is for people working on 256 color monitors. If you're using a monitor set to higher color settings, ignore this option. This option uses dithering to approximate colors that a 256 color monitor can't display.

- **Use Pixel Doubling**   This can speed up long processes on large images.

- **Painting Cursors**   You have three types of cursors to select from when you're using painting tools in Photoshop. The first is standard, which shows a symbol of the paint tool you're using, as shown in Figure 3-4. If you're using a pencil, you'll see a pencil cursor. If you're using an airbrush, you'll see an airbrush. Precise cursors show a crosshair for more precise positioning of your tool. The Brush Size cursor shows the size and shape of the brush you're using. If you're using a large rectangular brush to paint with, you'll see a large rectangular cursor.

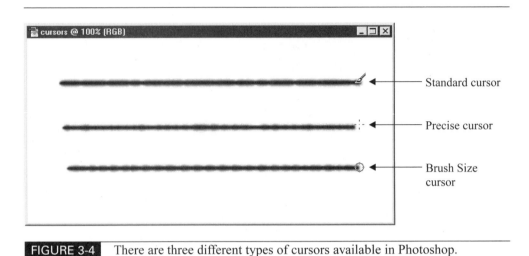

FIGURE 3-4   There are three different types of cursors available in Photoshop.

■ **Other Cursors**   Standard cursors, as mentioned in the preceding section, are a representation of the tool you're working with. Precise tools change the cursor to a crosshair for more exact positioning.

Setting Preferences for Transparency and Gamut

Transparency settings enable you to customize the way you see a transparent area within an image. Gamut settings control the way you see colors that are not printable, or are out of gamut. The Transparency and Gamut dialog is shown in Figure 3-5.

■ **Transparency Grid Size**   In a multilayered image, if you turn off the background layer, any transparent areas in your image show as a grid. You can set this grid size to suit your needs.

■ **Transparency Grid Colors**   You may want to change the default gray-and-white checkerboard pattern to something else if you're working on an image with a lot of gray or white in it and are having a difficult time discerning the image from the background grid. Otherwise, the gray-and-white pattern is a non-distracting background to work with.

■ **Gamut Warning Color**   If you produce a color in Photoshop that is visible on the screen, but is not printable, that color is said to be out of gamut. Computer monitors can display a wider range of colors than can be printed,

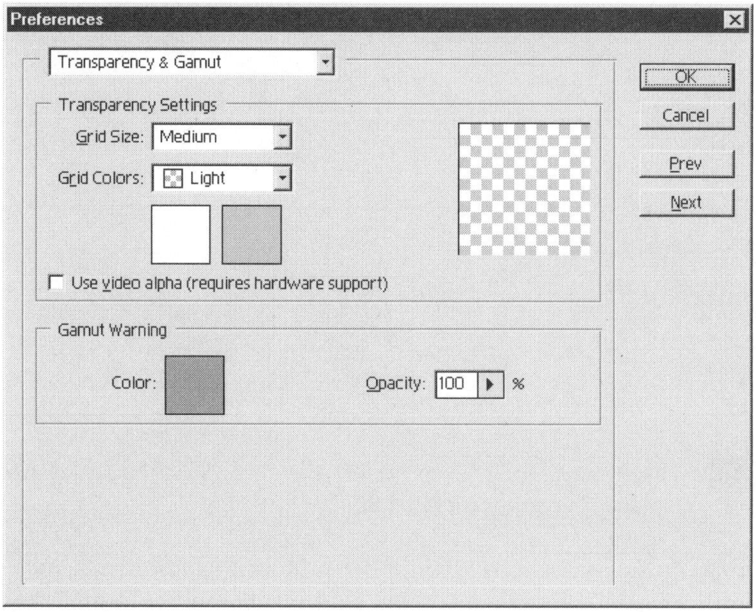

FIGURE 3-5   Transparency and Gamut dialog.

so this happens frequently. The gamut warning color replaces the unprintable colors in your image, alerting you so that you can replace the color with one that is printable. Figure 3-6 shows the original image, and the image with the colors that are out of gamut replaced by a light gray when View | Gamut is selected.

■ **Gamut Warning Opacity**   Changing the gamut warning opacity enables you to see more or less of the image beneath the out-of-gamut color, depending on the setting you select.

Setting Preferences for Units and Rulers

The settings for Units and Rulers affect not just type and rulers, but also many other settings, such as the default measurements for new images, resizing images, and so on.

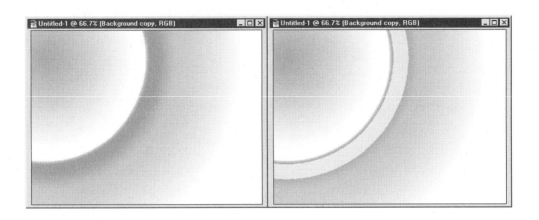

FIGURE 3-6 The original image is on the left; the image with the out-of-gamut color replaced by gray is on the right.

- ■ **Rulers** You can choose from pixels, inches, centimeters, millimeters, points, picas, and percentages for your measurement units. If you'll be working with web graphics or images for video, you will want to use pixels for your measurements. If you'll be creating images for print, use the measurement unit that best suits your needs as shown in Figure 3-7.

- ■ **Type** You can use a different unit of measurement for type than you do for rulers, if you wish.

- ■ **Column Width and Gutter** If you'll be working with a page-layout program, you may want to work with column widths as units of measurements.

- ■ **New Document Preset Resolutions** Select a resolution for new images. You'll discover more information about image resolution in Chapter 5.

Setting Preferences for Guides and Grids

Guides and grids are used for measuring and positioning your work in Photoshop. By clicking and dragging from the sides of an image window, you can create horizontal and vertical guides, as shown in Figure 3-8. You can also add guides by selecting View | New Guide. Grids are fixed to a set spacing.

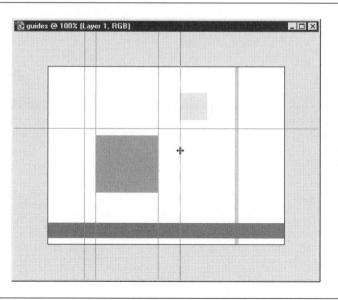

FIGURE 3-7   Unit preferences.

    Horizontal and vertical guides are useful for precise alignment.

■ **Guide Color** Customize the color you'd like to use for guides. The default is blue, but if you have a lot of blue in the image you're working on you may want to change this to something with more contrast.

■ **Guide Style** Select a line style—dashed, dotted, or solid—for your guidelines, as shown in Figure 3-9.

■ **Grid Color and Style** These settings enable you to choose a color and style for grids as you did for guidelines.

■ **Gridline every** This setting enables you to select a measurement for your grid.

■ **Subdivisions** You can divide your Guideline every setting into smaller increments with the Subdivisions setting. If you've set your guidelines to every 100 pixels, and the Subdivisions to 5, the guide will be made up of squares that measure 20 pixels by 20 pixels, because 100 divided by 5 equals 20.

■ **Slices** When you create large images for the Web, or create image maps for the Web, you will use the slice tool. In this preference area you can select a color for the slice lines and whether or not to number slices.

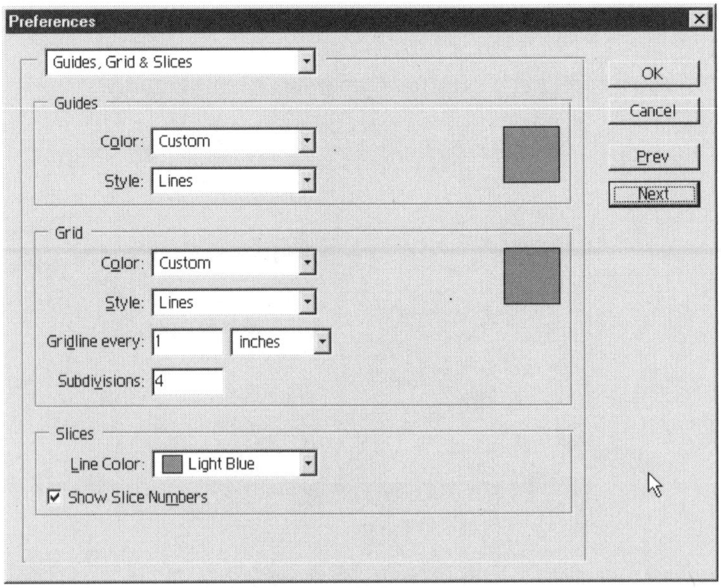

FIGURE 3-9 Selecting styles for guides, grids and slices so that they are easy to see and position is done throug the Guides, Grids, and Slices Preference dialog.

Setting Preferences for Plug-Ins and Scratch Disks

- **Additional Plug-Ins Directory**   One of Photoshop's best features is that you can keep adding onto it with plug-ins. Plug-ins add additional functions, such as filters, special effects, and export abilities. If you've installed plug-ins to any place other than the Photoshop Plug-Ins directory, you can have them load every time Photoshop opens by selecting the correct directory, as shown in Figure 3-10.

- **Scratch Disks**   Photoshop loves memory and it needs a lot of virtual elbowroom to work in. The general rule of thumb is that you need up to five times as much RAM as your image size in order to work in Photoshop. If you're working on a 40MB file, you'd better have at least 200MB of RAM available. Scratch disks are different from RAM in that RAM is memory and scratch disks are space on your hard drive that Photoshop uses temporarily while processing files. If you have multiple hard drives, use the drive with the most space available as your primary scratch disk.

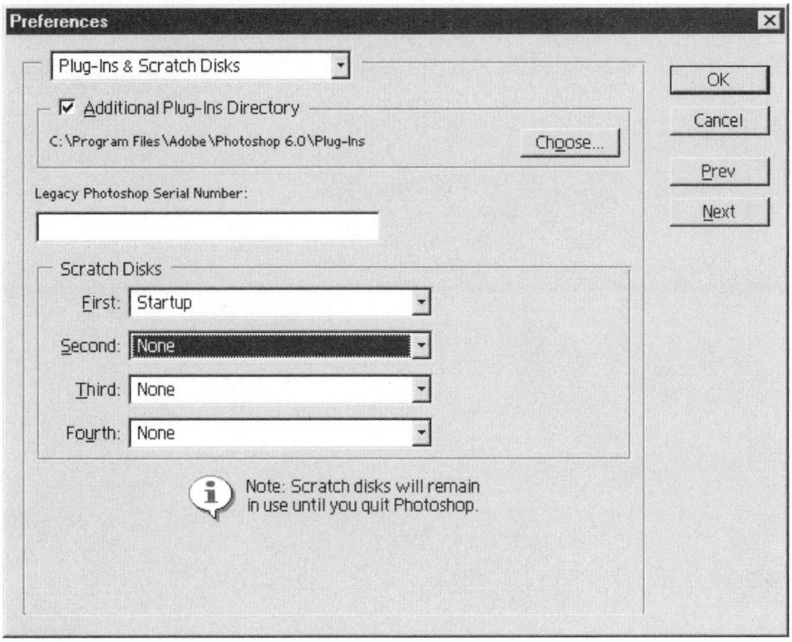

FIGURE 3-10   Scratch Disk Preferences.

Setting Preferences for Memory and Image Cache

When you apply a filter, or resize an image, Photoshop uses memory to complete the operation. You can change your memory settings as shown in Figure 3-11.

- ■ **Cache Settings** Photoshop generates your image at several zoom sizes (the default is four) to speed up your work when you zoom in and zoom out. Depending on how much memory you have, you may want to raise the number of cache settings to make your work go even faster.

- ■ **Physical Memory Usage** This setting determines how much of your RAM Photoshop can use. In most cases, it's best to leave this at the default setting.

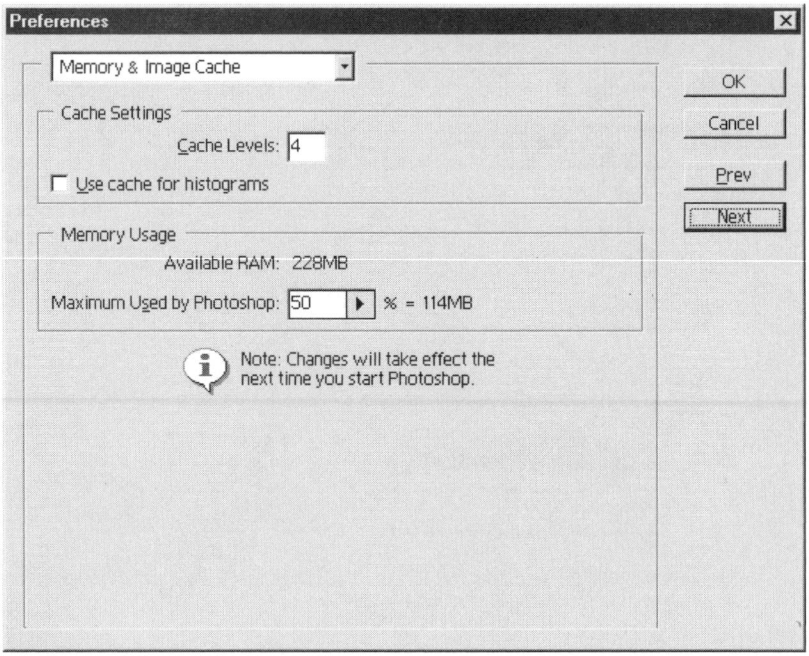

FIGURE 3-11   Memory and Image Cache.

Establishing a Working Color Space in Photoshop

One of the biggest challenges in computer graphics has always been getting what you see on your computer screen to match what comes out of the printer. The way an image appears on one computer monitor may vary wildly from the way it looks on another monitor. By customizing your color settings in Photoshop, you will be able to create a more predictable output for print.

When you first install Photoshop, you'll be given an opportunity to go through a step-by-step process to set up your color space in Photoshop. After the initial installation, you can customize your color settings by selecting Edit | Color Settings, as shown in Figure 3-12.

Within the Color Settings dialog box, you can select from several color management presets. If you're working with web graphics only, you'll want to select either Web Graphics Default or Color Management Off. Color management can actually create problems with web graphics, since it involves reinterpreting colors.

If you're creating graphics for print, you want to select either one of the print defaults from the color management presets, or choose to set the color management settings individually.

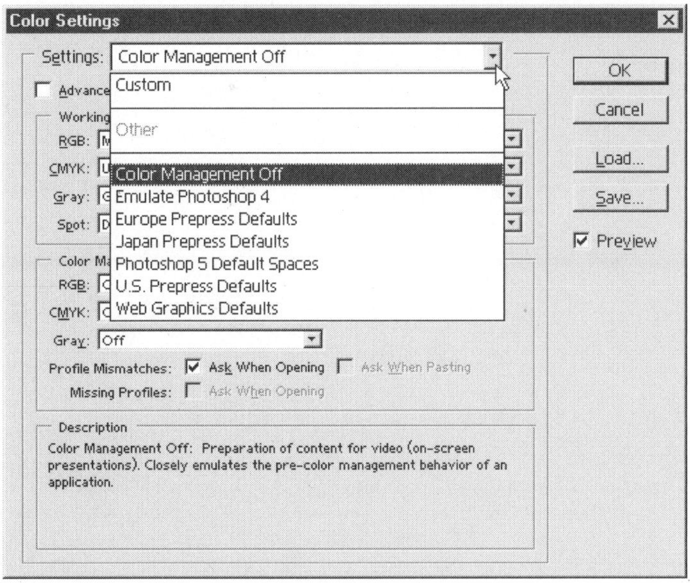

FIGURE 3-12   When creating web graphics, choose either Color Management Off or select Web Graphics Defaults.

Saving Your Workspace

If you share your computer with other users, or if you use different preference settings when you're working on different types of images, you can save your preferences. Saving your workspace enables you to save any custom settings and load them automatically. You can save preferences, which palettes are open on screen, and the location of the palettes.

Saving a Workspace

Once you've set everything up the way you want to work in Photoshop, select Window | Workspace | Save Workspace as shown here. Enter a name for the workspace.

Loading a Workspace

To load a saved workspace, select Window | Workspace and select one of the workspaces listed.

Chapter 4

Creating Selections

How to…

- Work with the Photoshop selection tools
- Work with the basic selection commands
- Modify a selection using the option bar
- Fill a selection
- Stroke a selection
- Move a selection
- Cut, copy, and paste a selection
- Crop a selection
- Modify a selection
- Save a selection
- Transform a selection

If you are like most Photoshop users, you'll spend more time with selection tools than with any other tools in Photoshop. Selection tools are important because they enable you to work with parts of an existing image. You can use selection tools to create complex, collaged images by copying and pasting from several photos into a single image. Selections are also useful for isolating part of an image that you want to adjust, paint, fill, or filter. You use a selection to work with part of a layer. You also use a selection to constrain an effect to a selected part of an image.

In this chapter you'll learn how to use a variety of selection tools, how to make complex selections, and how to use the Transform command to rotate, skew, or add perspective to an image.

Learning the Photoshop Selection Tools

There are three basic types of selection tools in the Photoshop toolbox, as shown in Figure 4-1. These include the marquee tool, the lasso tool, and the magic wand tool. Each type of selection tool works differently. Marquee tools select a geometric area. Lasso tools select a freeform, or irregular, area. And the magic wand creates selections based on color.

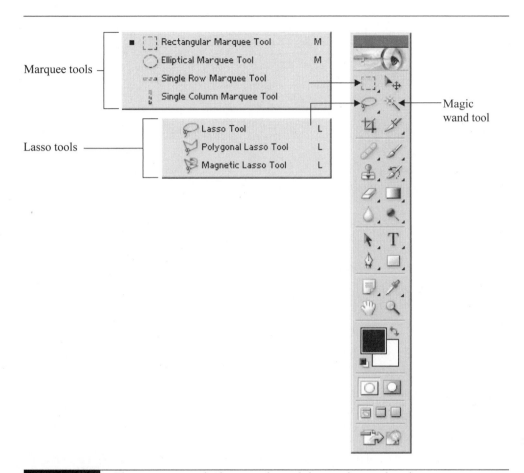

Marquee tools

Lasso tools

Magic wand tool

4

FIGURE 4-1   The marquee tools, lasso tools, and the magic wand tool.

The Marquee Tools

When you click and hold on the Marquee tool, four marquee tools are revealed, as seen in Figure 4-1. The marquee tools are used to create basic rectangular or elliptical selections in your image. These are, from left to right:

■ **Rectangular Marquee Tool**   This tool enables you to make a rectangular selection. If you'd like to create a perfectly square selection, hold SHIFT down while you click and drag this tool in the image window as shown in Figure 4-2.

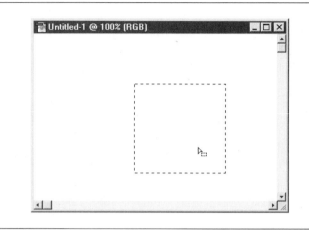

FIGURE 4-2   Holding SHIFT down while you click and drag creates a perfectly square selection.

- **Elliptical Marquee tool**   This tool enables you to create an elliptical selection. To create a perfectly round selection, hold the SHIFT key down while you click and drag this tool.

- **Single Pixel Row and Column Marquee Tools**   For those rare occasions when you want to select only a row or column that is a single pixel wide, you can use the single pixel marquee tool.

The Lasso Tools

Use the lasso tools to create freeform or complex selections. These tools are useful for tasks such as removing the background behind a person in a photo. The Lasso selection tools are a little trickier to use than the elliptical or rectangular marquee tool, and it may take some experimentation before you feel comfortable with them. Remember that you can eliminate a selection by using the keystroke CTRL-D/ COMMAND-D, or you can use CTRL-Z/COMMAND-Z to undo the last action you took in Photoshop.

Clicking and holding on the Lasso tool in the toolbox reveals the three types of Lasso selection tools as seen here.

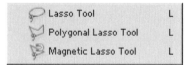

■ **Lasso Tool**   If you want to make a quick, freeform, hand-drawn selection, you can use the Lasso tool to draw your selection, much as you would use a pencil. This is a good tool for selecting a general area in an image. When you release the mouse, the selection automatically closes.

■ **Polygon Lasso Tool**   Use the Polygon Lasso tool to make a selection with straight edges. This tool is a little trickier to use. Click to create the first point of the selection, and click again to create a second point. A straight-line selection is automatically created between the two points, as shown in Figure 4-3. Click to create more points in your selection. When you're finished, you'll need to close the selection. Move the cursor back to the

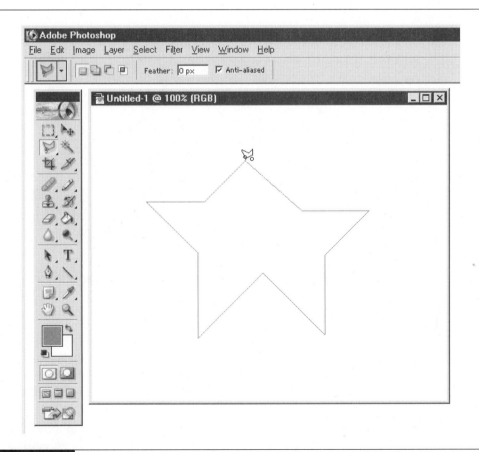

FIGURE 4-3   The Polygon Lasso tool creates a selection with straight edges.

first point you created, until a small circle appears next to the cursor, as shown in Figure 4-3. This circle indicates you're ready to close the selection. Click the cursor to close the selection. You can also double-click the mouse to close the selection.

When using the Polygonal Lasso tool, you can use SHIFT to constrain your lines to angles in increments of 45°.

■ **Magnetic Lasso Tool** Use the Magnetic Lasso tool to draw a selection that snaps to the edge of an area. The Magnetic Lasso tool is best used on areas that have edges with high contrast. Click and drag to use the magnetic selection tool, and it snaps the selection to the edge as shown here. You can also add points to the selection as you draw it by clicking the mouse to anchor the selection. You can remove previous points in the selection by pressing the DELETE key to remove the previous point. Double-click to close the selection. Changing the Frequency on the options bar to a lower number can help to create a more accurate selection.

The Magic Wand Tool

The Magic Wand tool enables you to select an area based on color. When you click the Magic Wand tool, you select adjoining areas of similarly colored pixels—pixels in the same color range. You can adjust the color range, or how closely the similarly colored pixels must much match the original color, by changing the Tolerance number in the options bar. The higher the Tolerance, the greater range of color you will select with the Magic Wand tool. You can enter a tolerance amount of 1, which would select only areas that have the exact same color value. The highest number you can enter in the Tolerance is 255, which would select every color. The default amount of Tolerance is 40. Once you've set the Tolerance, click the magic wand in the area that you want to select, as shown here.

Learning Basic Selection Commands

Since you'll be working with selections so often in Photoshop, it's worthwhile to memorize a few keystrokes that can make your workflow easier.

- **Deselect**   When a selection is active, you can paint, fill, or modify only within the selected area. You can't change anything outside the selection until you deselect the selection. To remove a selection, choose Select | Deselect, or use the keyboard shortcut of CTRL-D/COMMAND-D.

- **Hiding a Selection**   Sometimes it's hard to see what you're working on when the selection is visible. To hide the selection, use the keyboard shortcut CTRL-H/COMMAND-H. To make the selection visible again, use the same keyboard shortcut again to toggle the selection back into view.

> NOTE   *Using the* CTRL-H/COMMAND-H *also hides grids and guidelines until you toggle them back on by repeating the command.*

- **Inversing a Selection**   Sometimes the easiest way to select something is to not select it, but to select everything else. Although this may sound a bit enigmatic, this is useful when you're selecting a complex background from a simple object as shown in Figure 4-4. To inverse a selection, choose Select | Inverse.

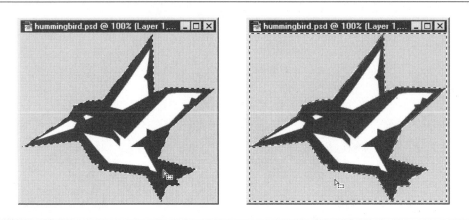

FIGURE 4-4   The original selection is on the left; the selection inverted, on the right.

Modifying a Selection Using the Options Bar

The options bar, at the top of the Photoshop screen, is context sensitive. Each time you select a tool from the toolbox your options for that tool display in the options bar.

Options for the Marquee Tools

You'll see the options for the Marquee tools shown in Figure 4-5. From left to right, these options are:

■ **New Selection**   This is the default for creating selections.

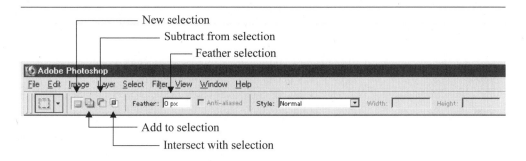

FIGURE 4-5   You can choose from a number of options for the rectangular marquee selection tool. These options are displayed on the Photoshop options bar once you select the marquee tool.

■ **Add to Selection**   This option enables you to add to an existing selection. You can also use the keyboard shortcut SHIFT to add to an existing selection while you use any selection tool. As shown here, you can make an initial selection and add to it using the Magic Wand tool.

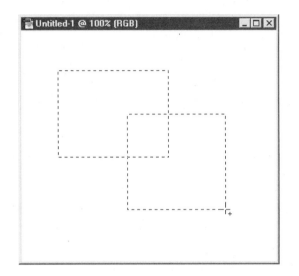

■ **Subtract from Selection**   This option enables you to subtract from an existing selection. You can also use the keyboard shortcut of ALT-SHIFT/ OPTION-SHIFT to subtract from an existing selection while you use any selection tool.

■ **Intersect with Selection**   With this option, only the areas of the existing selection and the selection you make will remain.

■ **Feather Selection**   Feathering a selection enables you to add a lovely soft edge to the entire selection. This is especially effective for creating soft vignette edges around an image. The larger the pixel number you enter, the softer the edges of your selection will be. To create a soft edge for a photo as shown here, select the area you want to keep, set the Feather command to create a soft edge. Inverse the selection by choosing Select | Inverse.

Next, cut away the excess area you've just selected by choosing Edit | Clear, as shown here.

- **Anti-aliased** Figure 4-6 shows the difference between an anti-aliased elliptical selection and one without anti-aliasing. Anti-aliasing softens the edges of a selection slightly, and is useful for web graphics, where you want the edges to look smooth.

- **Style** There are three types of marquee style options that have to do with the size of the selection you create:

  - **Normal** Normal is the default style for marquee selections.

  - **Constrained aspect ratio** This option enables you to create a selection that fits a certain aspect ratio. If you want to create a selection that is twice as high as it is wide, enter 2 in the width box and 1 in the height box.

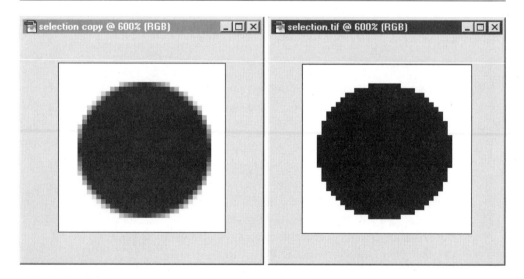

FIGURE 4-6 An anti-aliased elliptical selection on the left, and an elliptical selection without anti-aliasing on the right.

■ **Fixed**   If you need to crop an image to an exact size, you can enter the precise dimensions of your selection in the options bar as demonstrated here.

Style: | Fixed Size ▾ | Width: | 150 px | Height: | 150 px |

Options for the Lasso Tools

The option bar for the Lasso tools contains all of the options described for the marquee tools, with the exception of Style.

The Lasso Selection tool has a number of additional options to choose from, as you can see in Figure 4-7, including:

■ **Width**   This is the number of pixels the magnetic lasso tool samples to find an edge. The lower the number, the smaller the area that is sampled.

■ **Edge Contrast**   This controls the magnetic lasso tool's sensitivity to edges. In an image with low edge contrast, use a low number. In an image with high edge contrast, use a higher number.

■ **Frequency**   This is the number of points the tool creates to anchor the selection. The more complex the edge, the more points the selection needs to be accurate.

Options for the Magic Wand Tool

The function of the Magic Wand selection tool is to select areas of an image based on color. The options bar for this tool offers several additional options, as shown in Figure 4-8.

FIGURE 4-7   Choose from these options when you use the magnetic lasso tool.

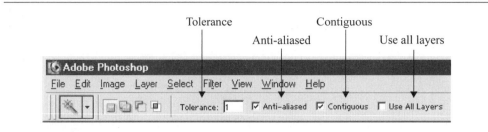

FIGURE 4-8 Use the options for the Magic Wand tool to customize your select-by-color workflow.

- **Tolerance** The tolerance setting determines how wide a range of colors you want to select. You can set the Tolerance from any number between 1 and 255. The Photoshop default setting is 40. Each image is different, and the higher you set the Tolerance number, the wider the range of colors you'll select.

- **Contiguous** If you select this checkbox, you'll select only areas that adjoin each other. If you don't select the Contiguous checkbox, the magic wand will create a selection that includes the color you've selected from anywhere in the layer you are working on.

- **Use All Layers** This option enables you to make a selection based on all visible layers in an image.

Filling a Selection

You can fill a selection using the paint bucket tool, the gradient tool, or the Edit | Fill command. These will all be described in greater detail in Chapter 6.

Stroking a Selection

When you stroke a selection, you create an outline. To stroke a selection, choose Edit | Stroke. The dialog box, as seen in Figure 4-9, appears.

You can set the width and color for the outline you'll be adding to your image. You can also position the stroke, as seen in Figure 4-10.

You can also set the Blending Mode and Opacity for the stroke, just as you can for a layer, as discussed in Chapter 2. If your selection is feathered, a feathered outline is created when you apply a stroke.

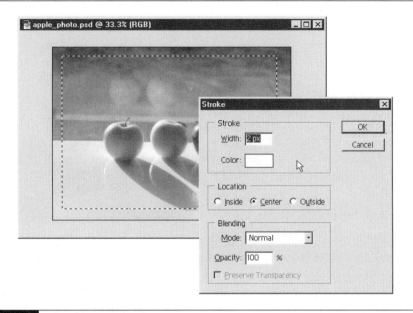

FIGURE 4-9 Stroking a selection.

Moving a Selection

You can move a selection using the move tool from the toolbox. Click and drag within the selection to move the selection.

You can also move the selection, without its contents, using the arrow keys on your keyboard to move it one pixel at a time. To move the selection with its contents, when the move tool is not selected, click inside the selection and drag it. To position a selection more precisely, use the CTRL/COMMAND key in conjunction with the arrow keys on your keyboard to nudge the selection one pixel at a time.

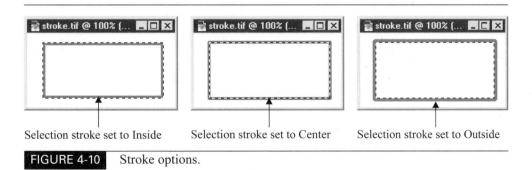

Selection stroke set to Inside   Selection stroke set to Center   Selection stroke set to Outside

FIGURE 4-10 Stroke options.

Cutting, Copying, and Pasting Selections

Photoshop uses the clipboard, or temporary memory, when you cut or copy a selection. The clipboard can hold only one image at a time. The last image you cut or copied is always on the clipboard.

Cutting a Selection

If you wish to delete the contents of a selection, select Edit | Cut, or use the keyboard shortcut CTRL-X/COMMAND-X. The selection is removed from the image, but is still available on the clipboard, and can still be pasted back into an image.

Copying a Selection

To copy the contents of a selection, choose Edit | Copy, or use the keyboard shortcut CTRL-C/ COMMAND-C. This pastes the contents of the selection to the clipboard.

Copying a Merged Selection

To copy all visible layers within a selected area, choose Edit | Copy Merged.

Pasting a Selection

Once you've copied a selection, you can paste into the same image within Photoshop by selecting Edit |Paste, or by using the keyboard shortcut CTRL-V/ COMMAND-V. This creates a new layer in your image.

Pasting into a Selection

You can paste a cut or copied selection directly into another selection in an image. This creates a new layer in your image, with a layer mask. Layer masks will be covered in Chapter 8. You'll be able to move the pasted image within the selection, as shown in Figure 4-11.

Cropping a Selection

To crop to a selection, choose Image | Crop. This crops the image to the edges of the selection.

TIP   *It's especially useful to use Image | Crop with a fixed-size selection if you are aiming to create an image with an exact size.*

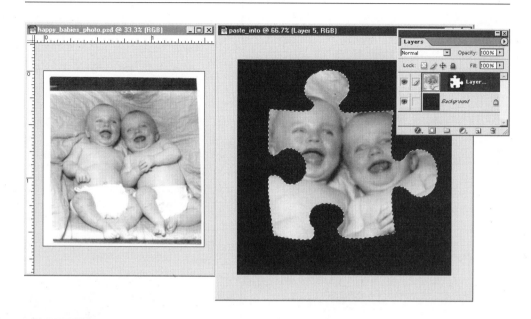

FIGURE 4-11 You can paste an image into another selection as shown here.

Modifying a Selection

Once you've created a selection, there are many ways to alter it in very precise ways, as demonstrated in Figure 4-12.

- **Border**   To create a border, choose Select | Modify | Border, and you will be able to enter a pixel value. The border is centered on your selection, so if you choose to create a border 10 pixels wide, 5 pixels of the border will fall outside the original selection and 5 pixels will fall inside the original selection.

- **Smooth**   If you've used the magic wand tool or the magnetic lasso tool and your selection is a little rough around the edges, you can use the smooth command to correct this. Choose Select | Modify | Smooth, and you can enter a pixel value for the Sample Radius. The smooth command adds or subtracts pixels from a jagged edge in order to smooth the selection.

- **Expand**   If your selection is just right, except for the fact that it's a bit too small, you can change your selection by choosing Select | Modify | Expand. Enter a pixel value for the amount that you want the selection to expand.

Original selection

Select | Modify | Border with a setting of
10 pixels applied

Select | Modify | Expand with a setting of
4 pixels applied

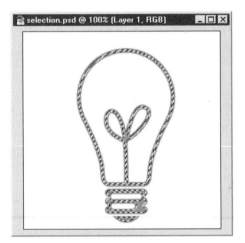

Select | Modify | Contract with a sample
radius of 2 pixels applied

FIGURE 4-12 Finesse your selections using the border, expand, and contract commands.

■ **Contract** If your selection is just a little too big, you can use the Contract command to shrink your selection. Choose Select | Modify | Contract, and enter a pixel value for the amount that you want to shrink your selection.

Selecting Color Range

When you use the Color Range command, you create a selection based on a range of colors. The Fuzziness slider in the Color Range dialog box controls the range, or variation, in color.

To create a selection based on a range of colors, choose Select | Color Range. Then use the eyedropper tool in the image window to select a color. Set the drop down Selection Preview menu to Quick Mask so that you can see what your selection will look like in the image window (it will appear as a red overlay). You can then adjust the selection you are creating in the following ways, as shown in Figure 4-13.

■ **Add color**   Click in the image window to add more colors to your selection.

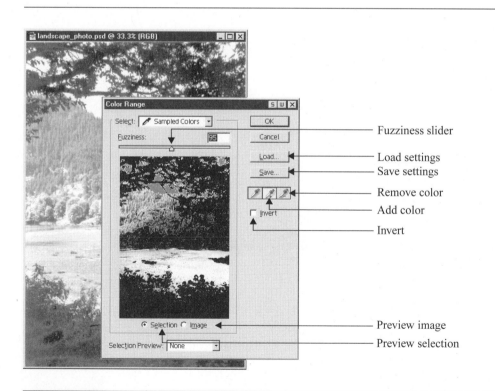

FIGURE 4-13   The Color Range dialog box offers tools to select a range of color, and then change that selection to a different color.

- ■ **Remove color** Click in the image window to remove colors from your selection.

- ■ **Fuzziness slider** Drag to increase or reduce the range of colors selected.

- ■ **Invert** Click this checkbox to invert your selection.

- ■ **Preview selection** This option enables you to preview the selection you are working on.

- ■ **Preview image** This option enables you to see a preview of the image you are working on.

- ■ **Save settings** This option saves the current settings for the Color Range tool to disk.

- ■ **Load settings** This option loads previously saved settings for the Color Range tool.

When you have finished with all of your adjustments, click OK to create your selection.

> TIP
>
> *First, make a loose selection of the area from which you want to select a color range. This eliminates the parts of the image you don't want to select with the Color Range command.*

Growing a Selection

Growing a selection is like using the Expand Selection command along with the magic wand. When you choose Select | Grow, your selection will grow to include pixels that fall within the tolerance range of the magic wand tool, as shown in Figure 4-14. By using Grow, your selection is increased based on the tolerance setting of the magic wand tool.

Selecting Similar Areas

The Select | Similar command is especially useful for creating a selection in an area of an image that is significantly lighter or darker than the rest of the image.

Create a selection using the marquee or lasso tool, based on the area you want to select. You can select multiple areas in your image by holding down SHIFT as you make multiple selections. Next, choose Select | Similar, and a selection of all areas of your image that are similar in color is automatically created, as shown in Figure 4-15.

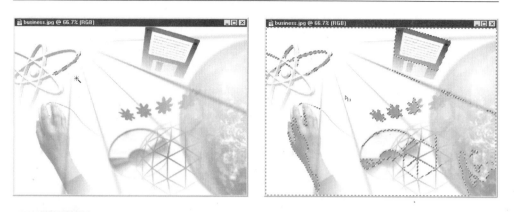

FIGURE 4-14   Growing a selection.

Saving a Selection

You can save the selection you have created for later use, as shown in Figure 4-16. Choose Select | Save Selection. Enter a name for the selection.

Loading a Selection

Once you've saved a selection, you can load it by choosing Select | Load Selection. In the drop-down menu labeled Channel, choose the name of your saved selection, as shown in Figure 4-17.

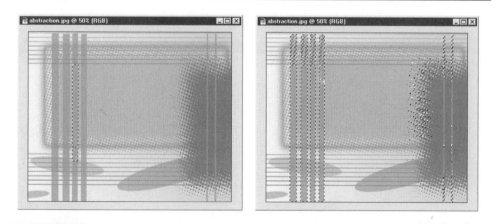

FIGURE 4-15   The original selection is on the left, and the selection after Select | Similar is applied is on the right.

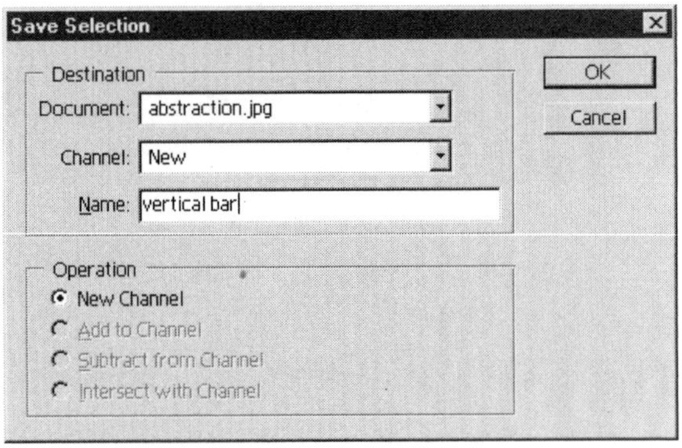

FIGURE 4-16 Saving a selection.

Selecting Everything on a Layer

To select everything on a layer, CTRL-click/COMMAND-click on the thumbnail of that layer in the Layers palette. This selects all non-transparent pixels on a layer.

Transforming a Selection

Once you have created a selection, you can transform it by rotating, skewing, or adding perspective to it.

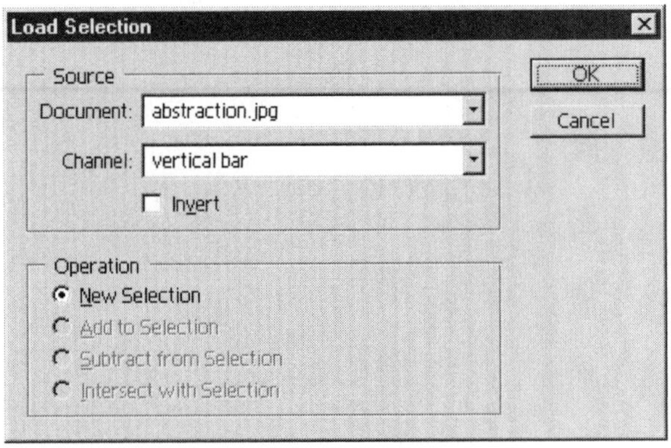

FIGURE 4-17 Loading a selection.

Photoshop offers two methods to transform a selection. You can transform only the selection, by choosing the Select | Transform Selection command, or you can ransform both the selection and the contents of the selection by choosing the Edit | Free Transform command. Once you've applied either of these commands, transforming the selection with or without its contents works in the same manner.

TIP *The keyboard shortcut for accessing the Free Transform command is* CTRL-T/ COMMAND-T.

4

Scaling a Selection

Once you've chosen Select | Transform Selection or Edit | Free Transform, your selection is surrounded by a bounding box, as seen in Figure 4-18. The bounding box has handles on the corners and on each side.

Click on any of the bounding box handles as shown in Figure 4-18 to scale your selection up or down. If you want to maintain the proportions of your selection, hold SHIFT while you drag the corner handle.

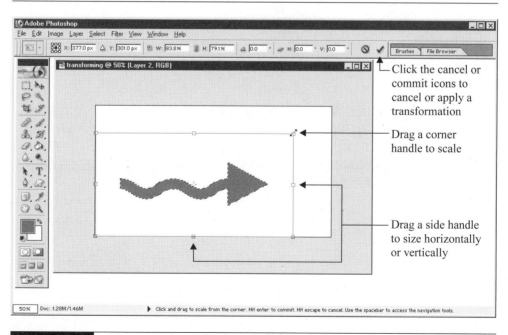

FIGURE 4-18 You can scale a selection by clicking and dragging on a handle of the bounding box that surrounds the selected area.

To resize the selection horizontally, drag a handle on the left or right side of the bounding box. To resize a selection vertically, drag a handle on the top or bottom side of the bounding box. When you are satisfied with your transformation, press ENTER, or click Apply on the options bar. If you want to cancel the transformation, press ESCAPE or click the Cancel icon on the options bar.

NOTE *Once you've chosen a Transform command, you cannot access any other tools or save your file until you either cancel or apply the transformation.*

Rotating a Selection

Rotating a selection is a little trickier than scaling a selection. To create a rotation, you'll need to move your mouse outside the bounding box until you see the rotation cursor, as shown here. Then click and drag to rotate the selection. If you want to rotate your selection in precise, 15-degree, increments, hold down SHIFT while you rotate the selection.

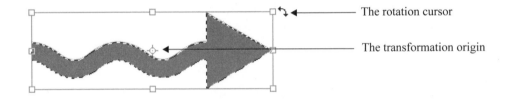

The rotation cursor

The transformation origin

You'll notice that, in addition to the bounding box and bounding box handles, there's a transform origin point in the center of the bounding box. This is the pivot point around which the rotation occurs. You can move the transform origin point by dragging it, as shown here, where the transform origin point has been moved to a corner of the bounding box, and the image is being rotated around that point.

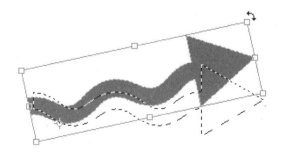

TIP
You can create any number of transformations before applying them. Just continue to transform your selection, and when you have finished, press ENTER, *or click the Checkmark icon on the options bar.*

Using the Transformation Option Bar

When you're using the Transformation command, the context-sensitive options change in the options bar, as shown in Figure 4-19.

The options on the options bar enable you to enter numeric values for the transformation point, scaling, rotating, and skewing of your selection. These settings are more precise than making transformations by clicking and dragging within the image window.

Creating Additional Types of Transformations

There's more to transformation than just scaling and rotating, although those are the most common. You can also skew, distort, add perspective, or flip a selection. To access these options, select Edit | Transform. There are several transformations that you can apply automatically without the use of the transformation bounding box. These are listed on the menu:

- Rotate 180°

- Rotate 90° CW (rotates your selection 90 degrees clockwise)

- Rotate 90° CCW (rotates your selection 90 degrees counter clockwise)

- Flip Horizontal

- Flip Vertical

Edit	
Undo Select Canvas	Ctrl+Z
Step Forward	Shft+Z
Step Backward	Alt+Ctrl+Z
Fade...	Shft+Ctrl+F
Cut	Ctrl+X
Copy	Ctrl+C
Copy Merged	Shft+Ctrl+C
Paste	Ctrl+V
Paste Into	Shft+Ctrl+V
Clear	
Check Spelling...	
Find and Replace Text...	
Fill...	
Stroke...	
Free Transform	Ctrl+T
Transform ►	
Define Brush...	
Define Pattern...	
Define Custom Shape...	
Purge ►	
Color Settings... Shft+Ctrl+K	
Preset Manager...	
Preferences ►	

Transform submenu:

Again	Shft+Ctrl+T
Scale	
Rotate	
Skew	
Distort	
Perspective	
Rotate 180°	
Rotate 90° CW	
Rotate 90° CCW	
Flip Horizontal	
Flip Vertical	

4

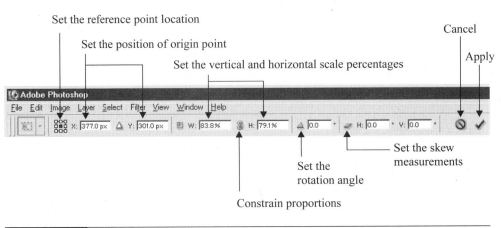

Set the reference point location

Set the position of origin point

Set the vertical and horizontal scale percentages

Cancel

Apply

Set the skew measurements

Set the rotation angle

Constrain proportions

FIGURE 4-19   Use the transformation options bar to make precise settings.

Skewing a Selection

When you skew a selection, you tilt the selected object in one direction. Select Edit | Transform | Skew, or right-click in the image window and select Skew.

Drag any corner to skew your selection, as shown here. Press ENTER to apply the transformation, or click Apply on the options bar.

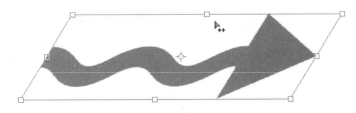

Distorting a Selection

Select Edit | Transform | Distort, or right-click in the image window and select Distort. As demonstrated here, drag any corner or side of the bounding box to skew your selection. Press ENTER to apply the transformation to the selection.

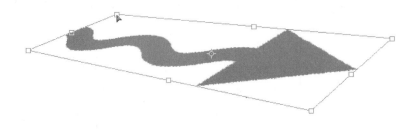

Adding Perspective to a Selection

You don't need a 3-D program to create the illusion of perspective. You can use the
Perspective transformation to create the sense that an object is receding into the
distance. Select Edit | Transform | Perspective, or right-click in the image window
and select Perspective. Drag a corner, as shown here, to add perspective to your
selection. Click ENTER to apply the transformation.

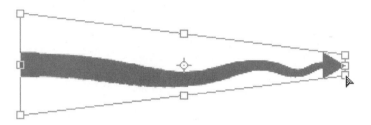

Chapter 5

Acquiring Images

How to...

- Target your image size and resolution
- Scan an image into Photoshop
- Resize an image
- Crop a scanned image
- Straighten a crooked scan
- Retouch a photograph using tools
- Retouch a photograph using filters and commands

One of the most common and powerful uses of Photoshop is the retouching of photographs. With tools in Photoshop, you can sharpen, replace, and repair existing images. This chapter will show you strategies you can use to correct and compensate for problems in an image. You will learn how to use your scanner to its best advantage, and how to fix common problems in scanned images. This chapter will use both selections and layers, which were covered in the preceding chapters, to help you build on your knowledge of Photoshop so you can achieve stunning results.

Targeting your Image Size and Resolution

Before you begin scanning, you'll want to consider how your final image will be used, because this will determine the size of your image. You'll be selecting a size based on resolution of an image, which is another way of saying how many pixels per inch make up your image. Figure 5-1 shows an image scanned at 72 pixels per inch, a typical resolution for the Web, and the same image scanned at 300 pixels per inch, a typical resolution for printing. The more pixels per inch, the higher the resolution and the better quality of the image. Another thing to keep in mind is that the higher the pixels per inch setting, the larger the file size. For print work, you'll want to work with a higher resolution for a good-looking image. For Web work, it's important to keep the file size smaller for a quicker download time.

Selecting an Image Size for the Web

Computer monitors are made up of a limited number of pixels per inch. If you are creating an image that will be displayed by a web browser, you'll want to keep the

FIGURE 5-1   Here, the same image is scanned at 72 pixels per inch and at 300 pixels per inch.

image small so that it downloads quickly. Resolution for web images is determined by the viewer's monitor. The important measurements for web images are the overall height and width of the image. As mentioned in Chapter 2, for an average monitor set to 640 × 480 pixels, the size of the viewing area within the web browser is actually 590 pixels wide by 325 pixels high. This measurement takes into consideration the area of the screen that is taken up by the edges and toolbar on the web browser. You'll want to make sure that your image is smaller than the viewing area. Use the default setting of 72 pixels per inch.

Selecting an Image Size for Video

As with scanning for the Web, the important issue for video is the width and height of the image rather than the resolution. There are two standards for video. The National Television System Committee (NTSC) standard is used in America and Japan. The Phase Alternation Line (PAL) standard is used in Europe, Australia, and China. Adobe suggests 720 pixels wide by 480 pixels high for NTSC video format, and 720 pixels wide by 576 high for PAL video. You can use the setting of 72 pixels per inch.

If you're creating artwork for a DVD or HDTV, you can select image preset sizes in the New Image dialog box as shown in Figure 5-2.

Selecting an Image Size for Print from the Desktop

In general, you'll want to scan at 300 pixels per inch for printing from a laser printer or inkjet printer. The documentation that accompanies your printer should give you advice on what is the best resolution for your images.

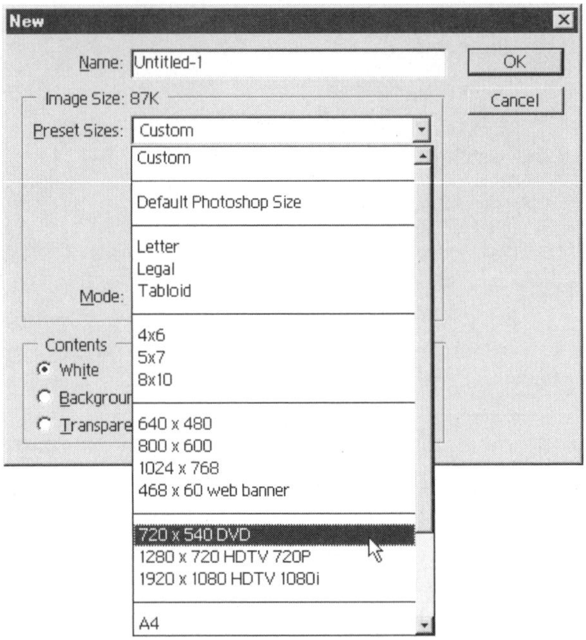

FIGURE 5-2 Select image preset sizes in the New Image dialog box.

Selecting an Image Size for Commercial Printing

You'll want to consult with your printer to find out what the final output will be for a commercial print job. Printers use lines per inch as a measurement, which are different from pixels per inch. Multiply the lines per inch by 1.5 to 2 to arrive at the correct pixel per inch setting for your image.

For example, if you're preparing a photo that will be printed at 133 lpi (lines per inch) determine the pixels per inch of the final image by multiplying 133 by 2. Your scanning target resolution is 266 pixels per inch.

Some typical lines per inch settings are:

- **Black-and-white newspaper**   85 lines per inch

- **Color newspaper**   100 lines per inch

- **Books, magazines, brochures**   133 to 150 lpi

- **High quality offset printing**   150 lpi and up

Scanning an Image into Photoshop

When you installed your scanner, software for scanning was installed for you to control your scans. This software varies from manufacturer to manufacturer, as you can see in Figure 5-3. In general, however, the software provides you with similar helpful options:

- **Resolution or pixels per inch**   You'll already know the pixels per inch setting from the preceding section. As a rule of thumb, when in doubt, scan at a higher resolution.

- **Image mode**   Your scanner and software may have labeled it something other than image mode, but you'll want to stick with RGB color, sometimes labeled 24-bit color. Although your scanner software can scan the image as grayscale, or black and white, Photoshop does a better job of converting images than most scanner software. First scan the image into Photoshop in full color. Next, in Photoshop, select Image | Mode and change color mode to grayscale, black and white, or indexed color.

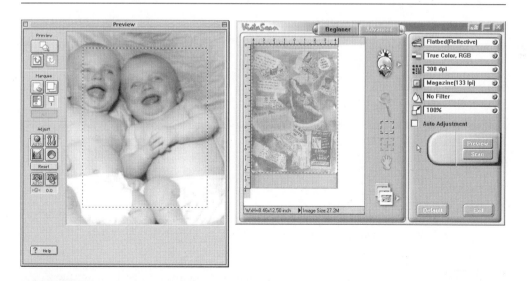

FIGURE 5-3   Scanning software interfaces from several manufacturers offer similar options.

■ **Descreening**   Screening applies a filter to compensate for artifacts that
come from the printing process. Use the screening filter when you scan
from a book, magazine, or other printed piece to eliminate these problems.
Your scanner software may offer a choice of screening for various printing
sources, such as magazines, books or newspapers. Figure 5-4 demonstrates
an image scanned with and without a descreening filter.

NOTE   *Be cautious of scanning images that you did not create. In the United
States, most work created in the last 95 years is copyrighted, meaning that
only the author of the work has the right to reproduce the work. For more
information and resources on copyright, see Chapter 14 for web sites with
more information.*

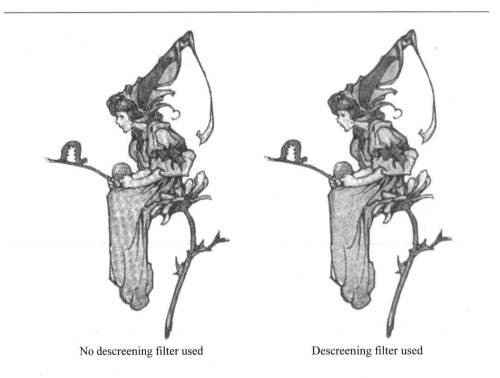

No descreening filter used   Descreening filter used

FIGURE 5-4   The image on the left was scanned without using a descreening filter.

Resizing an Image

It's always better to start larger than your intended image and then scale down rather than to start smaller and scale up. If you try to scale up, or increase the size of an image, Photoshop has to stretch the existing image. The result can be blurry, and the file size can be larger than the file size of an original scan to that size.

The exception to this is when you change the resolution of an image, or change only the pixel per inch value.

Changing the Size of an Image

To begin, choose Image | Image Size. The dialog box, as shown here, opens.

Before you change the size of any image, make sure that the Constrain Proportions checkbox is checked. This ensures that when you change the size of an image, it will change proportionately so that your work doesn't end up looking like a funhouse mirror. When you change the width, you'll want the height to maintain the same aspect ratio. Once you've clicked the Constrain Proportions box, you'll see a Link icon appear next to the Pixel Dimensions and Document Size measurements, indicating that the dimensions will change in proportion to each other.

If you want to change the size of an image, check the Resample Image checkbox, also located at the bottom of the Image Size dialog box. Remember that when you click the Resample Image box, your image will be permanently changed. It's a good idea to make a backup copy of your image before you resample if you think you may ever need to edit the original image.

Once you've clicked both the Constrain Proportions and Resample Image checkboxes, all you need to do is to change either the Width or Height value in either the Pixel Dimension or Document Size areas. All of the other measurements automatically resize to match the Width or Height value that you have changed.

Changing the Resolution of the Image

To change the resolution, or pixels per inch, of an image follow these steps:

1. Make sure the Resample Image checkbox is unchecked.

2. Enter the value of the resolution you wish to use. As you see below, the Document Size information changes but the Image Size information does not change. This means that the image will print out at a higher pixel per inch setting, but the resulting image will be dimensionally smaller.

3. Click OK.

Cropping a Scanned Image

Often you'll want to crop in on a specific part of an image in order to reduce the size of your image or to eliminate extraneous detail. Cropping is a good way to create a focal point in an image so that the main subject stands out.

Cropping Using the Crop Tool

Click and drag the crop tool from the Photoshop toolbox. You'll see a bounding box, as shown in Figure 5-5. This bounding box works exactly the same as the free transform bounding box discussed in the preceding chapter. You can scale, move, or rotate the crop area without changing the image itself. When you're ready to apply the crop to the image, either double-click within the cropped area, press ENTER, or click the COMMIT icon on the options bar.

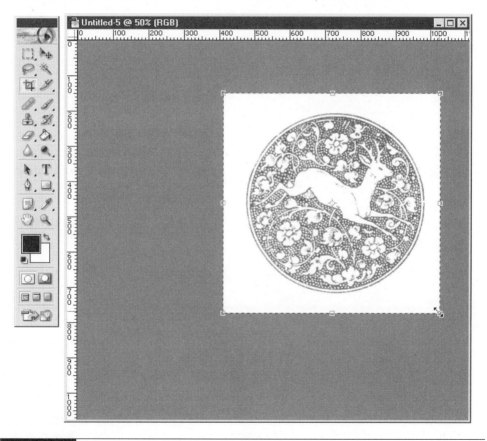

FIGURE 5-5   Use the crop tool to extract the portion of an image you want to keep.

Cropping Using a Selection

You can crop to any selection you've made using any of the selection tools, including any of the marquee or lasso tools. Simply chose Image | Crop.

Straightening a Crooked Scan

If you've ever tried rotating a crooked scan to straighten it, you'll know how frustrating it can be to try to do this by trial and error. Luckily, Photoshop provides a relatively painless way to straighten a crooked scan.

1. Click and hold the eyedropper tool as shown here to reveal the Measure tool.

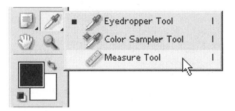

2. Click and drag the measure tool along the top edge of the scan you wish to straighten, as shown in Figure 5-6.

3. Choose Image | Rotate Canvas | Arbitrary, and the correct value will already be entered for rotation.

4. Click OK, and your scan will automatically be rotated to the correct degree.

Retouching a Photograph Using Tools

Photoshop is filled with tools and filters aimed at correcting everything and anything that can go wrong with a photograph. Since each photograph is unique, you'll want to experiment to become familiar with these correction tools.

FIGURE 5-6   With the measure tool, click and drag along the top edge of the scan to straighten the image.

FIGURE 5-7   The result of rotating the image to straighten it.

Using the Clone Tool

Use the clone tool to copy part of an image from one area to another area, or to a second image. Cloning is great for correcting small areas of a photo, such as removing a spot from a face, or a telephone line from a landscape. Cloning is also a good way to fill in information in an image that may be obscured or damaged, as shown in Figure 5-8.

When you use the clone tool, you copy information from one part of an image to another part of the same image, or a different one. Select the clone tool from the Photoshop toolbox. You'll notice that the options bar changes to give you options for your brush. These options include:

- **Brush Size**   Select a brush of the appropriate size and shape.

- **Mode**   As discussed in Chapter 2, you can set the mode of the cloning brush just as you would set the mode of a layer.

- **Opacity**   Adjust the opacity of the cloned image.

FIGURE 5-8   Cloning provides a great way of removing or copying a portion of the image.

■ **Aligned**   When the Aligned checkbox is checked, each time you use the clone brush, it will clone from the source image continuously as you move the tool. When the Aligned checkbox is unchecked, every time you use the clone brush it will clone from the same place in the image, over and over again.

■ **Use All Layers**   With this option you can clone from all layers in an image, instead of just the layer you are currently working on.

Decide which part of the image you will copy from, and ALT-click/OPTION-click the clone tool in that area. Click where you wish to clone to, and paint until you're satisfied with the result. You'll find that your best results come with cloning from an area that is very similar to where you are cloning to in texture and color.

As demonstrated in Figure 5-9, you can achieve some very painterly effects using the clone tool. This figure was created by cloning from an original image into a new image, using a large, soft brush with the opacity set to a low amount, and the Aligned checkbox checked.

FIGURE 5-9   Use the cloning tool to create painterly effects.

Using the Healing Brush Tool

The healing brush tool works much the same as the clone tool. You can use the healing brush to copy from one area of an image to another, or to copy from one image to another. As with the clone tool, you'll want to select the area you'll copy from, using ALT-click /CTRL-click. Then move to the area you wish to copy to and drag the healing brush to fill the area.

Using the Patch Tool

If there's an area of your image that has scratches or other flaws you'd like to remove, you can use the patch tool. The patch tool enables you to create a selection which it then repairs using a source you've defined.

If you click and hold on the Healing Brush icon in the toolbox, you'll see the patch tool. Select the patch tool, which changes into the lasso selection tool. Select Destination from the options bar. Select the area you wish to remove scratches and tiny defects. Then, drag the selection that you've created to the spot that you wish to use as a sample to correct the destination area. Click the Source radio button and the destination area is patched with the information from the source area you've defined.

Using the Dodge Tool to Lighten

You can use the dodge tool to lighten an area or highlight an area you'd like to draw attention to, as shown here. If the entire image is too dark, you'll want to use another approach. See the following section on Adjusting Contrast.

Use the dodge tool as you would a paintbrush, and use the original image as a source to lighten from. Once you select the dodge tool from the toolbox, you'll see the option bar change to display the following options:

- **Brush**   Select the type of brush you'd like to use.

- **Range**   Choose from lightening the shadows, midtones, or highlights in your image.

- **Exposure**   This setting determines how much you'll be lightening the image with each application of the Dodge tool.

TIP   *Holding down* SHIFT *while clicking or dragging any tool causes the tool to move in a straight line.*

5

Using the Burn Tool to Darken

The burn tool is very similar to the dodge tool, except that it darkens your image instead of lightening it. Click and hold on the dodge tool to reveal the burn tool. The options bar reveals the same choices of Brush, Range and Exposure that it does for the dodge tool.

Using the Sponge Tool to Intensify or Desaturate Colors

You can use the sponge tool to change the saturation, or intensity, of color in an area. The sponge tool doesn't affect the lightness or darkness of an area, only the color. Click and hold on the dodge tool to reveal the sponge tool. After you select the sponge tool, the options bar enables you to select a Mode. You can choose Desaturate, which reduces the intensity of the colors you apply the tool to, or Saturate, which intensifies the colors.

Using the Smudge Tool to Blend

The smudge tool is useful for blurring edges, and can be helpful for cleaning up a ragged edge, as shown here.

The following options are available with the smudge tool:

- **Brush**   Select the type and size of brush you'd like to use for smudging.

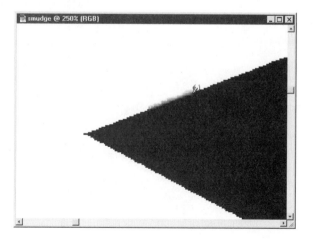

- ■ **Mode**   Select a mode for how the smudge tool interacts with the areas you smudge.

- ■ **Strength**   This setting controls how much smudging the tool does.

- ■ **Use All Layers**   This option enables you to smudge all layers in the image.

- ■ **Finger Painting**   This option enables you to use the foreground color to smudge with the image

Using the Sharpen Tool

If you have a small area to sharpen, you can use the sharpen tool to adjust the sharpness of edges. Click and hold on the smudge tool to reveal the sharpen tool. Drag the sharpen tool across the area of the image you'd like to sharpen.

Using the Blur Tool

Sometimes it's useful to blur a small area of an image that contains too much noise, artifacts from scanning, or other unwanted details, as shown here. You can use the blur tool to eliminate these defects. Click and hold on the smudge tool to reveal the Blur tool. From the options bar, you can adjust the Brush, Mode, and Strength of the tool.

Retouching a Photograph
Using Filters and Commands

Photoshop offers a variety of filters and menu commands you can use to adjust scanned images. You can choose to apply the filter to the entire image, or to just part of an image.

If you want to sharpen only part of an image, create a selection for the portion of the image you want to correct. If you create a selection, you may want to use a feathered edge to lessen the contrast between the adjusted area and the rest of the photo, as shown here.

You'll want to use filters rather than tools to correct large areas of an image. For instance, if the entire photo is blurry, apply the Unsharp Mask filter rather than use the sharpen tool from the toolbox. Filters and commands are good choices to correct images where the overall color balance or contrast needs to be corrected.

One Hit Wonders – Auto Levels, Contrast, and Auto Color

There are three adjustment commands you can use if the overall contrast or color of an image is off. These are single-click adjustments that can often save an image that seems hopelessly overexposed, or has a color cast. They're worth a try since you can always use CTRL-Z/COMMAND-Z to undo them.

- ■ **Image | Adjustments | Auto Levels**   This corrects an image that is too light or too dark.

- ■ **Image | Adjustments | Auto Contrast**   This corrects an image that may be lacking in contrast, or punch, by further lightening light areas and darkening dark areas. A washed-out image is a good candidate for the Auto Contrast command.

- ■ **Image | Adjustments | Auto Color**   If you have an image with a color cast, where the colors seem to be too red or yellow for instance, use the Color Balance command to correct them.

Applying the Unsharp Mask Filter

One of the most common problems with a scan is that it is blurry. There's a filter designed especially for this, cryptically named the Unsharp Mask filter. Contrary to its name, the Unsharp Mask filter actually sharpens the edges in an image. The results of unsharp masking is shown in Figure 5-10.

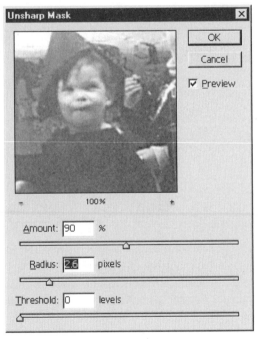

Choose Filter | Sharpen | Unsharp Mask. Make sure the Preview checkbox is selected so that you can see the effect your changes have. You can click and drag within the Preview window, as shown here, to view a particular portion of the image. You can also use the plus and minus controls below the preview window to change how much or how little the preview is zoomed.

You'll have three settings to experiment with:

- **Amount**   This controls how much sharpening to apply.

- **Radius**   This determines the number of pixels surrounding an edge to sample. The larger your image, the higher the number you want to use.

Original image

Amount, 50%; Radius, 1 pixel; Threshold, 5

Amount, 100%; Radius, 10 pixels;
Threshold, 0

Amount, 200%; Radius, 3 pixels;
Threshold, 5

FIGURE 5-10   The Filter | Sharpen |Unsharp Mask is applied here with different settings.

5

■ **Threshold**   This determines the amount of difference there must be between parts of the image in order for sharpening to take place, rather like the magic wand in reverse. The default value, 0, applies sharpening to all of the pixels in an image.

Applying the Dust and Scratches Filter

If you have an area of a photo with dust or scratches or any other type of small defect, you may want to experiment with the Dust & Scratches filter. Select the area you wish to correct, and choose Filter | Noise | Dust & Scratches. As with the Unsharp Mask filter, you can also experiment with the Radius and Threshold amounts for the best output for each image.

NOTE   *Make sure you're not adding your own dust to images as you scan! Follow your manufacturer's instructions for cleaning the scanner glass regularly.*

Adjusting Contrast and Color in a Photograph

Although a photograph may have major problems—overexposure, a color cast, a portrait of Grandma with blazing red eyes—you can adjust these and other problems using several different methods in Photoshop.

Adjusting Contrast in a Photograph Using Levels

When a photograph has an overall problem with contrast—it's either too dark, too light, or washed-out looking—you can adjust the light and dark values using the Levels command.

Select Image | Adjustments | Levels. Check the Preview checkbox so to view the changes in your image as you adjust the levels. The graph that looks like a mountain range is called a histogram. It's a record of lights and darks in your image, as you see in Figure 5-11.

The triangles below the histogram represent shadows (the black triangle on the left) and highlights (the white triangles on the right). In this example, you can see that most of the graph is weighted towards the right side. By dragging the left triangle towards the center, you increase the amount of shadow, and thus contrast, in your image. By dragging the middle slider, which represents midtones, you to darken the midtones. Adjusting levels is one of the quickest and most powerful ways to correct a photo in Photoshop, as shown in the corrected photo (Figure 5-12).

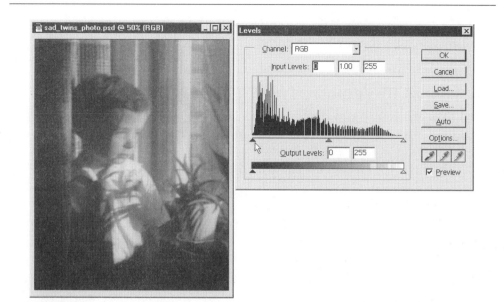

FIGURE 5-11   Use levels to adjust the contrast while previewing the changes in the image.

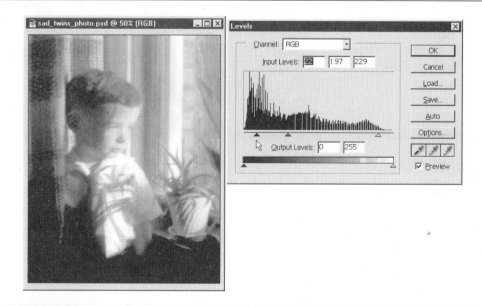

FIGURE 5-12   Adjusting the highlight and midtone triangle sliders to correct this photo.

Adjusting Contrast in an Image with Layer Modes

Another technique you can use to correct a photograph that has problems with contrast is to use Layer modes.

Adjusting an Overexposed Photo Using Layer Modes

If you have an overexposed photograph, or one that is overall too light, you can adjust the contrast by using Layer modes as shown here.

1. Duplicate the layer you want to adjust.

2. Set the Blend Mode for the new layer to Multiply.

3. Adjust the Opacity slider on the Layers palette to create the amount of contrast you want.

Adjusting an Underexposed Photo Using Layer Modes

An underexposed photograph is one that is too dark throughout the image. You can improve the contrast of an underexposed photograph using layer modes.

1. Duplicate the layer you want to lighten.

2. Set the Blend Mode for the new layer to Screen.

3. Adjust the Opacity slider on the Layers palette to create the amount of contrast you want, as shown here.

Adjusting Color and Saturation in a Photograph Using Variations

Often, a photograph will have a color cast, or an overall tone, that is not pleasing. You can easily experiment to find a correct color balance for such an image using a Photoshop command called Variations. Variations shows you a number of different options for your image, as shown in Figure 5-13.

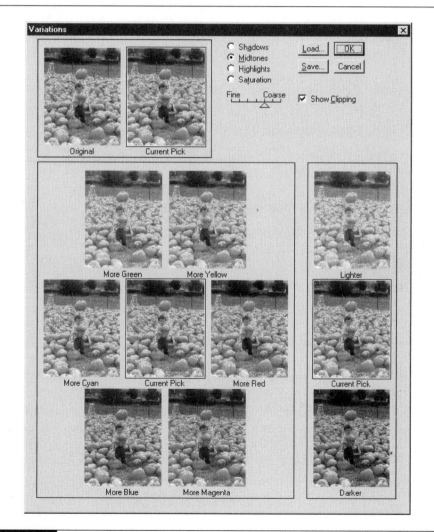

FIGURE 5-13   You can use the variations command to correct color balance.

Select Image | Adjustments | Variations. The Variations dialog box shows you previews of your image mixed with other colors. It also shows you a preview of your image adjusted so that it is lighter and darker. At the top of the dialog box, you'll see your original image, along with your current choice of Variations on that image. If you select adjustments, all of the thumbnails update each time you click.

The slider labeled Fine and Coarse in the Variations dialog box controls how much color shifting is shown in the previews for color and light and dark changes. If the slider is set to Fine, you'll see very minor changes. If the slider is set to Coarse, you'll see major changes between the current pick and the variations. The Show Clipping checkbox shows you the area of your image that is out of Gamut, or producing unprintable colors. If you're working for video or the Web, you'll want to uncheck this checkbox.

Correcting Red Eye

One of the more alarming things that can go wrong with a photograph is called "red eye." This happens when a camera's flash reflects on the subject's retina, but it is easily corrected in Photoshop. Simply use the sponge tool to desaturate the red area, as shown in Figure 5-14.

Colorizing a Black-and-White Photograph

If you're looking to create a vintage photograph look, you can colorize a black-and-white photograph to give it a soft, aged look.

1. Create a new layer in the image by clicking the New Layer icon at the bottom of the Layers palette.

2. Set the Blending Mode on the Layers palette for the new layer to Color.

3. Select the paintbrush tool, and select a large brush size in the options bar. Set the Opacity for the brush to a low amount, such as 10%, so that you can build up color. Enable the Airbrush capabilities for the brush by clicking the Airbrush icon in the options bar, as shown in Figure 5-15.

4. Begin painting over the areas you wish to tint, using whatever colors you like.

5. Adjust the Opacity slider on the Layers palette to adjust the amount of color you apply.

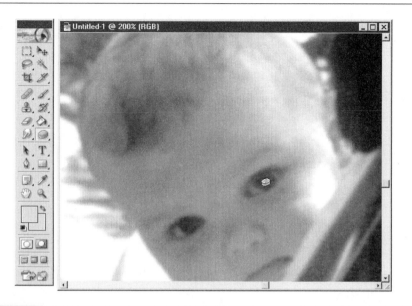

FIGURE 5-14   Use the sponge tool to desaturate and fix a case of red eye.

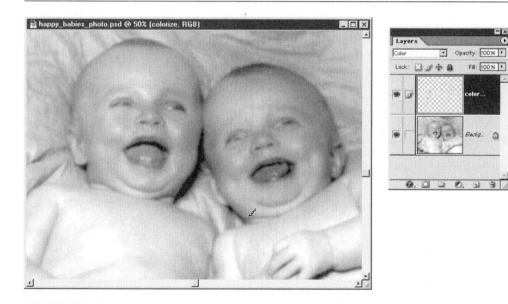

FIGURE 5-15   Selecting Color Blending Mode in the Layers palette allows you to airbrush color into the black-and-white photograph.

Chapter 6

Using the Paint and Fill Tools

How to...

- Use the paint and eraser tools
- Select options for the paint tools
- Adjust options for eraser tools
- Use the liquify tool
- Create gradients
- Create custom pattern fills
- Use the history palette

Paint tools enable you to express your inner Michelangelo, giving you the freedom to paint in an infinite variety of ways. Photoshop's paint tools can mimic traditional artists' tools ranging from pencils to airbrushes.

You can fill any layer or selection with a fill. Fills can be made up of solid colors, gradients, or patterns. Gradients are smooth transitions of colors, and they're a wonderful tool for adding shiny or metallic effects to type or objects. Gradients and patterns can add texture and depth to your image. You can also create custom gradients and patterns and save them for later use.

What would the world be like if you never had to worry about making a mistake? Well, it's possible in Photoshop. By using the History palette, you can move backward and forward through the steps you've taken with your image, undoing and redoing your work without losing steps in between.

Using the Paint and Eraser Tools

Photoshop offers two painting tools—the paintbrush and the pencil—as seen in Figure 6-1. To access the pencil tool, click and hold on the paintbrush tool to reveal the pencil. For each of these tools, you can select brush size and you can control various options to create different effects as you paint.

Use the eraser tool and the magic eraser tool to remove areas from your image. As with other Photoshop tools, there are many options you can choose to tune exactly how each tool works for you.

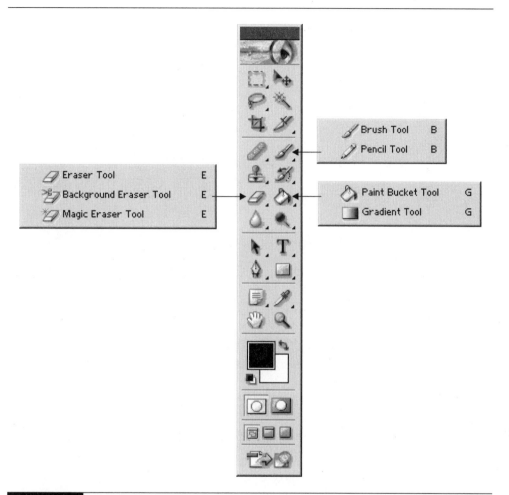

FIGURE 6-1   You can access various paint tools from the Photoshop toolbox.

6

> **TIP**   *To constrain any brush to a straight line,* SHIFT-*click. To create a straight*
> *horizontal or vertical line,* SHIFT-*drag your brush.*

Using the Paintbrush Tool

The paintbrush works like a real paintbrush, enabling you to create brush strokes
and painterly effects, as shown in Figure 6-2. You can use the paintbrush to create
impressionistic daubs or sweeping strokes of color.

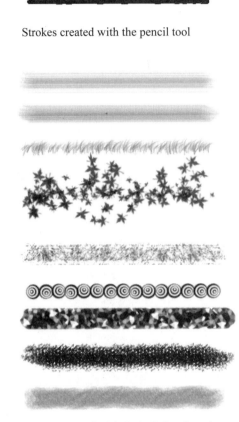

Strokes created with the pencil tool

Strokes created with the paintbrush tool

FIGURE 6-2   The appearance of brush strokes varies depending on whether they have been created with the brush tool or the pencil tool.

Using the Pencil Tool

The pencil tool produces hard, rectangular edges with the brush as shown in Figure 6-2. It's generally used to draw geometric shapes. The very smallest pencil brush, a 1 pixel brush, is useful for cleaning up small areas in an image, especially for low-resolution web work.

Using the Eraser Tool

The eraser tool removes color from a layer within an image. Use it by clicking and dragging the tool across the area that you want to erase. You can set the type of brush stroke to use for the eraser so it works like the airbrush, paintbrush, or pencil tool, giving you softer or harder edges, depending on which option you select.

NOTE *Be sure the layer you're working on doesn't have the transparency checked. A layer with locked transparency can't be erased.*

Using the Background Eraser Tool

The background eraser tool erases areas of similar color as you drag over them. This is useful, as the name implies, for erasing backgrounds from around an object.

Using the Magic Eraser Tool

The magic eraser tool erases areas of a similar color range. It's a little less flexible than the background eraser tool, since it offers fewer settings to change the way it interacts with your image.

Selecting Options for the Paint Tools

When you click on any of the paint tools, the Options bar displays several options for the brush tool, as shown in Figure 6-3.

The Options bar for the brush and pencil tools enables you to access and control a number of options for painting tools.

Tool presets   Brush preset picker   Enable airbrush   Brushes palette

FIGURE 6-3   The Options bar for the brush tool gives you access to Brush presets, Brush Mode, Opacity, Flow, and Airbrush controls.

- ■ **Brush Preset Picker**   Browse a variety of brush presets, from simple, round shapes to photographic images. You can also save, load, and edit brushes with this drop-down.

- ■ **Brush Mode**   You can set the mode of your brush just as you can set the mode of layers, as discussed in Chapter 2. Experiment with brush modes to yield some surprising and interesting effects.

- ■ **Opacity**   Opacity controls the maximum opacity of brush strokes.

- ■ **Flow**   Flow controls how quickly the painting tool applies the paint. Setting flow and opacity for a brush to a lower number can be helpful if you're working in a painterly manner, building up brush strokes as you work. Each time you apply another brush stroke over a previous stroke, the color builds up.

- ■ **Enable Airbrush**   With this option you can use the paintbrush as an airbrush, so you can add color slowly with a very soft brush.

- ■ **Brushes Palette**   The brushes palette enables you to create and edit many aspects of how a particular brush works. You can add texture to create realistic rough chalk effects, alter the range of color a brush produces, or create many more effects.

Using the Brush Preset Picker

To select from a variety of brushes, first select the paintbrush tool from the toolbox. Then click on the brush icon, as shown here, to open the Brush Preset picker, which displays all the available brushes you can choose from. You'll find that some brushes give soft effects and some give textured effects. To select a different brush, simply click on the brush you want to use. At the top of the Brush Preset picker, there is a slider that controls the size of the brush. Click anywhere outside the Brush Preset picker window to close it.

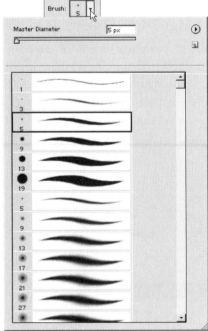

Brushes are stored in groups that Photoshop calls sets. Brush sets can be edited, saved, and loaded. You can create your own custom brushes and brush sets. Chapter 14 lists Internet sources that provide brush sets you can download.

The Brush Preset Picker Menu

You can do much more with the Brush Preset picker than simply select a brush. Click on the arrow in the upper right corner of the Brush palette to view a menu with more options for organizing, saving, and creating brushes, as shown in Figure 6-4.

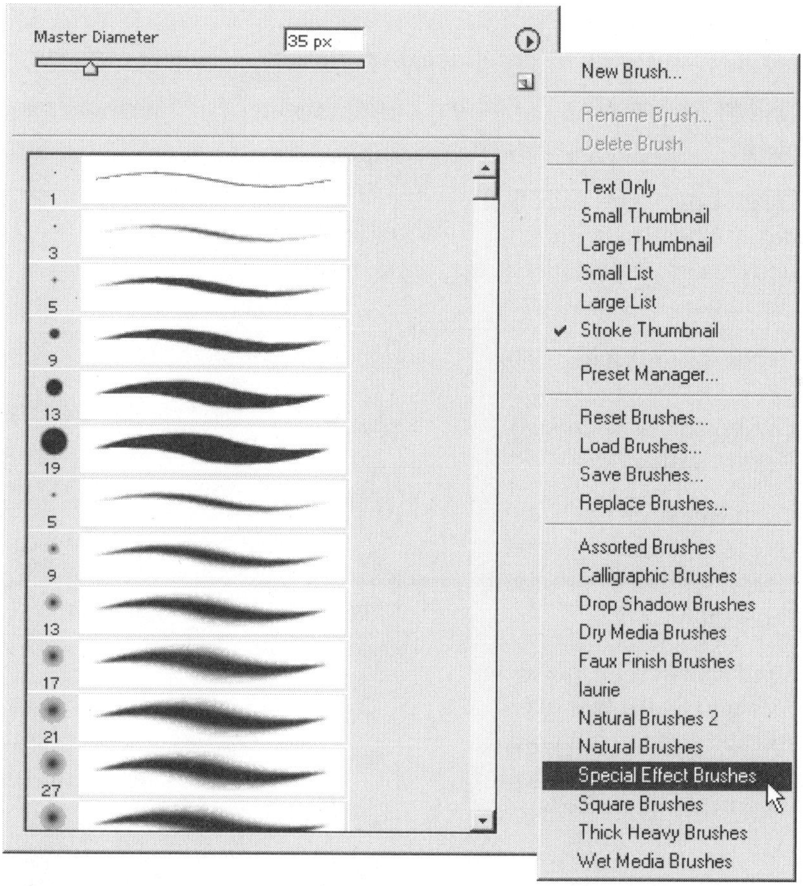

FIGURE 6-4   Brush palette options for organizing, saving, and creating brushes.

- **New Brush**   You can create a new brush based on the currently selected brush.

- **Rename Brush**   Since you can choose to display brushes with text, you may want to give your brushes distinctive names.

- **Delete Brush**   This option deletes the currently selected brush from the brush set.

- **Text Only**   This option displays text labels instead of a preview of the brush in the brush preset picker.

- **Small Thumbnail**   This is the default display of brushes in the brush preset picker.

- **Large Thumbnail**   This option displays a larger preview of your brushes.

- **Small List**   This option displays brushes with small thumbnails and text labels.

- **Large List**   This selection displays brushes with large thumbnails and text labels as shown here.

- **Stroke Thumbnail**   This option shows a preview of a paintbrush stroke created with the brush.

- **Reset Brushes**   Select this to reset the brushes to the default set that ships with Photoshop.

- **Load Brushes**   Choose this option to load a new set of brushes. Several additional brush sets are automatically installed with Photoshop.

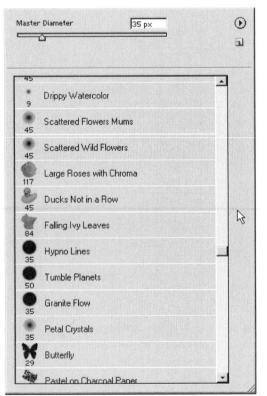

- **Save Brushes**   Select this to save your current brush set to your hard drive.

- **Replace Brushes**   This option enables you to replace the currently displayed brushes with a new set.

- **List of available brushes**   At the bottom of the brush preset picker menu, you'll see a list of available brushes. If you click on one of these brush sets, you'll be asked if you want to replace or append the new brushes to your current brush set as shown here. Replacing the brushes removes your current brush set and replaces it with the new brush set. Appending new brushes adds them to your current brush set, listing them at the end.

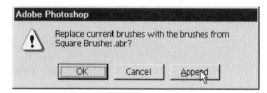

Adjusting Brush Presets

If you open the Brushes palette, located in the palette well or by selecting Window | Brushes, you will be able to adjust a vast number of settings that affect the way brushes works. To adjust the full range of brush attributes, make sure you have the paintbrush tool selected and an image open. Select the title of a brush variation on the left of the Brush Presets dialog box to edit attributes for that setting. Once you select a preset to begin with, you can experiment with options to create the type of brush you would like to use in your work.

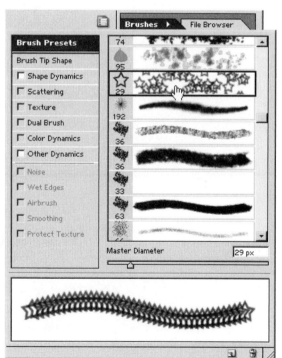

Brush Tip Shape

By selecting this option, you can choose a brush shape, the diameter size, angle, and roundness, hardness, and spacing for the brush shape.

- **Diameter Size**   Drag this slider to change the size of the brush, measured in pixels.

- **Angle**   This setting adjusts the angle for the brush. You won't see any change to your brush unless you also change the Roundness setting.

- **Roundness**   This changes the shape of a brush from a circle to an ellipse, as shown here.

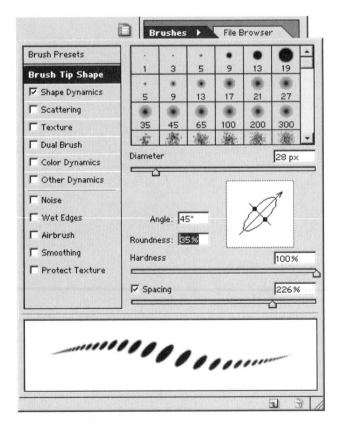

- **Hardness**   The lower the hardness setting, the softer the brush will be.

■   **Spacing**   For scatter brushes, you can determine how much spacing exists between each brush by changing this slider.

Shape Dynamics

When you select the Shape Dynamics option, you can change the Size Jitter, Minimum Diameter, Angle Jitter, Roundness Jitter, and Minimum Roundness of your brush. The jitter settings control the randomness of the brush strokes.

Scattering

When you create a scatter brush, you can alter the Scatter, Count, and Count Jitter to control the number of brush marks that are created with each brush stroke, as shown here. Scatter brushes are good for creating texture and backgrounds.

Texture

For realistic brushes that paint like watercolor, chalk, crayon, or oil paint, you can apply a texture to add to the depth and realism. In the Texture option, you can choose a texture from the preview, select a mode for the application, and experiment with the depth settings to find a pleasing combination of textural appearance.

Dual Brush

A dual brush uses two brush tips to create a stroke. You can alter the Blending mode, Diameter of the brushes, Spacing, Scatter, and Count to create infinite varieties of paintbrushes.

Color Dynamics

By changing the color dynamics of a paintbrush, you can add randomness to the range of color that a particular brush applies. You can change the Foreground/ Background Jitter, Hue Jitter, Saturation Jitter, Brightness Jitter, and Purity as

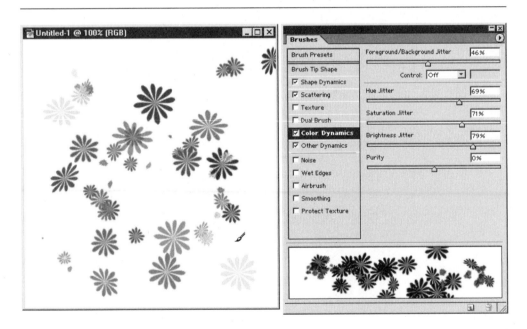

FIGURE 6-5   Use Color Dynamics to adjust the jitter and purity.

shown in Figure 6-5. All these controls affect the randomness of one aspect of color as the brush applies it. By adjusting these controls, you can create brushes that apply paint in daubs that vary slightly from stroke to stroke, adding a more handcrafted look to your work.

Other Dynamics

You can set the variation amount of the opacity and flow of paint as it is applied by selecting Other Dynamics as shown here.

More Brush Features

- **Noise**   Use noise to add a grainy effect to the edges of a brush.

- **Wet Edges**   The Wet Edges option gives a darker outline at the edge of a brush stroke. This mimics the way a watercolor brush stroke would appear, with the pigment settling along the outside edges.

- **Airbrush**   This option enables you to make uniformly smooth strokes, with soft edges. Choosing this option has the same effect as clicking the Enable Airbrush icon in the brushes Options bar.

- **Protect Texture**   Use this option when you want the same texture to be applied to all brush presets; for example, if you want to create the consistent look of painting on the same textured background in an image, no matter which brush you work with.

- **Smoothing**   The Smoothing option enables you to create smoother curves in brush strokes.

Creating a Custom Paintbrush

Any area of any image can become a custom brush. This allows you to create brushes that can save you time, or add texture. If you use a particular shape or symbol over and over again in your work, you can change it into a brush so that you can use it anytime you need it. You can also make patterned or textured brushes, as shown in Figure 6-6.

To create a custom brush:

1. Select an area of an image you'd like to use as a brush. For strong effects, use black or dark colors to create your brush. For subtler effects, use pale colors. For soft effects, you may wish to apply a blur filter to your image before defining a brush.

2. Choose Edit | Define Brush.

3. To edit spacing and the name of your new custom brush, click on its preview in the Options bar.

Adjusting Options for Eraser Tools

Because the eraser tools work differently from paint tools, you'll have different options on the options bar to choose from for the three eraser tools. If you've selected the Lock Transparency or Lock All setting for a layer on the Layers palette, you won't be able to erase.

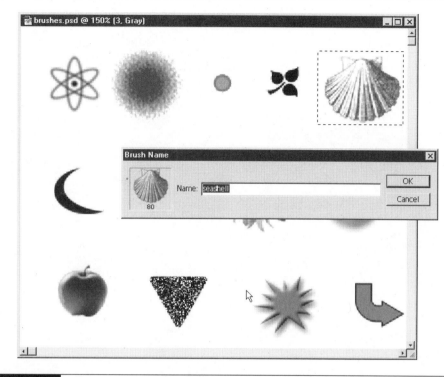

FIGURE 6-6   Create a custom brush from any area of any image.

Options for the Eraser Tool

■ **Brush**   Just as with the paint tools, you can select a brush size and shape for the eraser tool.

■ **Mode**   Choose from Paintbrush, Airbrush, Pencil, or Block tools to erase with. The Block is a square as shown in Figure 6-7.

■ **Opacity**   You can choose to adjust how much you erase with the Opacity setting.

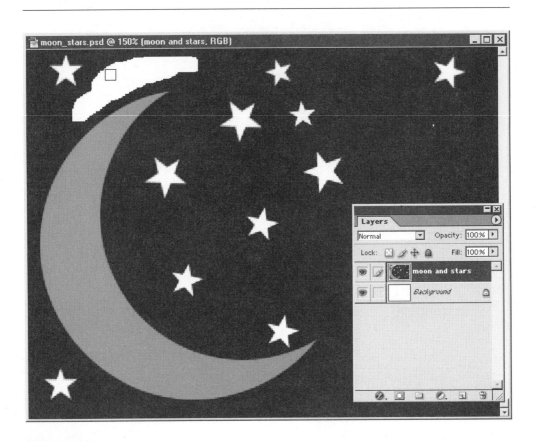

FIGURE 6-7   Erasing a portion of the black fill with the block eraser tool.

Options for the Background Eraser Tool

- **Brush**   You can select a type and size of brush from the Brush Preset picker for erasing, just as you can select a type of brush for painting

- **Limits**   When you select Contiguous, areas that are adjacent, or next to each other, are erased. When you select Discontinuous, all pixels, whether or not they are adjacent, are erased. Find Edges searches for edges.

- **Tolerance**   Setting the Tolerance to a higher number causes a wider range of colors to be erased.

- **Protect Foreground Color**   Check this checkbox if you want to avoid erasing the current foreground color.

- **Sampling**   Select Continuous to continue to sample as you drag the eraser. If you select Once, the first click of your brush determines what gets erased. Select Background to erase only the currently selected background color.

Options for the Magic Eraser Tool

The magic eraser tool works to erase pixels of a similar color value, similar to the way the magic wand tool creates a selection based on color range. This is a good tool to use if, for instance, the background you are erasing is different in color from an object in the foreground.

- **Tolerance**   As with the eraser tool, set the Tolerance to a higher number to erase a wider range of colors.

- **Anti-aliased**   Select Anti-aliasing to give the edge of the erased area a softer edge.

- **Contiguous**   Check this checkbox to erase colors that are adjacent to each other.

- **Use All Layers**   If you check this checkbox, you'll erase across all layers, not just in the currently selected layer.

Learning the Liquify Tool

The Liquify tool enables you to turn your image into a fun house mirror. You can bend, twirl, warp, or bloat your image using paint-like tools.

To open the Liquify dialog box, select Filter | Liquify. This displays the options and preview for the Liquify command, as shown in Figure 6-8.

You can select from any of the tools on the left, with the exception of the Freeze and Thaw tools, to start pushing and pulling your image right away. Just click and drag to distort the image. On the right side of the dialog box, you'll see settings you can tweak, including brush size and opacity.

The Freeze tool enables you to protect portions of your image from distortion. Click the Freeze tool and paint the area you want to protect. The protected area will appear as a semitransparent red mask. To undo the Freeze tool, select Thaw, which erases from the red mask.

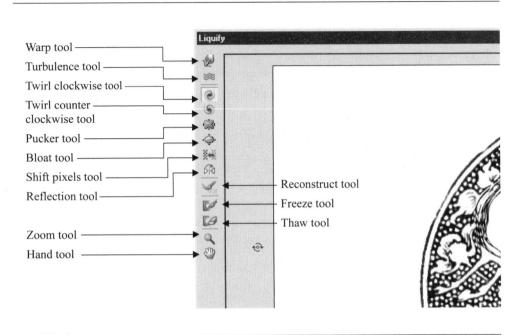

Warp tool
Turbulence tool
Twirl clockwise tool
Twirl counter
clockwise tool
Pucker tool
Bloat tool
Shift pixels tool
Reflection tool

Reconstruct tool
Freeze tool
Thaw tool

Zoom tool
Hand tool

FIGURE 6-8   The Liquify command

Creating Gradients

A gradient is a fill created of a smooth transition of colors. You can use a gradient to fade from one color to another, or you can create a multicolored gradient. Gradients are also useful for fading one area of an image into another.

Photoshop has a flexible gradient tool that enables you to create custom gradients that you can save and reuse. You can also apply gradients in several shapes, expanding the possibilities even further.

To create a gradient, click and hold on the paint bucket tool and select the gradient tool as shown here.

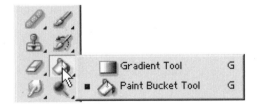

The Gradient Editor

On the options bar for the gradient tool, you'll see a preview of the currently selected gradient. This tool works much the same as the Brush palette works, providing you with access to saved presets and an editor for customizing. Click on the gradient swatch and the Gradient Editor appears as shown in Figure 6-9. Use this editor to create custom gradients, or to edit gradients. You can even create multicolored gradients that include transparent areas.

- ■ **Presets**   This displays a thumbnail of all of the currently loaded gradients. If you let your mouse hover over the gradients, you'll see the gradient name pop up. Click on any preset to load it.

- ■ **Name**   This is the name of the gradient. You can change the name here by typing in a new name. Click the New button to the right of the Name field to create a new gradient based on the currently selected gradient.

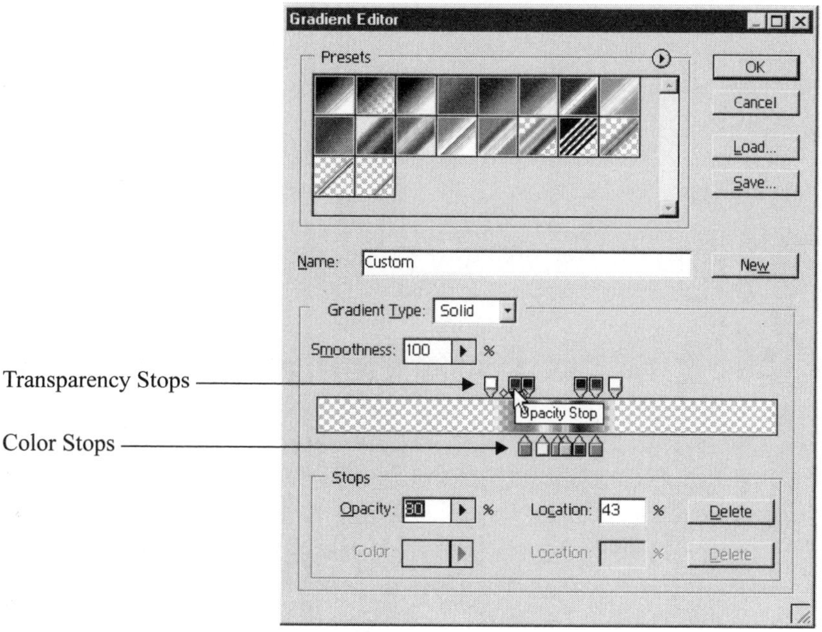

FIGURE 6-9   The Gradient Editor allows you to create custom gradients.

- **Gradient Type**   You can choose to have a gradient that is made up of solid color, or with noise added. Noise creates a gradient made up of narrow strips of color.

- **Smoothness**   The default smoothness level is 100%, and there's no compelling reason to change that.

- **Stops**   In the center of the Gradient Editor is a preview of the gradient you're editing. On top of the gradient are small squares called Transparency stops. These determine the transparency of the gradient at that location, as shown in Figure 6-9. When you select a Transparency Stop, the Opacity and Location of that stop become editable. The Opacity determines how transparent that portion of the gradient is. The Location is the position of the transparency stop. Below the gradient preview are the color stops. These determine the color and location of the gradient colors. When you select a Color Stop, the Color and Location become editable. The Color is the currently selected color of the color stop in the gradient. The Location is the position of the color stop within the gradient.

Creating a Custom Gradient

You create custom gradients in Photoshop by tweaking an existing preset to create a new gradient. To create a custom gradient:

1. Click on the gradient swatch in the option bar to open the Gradient Editor. From the presets presented, select a gradient to base you custom gradient on.

2. Type a name in the Name field, and click the New button, and as shown in Figure 6-10.

3. In the gradient preview, click a color stop. You can change the color by double-clicking on the swatch, which will open the Photoshop Color Picker. You can also move your mouse, which will turn into the eyedropper tool, over an open image and select a color from there. You can drag the color stop to a new position as shown here.

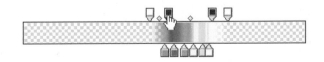

Gradient Editor

Presets

OK
Cancel
Load...
Save...

Name: rainbow-transparent   New

Create a new gradient preset

Gradient Type: Solid

Smoothness: 100 ▸ %

Stops

Opacity: ▸ %   Location: %   Delete

Color: ▸   Location: %   Delete

6

FIGURE 6-10   Create a new gradient by typing a name and clicking the New button.

4. To add a new color stop, click anywhere below the gradient preview. This adds a new color stop that you can adjust.

5. To add a transparency stop, click above the gradient preview. In the section marked Opacity, set the opacity to the percentage you want to use. A setting of 0% makes the gradient completely transparent, and a setting of 100% makes the gradient completely opaque, as shown here.

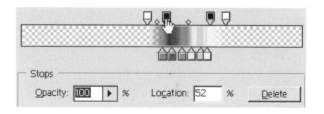

Stops

Opacity: 100 ▸ %   Location: 52 %   Delete

6. To delete a stop, select the stop and click the Delete button. You can also drag a stop away from the gradient to delete it.

7. To save the gradient, click Save. This enables you to create a new gradient set.

Applying a Gradient

To apply a gradient, select the gradient tool. Click and drag the gradient to apply it to your image. Where you begin and stop clicking and dragging the tool determines how smoothly or abruptly the gradient transitions from one color to another, as shown in Figure 6-11.

Loading New Gradient Sets

You can load gradient sets from your hard drive. Select the arrow to the right of the gradient to reveal the Gradient palette menu. You can select from a preset name, as shown here. You can also browse your hard disk by selecting Load from the menu. Photoshop asks you if you wish to Append or Replace your current gradient set. Append adds the new set to your current set. Replace removes your current set and replaces it with the new gradient set.

Gradient Options

Once you've selected or created a gradient, you can select different options from the options bar that will affect how the gradient will be applied to your image, as shown below.

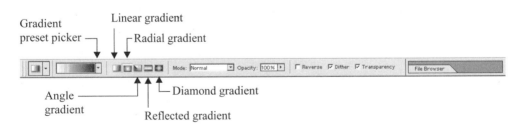

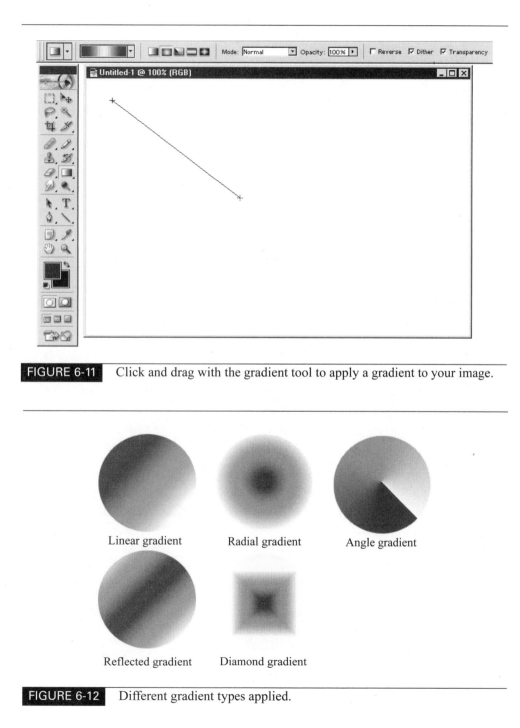

FIGURE 6-11   Click and drag with the gradient tool to apply a gradient to your image.

Linear gradient   Radial gradient   Angle gradient

Reflected gradient   Diamond gradient

FIGURE 6-12   Different gradient types applied.

6

- **Gradient Shape** You can apply gradients in a number of shapes. From left to right, these shapes are Linear Gradient, Radial Gradient, Angle Gradient, Reflected Gradient, and Diamond Gradient. You can see each of these differently shaped gradients applied to the same shape in Figure 6-12.

- **Mode** Changing the mode of a gradient can yield some surprising and exciting results. In Figure 6-13 a simple radial gradient was applied to the same image four times. The mode of the gradient was set to Difference.

- **Opacity** You can adjust the opacity of the gradient you apply, creating more subtle effects.

- **Reverse** To reverse the order of the colors in your gradient fill, select the Reverse checkbox.

- **Dither** To create a smoother blend of colors, select Dither.

- **Transparency** To eliminate transparency from a gradient you're using, deselect the Transparency checkbox.

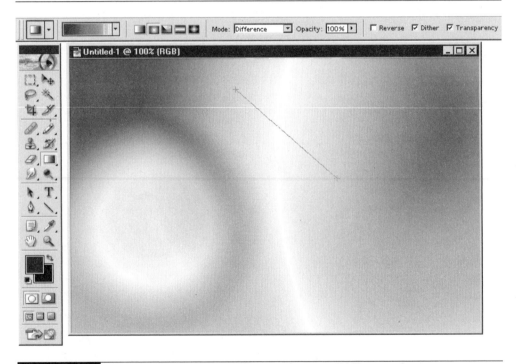

FIGURE 6-13 Experiment with a gradient mode set to Difference for some surprising results.

Creating Custom Pattern Fills

You can create unique patterns and textures in Photoshop to add interest to your image. Photoshop also comes with a number of pattern sets. You can also create your own custom fills.

To create a custom fill:

1. Select an area of an image you'd like to use as a fill. If you want to use an entire image as a fill, you don't need to create a selection.

2. Choose Edit | Define Pattern. This opens the Pattern Name dialog box. Enter a name for your pattern, as shown below.

3. Next, select an area of your image you want to fill with the pattern using a selection tool.

4. Select Edit | Fill. In the box marked Use, select Pattern. Click the down arrow to browse the Pattern picker and select the pattern you want to use, as shown in Figure 6-14. Click OK, and your pattern is applied to the selected area.

The custom fills you create are useful, not only for creating patterned areas in your image, but for creating textured brushes. To use a pattern in a brush, open the Brushes palette, select the Texture option, and click the Pattern picker to select a pattern to use with a brush.

Using the History Palette

We've all experienced that moment when we wish we could turn back the clock and return to an earlier state of working on an image. The Photoshop History palette enables you to do exactly that. You can use the History palette to go back to a previous state, and to delete things you've done to an image. If you decide that applying that filter three steps back was a bad idea, the History palette enables you to delete that step and the steps following it. With the History palette you can also create a new image from states of an image. This new image is called a snapshot.

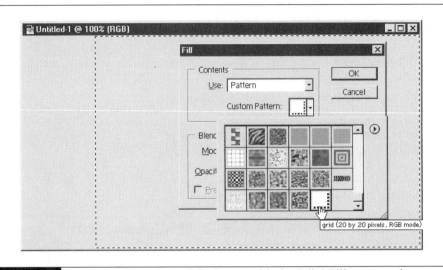

FIGURE 6-14 You can fill an area of the image with the Edit | Fill command.

The History palette does have limitations. Once you close Photoshop, or the image you're working on, the History palette is cleared. You can't access the History from a previous session. The History palette is a memory hog, so it lists only the previous 20 states. Photoshop automatically deletes older states in order to free up memory.

Going Back in Time with the History Palette

To open the History palette, choose Window | History. As shown in Figure 6-15, every alteration you've made to the current image is shown in the History palette.

At the top of the History palette is a thumbnail of a snapshot of the image you're working on. A snapshot is a temporary copy of any state of the image. Select a snapshot to work from that state of the image.

> **NOTE** *Histories and snapshots aren't saved with your image. When you close an image the snapshot is deleted.*

When you select a History state, the states below it become grayed out. If you click the Delete icon, you delete that state and all states following that state.

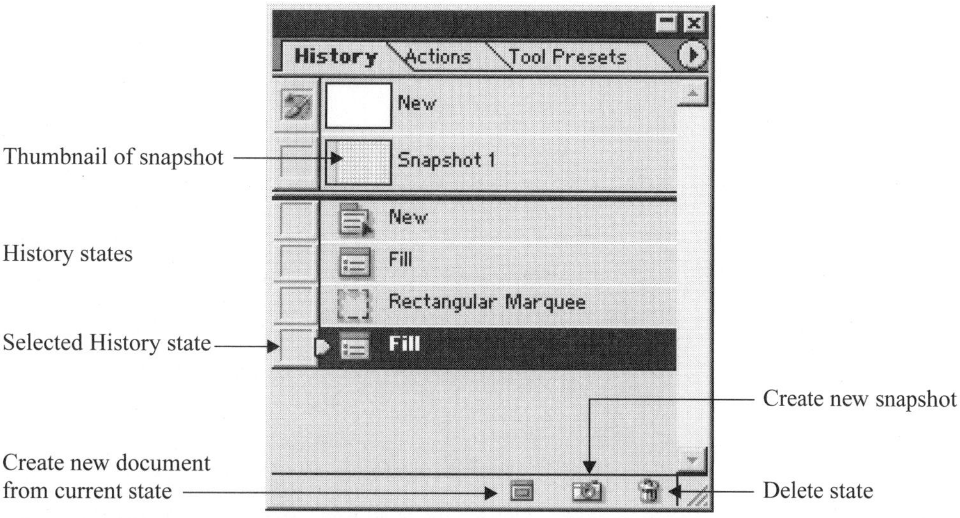

Thumbnail of snapshot

History states

Selected History state

Create new document
from current state

Create new snapshot

Delete state

6

FIGURE 6-15   The History palette.

Deleting a Single History State

There are times when you may want to go back and undo a single step without
affecting the steps that follow it. To delete a single history state, and not the
following states, do the following:

1. From the flyout menu on the History palette, select History Options, then
   Allow Non-Linear History as shown below.

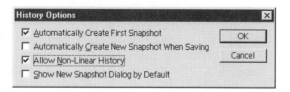

2. Select the state you wish to delete in the History palette.

3. Click the Delete icon at the bottom of the History palette.

Chapter 7

Adding Type

How to...

- ■ Edit type
- ■ Use the character palette
- ■ Create paragraph text
- ■ Copy and paste type from another application
- ■ Find and replace text
- ■ Spell check text
- ■ Rasterize type
- ■ Rotate type
- ■ Change the opacity and blending mode of type
- ■ Exchange files with editable type

Adding type to an image in Photoshop is simple and easy. In this chapter, you'll learn how to add distortions to type—bending and twirling the letters to a number of fascinating shapes. You'll learn how to control the spacing between and around type with precision.

Type layers are different from regular layers in Photoshop, because type remains editable. You can change the font, size, color, and spacing of your type at any time as long as you save your image in the native Photoshop PSD format.

Editing Type

When you click the type tool on your image, you can start typing and immediately create type. The type is automatically created on its own new layer. You'll notice a T next to the layer preview in the Layers palette, indicating that it is a type layer. Type layers are different from regular layers, and type layers have some limitations. You can't add anything to a type layer other than type. You can't apply a gradient or fill to a type layer, unless you use the Layer Effects, which we'll cover in the next chapter.

One of the biggest bonuses to Adobe's type tool is that the text remains editable. This gives you great flexibility. Type is created in a vector format, which means if you decide to change the typeface, color, or spelling, you can do so quickly and easily. If you resize your image, the type is automatically resized without loss of quality.

Vectors are outlines, while bitmaps are made up of pixels. Vectors are more flexible, since they scale without loss of quality. You can change type from vector format to bitmap format by rasterizing it. There are several reasons why you might want to change type from its editable vector form into a bitmap. If you're saving a file to anything other than the Photoshop PSD format, the type is automatically rasterized when you select Layer | Flatten Image. There are also limitations to what you can do to a vector type layer. For instance, you can't apply a filter to a type layer, or use any of the paint tools on a type layer.

While you're using type, remember that you aren't limited to just letters and numbers. There's a universe of dingbat, or symbol, typefaces available that you can use to add everything from professional looking bullets to funky, hand drawn sketches to your image, as shown here. In Chapter 14 you'll find a list of places on the Web to find downloadable fonts.

Type Options Bar

Once you click the type tool on your image, you'll see the options bar, as shown in Figure 7-1. You'll be able to control a number of features for your type from the options bar.

- ■ **Create a Text Layer**   This is the default for the type tool. With this button selected, you'll create a new type layer when you click on your image with the type tool.

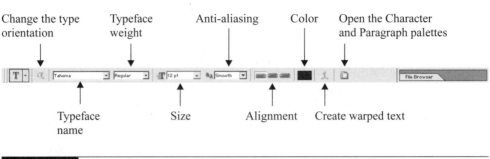

Change the type orientation — Typeface weight — Anti-aliasing — Color — Open the Character and Paragraph palettes

Typeface name — Size — Alignment — Create warped text

FIGURE 7-1 The type options bar offers unlimited formatting options.

- **Change the Type Orientation** Horizontal type is the default orientation for type. If you want your type to be oriented vertically, click this button. Vertical type is more difficult to read than horizontal type, so you'll want to keep it to a minimum. This is a useful option for creating a border using characters from a dingbat typeface.

- **Typeface Name** Click on the arrow next to the currently selected typeface name and you can scroll through a list of all of the fonts you have installed on your system. If you install new fonts, they won't show up until you restart Photoshop.

- **Typeface Weight** If you have more than one style of a typeface installed, such as bold or italic, you can select the style here by clicking on the arrow that points down as shown in Figure 7-2.

- **Size** Select a size for your type here. The units of measurement are set under Edit | Preferences | Units & Rulers. If it seems like you're getting inconsistent type sizes in relationship to your image, it might be useful to know that type sizes are related to the resolution of an image.

- **Anti-Aliasing** If you're using type at a low resolution, you'll want to experiment with the Anti-aliasing settings to find what works best for you. You can choose from None, Sharp, Crisp, Strong, or Smooth, as shown in Figure 7-3.

- **Alignment** Click an icon to center your type or to align it to the left or to the right.

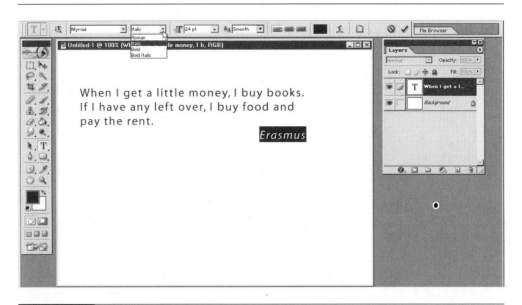

FIGURE 7-2   Select the typeface style by clicking the typeface weight drop-down arrow.

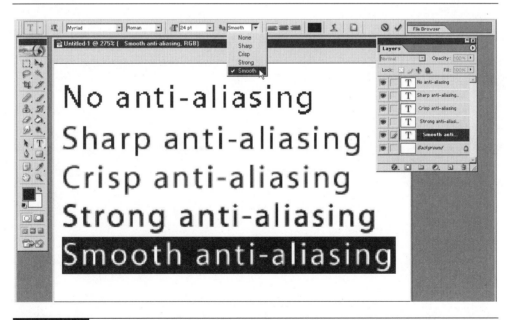

FIGURE 7-3   Choosing an Anti-aliasing setting may improve the text quality dependent upon the text's font and size.

■ **Color** Click the color swatch to bring up the Photoshop Color Picker to change the color of the type. You can even make each letter a different color if you like.

■ **Create Warped Text** In order to create warped text, you first need to create text. Make sure the text is selected, and click the icon on the options bar for Create Warped Text. As shown in Figure 7-4, you have a variety of shapes that you can use to distort your text. Once you've selected a shape for the distortion, you can tweak the amount of Bend as well as Horizontal and Vertical Distortion.

■ **Palettes** Click this icon to open the Character and Paragraph palettes. You can edit more type attributes with these palettes, which are described later in this chapter.

FIGURE 7-4   Examples of experimenting with the warp text feature.

Editing Existing Type

Once you've made the adjustments to your type using the options bar, you may find yourself stuck. You are limited to what you can do to your image until you exit the type editing mode. This can be a little disconcerting, but it's easy to exit the editing mode. Press ENTER, or check the Commit checkbox, located in the options bar.

To edit existing type, select the type layer you want to edit. Select the type tool from the toolbox, and use it to highlight the portion of the type you want to edit. You can edit all of the type or just a portion of the type, as shown here. You can change the color, alignment, spacing, or font of individual letters or words.

7

TIP   *To select all the type on the layer, double-click on the thumbnail of the type layer in the Layers palette.*

Using the Character Palette

The Character palette duplicates some of the functions from the options bar, including font name, weight, size, and color. But it also offers you ways to tweak settings for spacing and scale of type that can add elegance and precision.

- **Leading**   Leading is the amount of space between lines of text. The default setting is Auto. Generally, leading is set to a slightly larger size than the type, so 12-point type would have about 14 points of space between lines of type. To add more "breathing room," it's sometimes a good idea to add extra space between lines of type by increasing the leading.

- **Tracking**   Tracking is the overall spacing between letters. You can add more space between letters by changing this value to a higher number. To decrease the spacing between letters, you can use a negative number, as shown in Figure 7-5.

- **Vertically Scale**   You can scale your typeface in height by adjusting this number. Most typefaces are carefully created to read well without changing the scale, so use the Vertical and Horizontal scale with care.

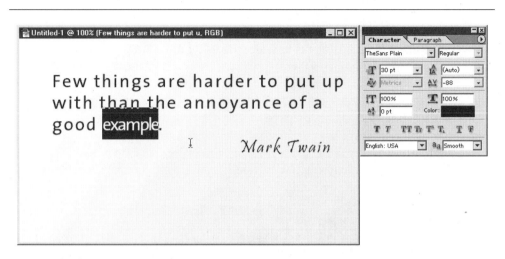

FIGURE 7-5 Tracking letters.

- **Horizontally Scale**   You can choose to scale your type horizontally with this setting.

- **Baseline Shift**   For mathematical formulas, adding a trademark symbol, or other special effects, you can set the Baseline Shift to a positive number to shift the type upwards, or a negative number to shift the type downwards.

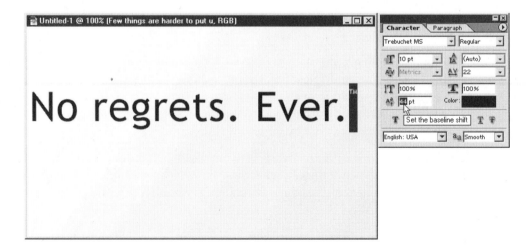

In addition to using the options on the Character palette, you can use several additional and often overlooked type options on the menu for the Character palette. These options are displayed below.

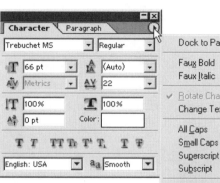

- **Faux Bold**   If you don't have the bold version of a font installed, you can fake it by selecting Faux Bold from the Character menu.

- **Faux Italic**   Faux Italic tilts your font to the right, as shown in Figure 7-6.

- **All Caps**   This option changes all type to uppercase letters.

FIGURE 7-6   Faux italics skews your text to give it a slanted look.

- ■ **Small Caps** This option changes lowercase letters to small uppercase letters, as shown in Figure 7-7.

- ■ **Superscript** This option automatically creates a baseline shift and sizes the type up.

- ■ **Subscript** Select this option to create a baseline shift downwards.

- ■ **Underline** Add a line beneath your type with this option.

- ■ **Strikethrough** Strikethrough adds a line through the selected type.

Creating a Type Mask

If you want to create a mask or selection for your type, rather than create type filled with the current foreground color, select this tool, available when you click and hold on the text tool. The type mask tool does not create a new layer for your text, but adds a selection in the shape of type, as shown in Figure 7-8.

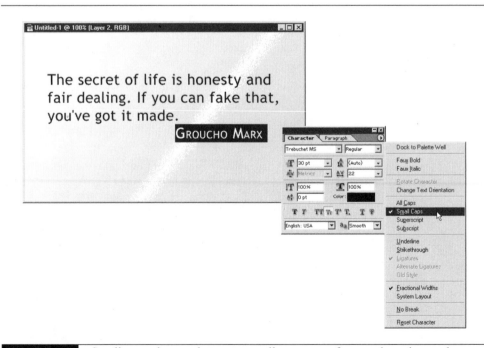

FIGURE 7-7   Small caps changes letters to small uppercase form and can be used effectively as in this example to list a person's name.

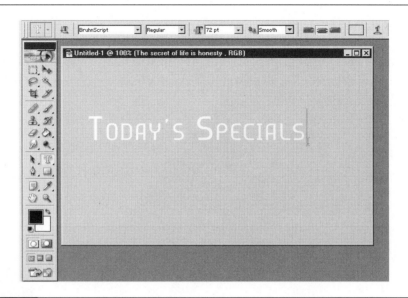

FIGURE 7-8   The type mask tool adds a selection in the shape of type.

Creating Paragraph Text

Paragraph text is useful for large blocks of type. You can set indents and paragraph spacing in addition to the type attributes that you can set through the Character palette and options bar.

To add paragraph type to an image, select the type tool, then click and drag to create a rectangle, or frame, that the text will flow into. To change the size of the frame for the paragraph, drag any of the handles located on the sides of the frame, as shown here. The text flows into the adjusted frame size.

The Paragraph Palette

If you will be adding large blocks of text to an image in Photoshop, you'll find the options on the Paragraph palette helpful. You can adjust the formatting for a single paragraph by highlighting it with the text tool. Otherwise, paragraph formatting is applied to all text on a layer.

- ■ **Alignment** You can choose to align your text left, center, or right by clicking one of these icons.

- ■ **Justification** Justification forces type to the left and right edges of the paragraph frame. The justification icons control how the last line in a paragraph is handled. Left aligns the last line with the left edge of the paragraph frame, right justify does the opposite. Center centers the last line, and Justify all forces the last line to span the entire frame.

- ■ **Indent** This option enables you to control the indentation of a paragraph from the left and right edges of the frame, which is useful if you're creating bulleted lists or tables. You can also set how much the first line of a paragraph is indented.

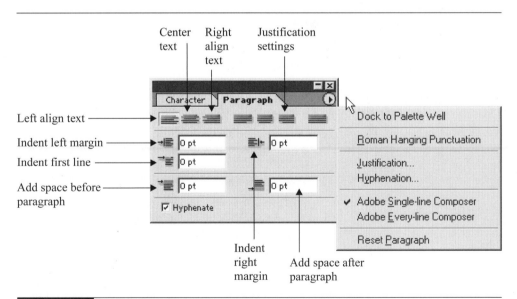

FIGURE 7-9 The settings on the Paragraph palette enable you to control how blocks of text appear in your image.

Copying and Pasting Type from Another Application

You can add large blocks of type from another application, such as Microsoft Word, or a web browser.

1. Highlight the text, then use CTRL-C/COMMAND-C to copy the text to the clipboard, or the computer's temporary memory.

2. Open Photoshop, click and drag the text tool to create a place for the text, and click within the rectangle.

3. Finally use CTRL-V/COMMAND-V to paste the copied text into the paragraph text block, as shown in Figure 7-10.

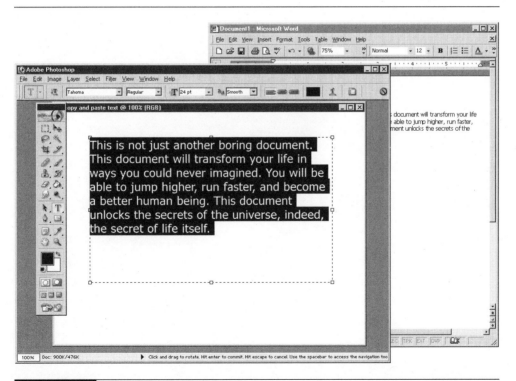

FIGURE 7-10   Here, we've copied text from Microsoft Word and pasted it into Photoshop.

Finding and Replacing Text

If you need to find and replace text, it's easy to do. Select Edit | Find and Replace. Enter the text you want to find, and what you would like to replace it with. This is especially helpful if you've used placeholder text or when you're working in a production environment where you are generating many similar graphics with text, such as banner ads for web sites.

Spell Checking Text

If you'd like to check your spelling, select the Type layer you want to check. Select Edit | Check Spelling to check the spelling of the text on that layer. If a spelling error is found, you can choose to ignore it, change it, or add the word to your Photoshop Dictionary, as shown in Figure 7-11, so that next time the word is spell checked it won't show as misspelled.

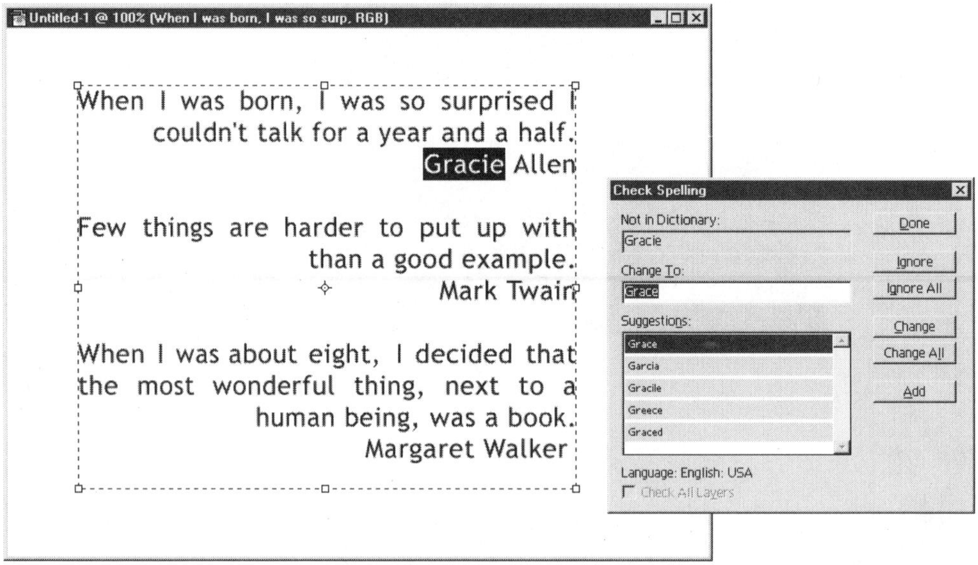

FIGURE 7-11   Checking the spelling within Photoshop is a similar process when compared to other application programs.

Rasterizing Type

If you want to paint within type, or apply a filter to a type layer, you'll need to rasterize the type layer first. Once you rasterize a layer, it will no longer be editable.

To rasterize a type layer, you can select Layer | Rasterize | Type, or right-click/CTRL-click on the layer name in the Layers palette and select Rasterize from the popup menu as shown here.

The T (type) label from the layer preview disappears, as shown here, to let you know that the type has been bitmapped and is no longer editable as type. Type is automatically rasterized and flatten with any other layers in your image if you select Layer | Flatten Image.

Rotating Type

In order to rotate type, you'll need to be out of type editing mode. Select Edit | Free Transform, or use CTRL-T/COMMAND-T and rotate the type as shown here. If you wish to apply a Distort or Perspective transformation to your type, you will need to rasterize the type layer first.

7

Changing the Opacity and Blending Mode of Type

You can quickly add interesting effects to your image by changing the Blending Mode of your type. Multiply, Screen, Soft Light, and Hard Light are especially effective applied over photographs or other background elements.

Changing the Opacity of the type layer can also add interest and excitement to your image by enabling background elements to show through the type, as shown in Figure 7-12. The type for this image was warped using the Create Warped Text icon on the type options bar. Then the opacity and mode settings were changed.

Duplicating type layers and offsetting them is an effective method of creating interesting type effects, as shown in Figure 7-12.

Experimenting with different layer modes and colors can produce some interesting results. In the example shown in Figure 7-12, the type layer behind was changed to a mode of Normal, and the color was set to white. This produced a three dimensional effect without the use of any special filters or layer effects.

Sharing Files that Contain Editable Type

In order to use a layer with editable type, you must have the typeface used to create the type layer installed on your computer. If you'll be sharing a Photoshop file with others, and want the type to remain editable, you will want to make sure that they have the same font installed.

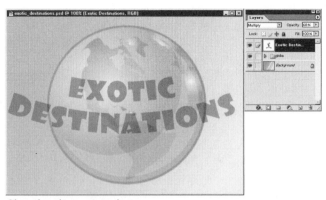

Changing the text opacity

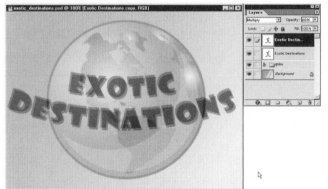

Duplicating and offsetting type layers

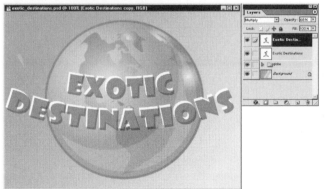

Creating a 3-D look by experimenting with different layer modes and colors

FIGURE 7-12   Creating special text effects by changing the opacity, duplicating and offsetting type layers, and producing a three-dimensional look.

Chapter 8

Creating Wow with Layer Effects

How to...

- Create layer effects
- Manage layer effects
- Apply a layer style
- Create a layer style

If you've been wondering how to achieve eye-popping effects for your images in Photoshop, then you'll want to learn more about layer effects. Layer effects include strokes, gradients, textures, bevels, drop shadows, and contours. You can adjust the color, size, and blending mode of layer effects to achieve results that are exciting and unique.

Once you've tweaked the settings for a layer effect, until you get exactly the result you want, you can save it as a layer style. You can save and load layer styles and use them again and again. Layer styles are useful, for example, if you want to create a consistent set of buttons for a web site. You can create layer effects that make a button look embossed, highlighted, or three-dimensional.

Creating Layer Effects

Layer effects are one of the coolest tools in Photoshop. With a few mouse clicks, you can add professional looking drop shadows, bevels, glows, and much more. These effects can be easily changed, copied to other layers, or saved for use on other images. Layer effects scale with an image, without a loss of quality. They also remain editable as long as the file is saved in Photoshop PSD format, which is a big benefit.

When you use a layer effect, it is applied to everything on the selected layer. You can add multiple layer effects to a layer.

NOTE *Layer effects cannot be applied to the Background layer in an image.*

To create a layer effect, you must first create a layer. Then click the first icon at the bottom of the Layers palette. A drop-down menu appears, displaying a list of all the different layer effects, as shown in Figure 8-1. Select any layer effect.

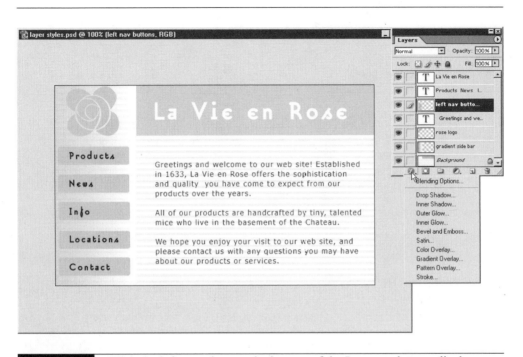

FIGURE 8-1   Click the left-most icon at the bottom of the Layers palette to display various layer effects in the drop-down menu.

When you select a layer effect, the Layer Effects dialog box opens, as seen in Figure 8-2. This is a large dialog box that may take up most of your screen, so you'll want to move it, by clicking and dragging on its title bar, so that you can see your image change while you experiment with various settings in the Layer Effects dialog box.

As you can see in Figure 8-2, on the left pane of the dialog box is a list of the various effects that you can apply. On the right pane are the settings that affect the layer effect, such as Blend Mode, Opacity, Angle, Distance, and Size. To the right of these settings are the OK, Cancel, New Style, and Preview buttons. You can also preview the settings in your image as you edit various styles.

Once a layer effect is applied, it appears in the Layers palette below the layer, as shown in Figure 8-3. If you've applied multiple effects, they will be listed individually.

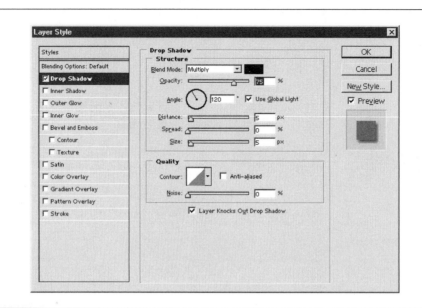

FIGURE 8-2 The Layer Effect dialog box enables you to select from a variety of different effects quickly and easily.

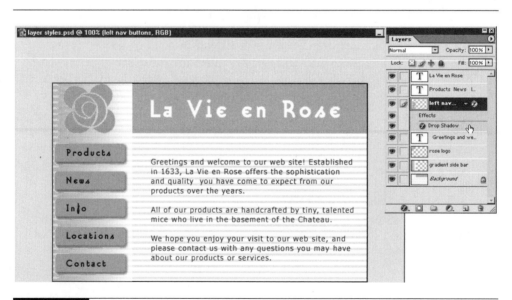

FIGURE 8-3 The layer effect is listed below the layer in the palette.

There are ten layer effects to choose from. You can combine and edit layer effects without changing your original image. While you're working in the layer effects dialog box, you can move between different effects by selecting them on the left side of the Layer Effects dialog box. You can toggle an effect on and off by selecting the checkbox next to its name on the left pane in the Layers Effects dialog box. The layer effects are:

- ■ **Drop Shadow** Adding a drop shadow is an easy way to create a three dimensional effect for images. You can change the color of the shadow from the default of black to any color by clicking on the color swatch to the right of the Blend Mode label. The default setting for drop shadows is 75% opacity, which can be a little dark and heavy, as shown in Figure 8-4. You may want to lighten the effect. Angle sets where the imaginary light source originates from—if you drag the angle to the upper right area of the circle, the drop shadow falls to the lower left. Use Global Light to link all effects in an image. If you change the Angle setting for any layer effect in an image, all the other Angle settings for which you have checked the Use Global Light checkbox also update to match that angle. This is useful for creating consistent three-dimensional effects across several layers. Distance is how far away the shadow is from the object on the layer. Moving a shadow away from an object can give the illusion that the object is farther away from the background as shown in Figure 8-4.

Default drop shadow
Opacity 75%; Distance 5 pixels;
Size 5 pixels

Opacity 50%; Distance 10 pixels;
Size 10 pixels

Opacity 30%; Distance 20 pixels;
Size 20 pixels

FIGURE 8-4   You can change various settings to create different shadowing effects.

8

You can also experiment with the Distance setting dynamically by dragging the shadow in the image window itself as shown here.

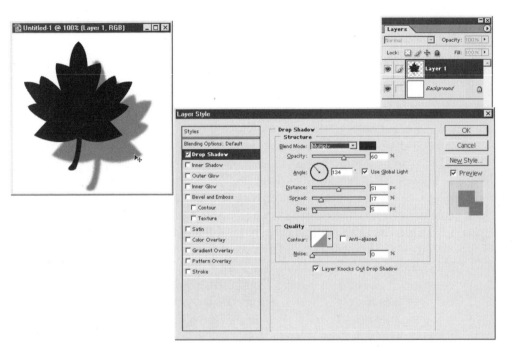

Spread sets how much bigger the shadow is than the original object, and Size sets how far the blur extends in the shadow. Contour governs the shape of the effect. Contour isn't very helpful for creating realistic drop shadows, but it can create some exciting effects for bevels. Noise adds noise, or dithered pixels, to the shadow to create a grainy effect, as shown on the right.

- **Inner Shadow** By selecting Inner Shadow, you can create a cut-out effect, as shown in Figure 8-5, where the Inner Shadow is applied to text. You can adjust the Angle, Size, and Opacity to create realistic results.

FIGURE 8-5   Creating an inner shadow gives dimension to the text at the top of the image.

- **Outer Glow** If you have been wondering how those glowing web site buttons are created, this is the effect that's most often used. In Figure 8-6 the effect is applied to text.

You can change the color of the Outer Glow by clicking the color swatch, or you can even apply a gradient by clicking on the gradient preview, which opens the gradient editor, as shown in Figure 8-7.

- **Inner Glow** Inner Glow is very similar to Inner Shadow, but you can't set the angle of the glow. The inner glow applies color equally from all sides of the object. In the example shown in Figure 8-8, an inner glow has been applied to the rose, and the Source, Choke, and Size settings have been adjusted.

- **Bevel and Emboss** If you'll be creating buttons for web pages, this is the effect you'll want to select to create a three-dimensional button. Bevels are also great for text. Click the Style button to see a drop-down list of the types of bevels that you can apply. An Outer Bevel creates a beveled edge outside

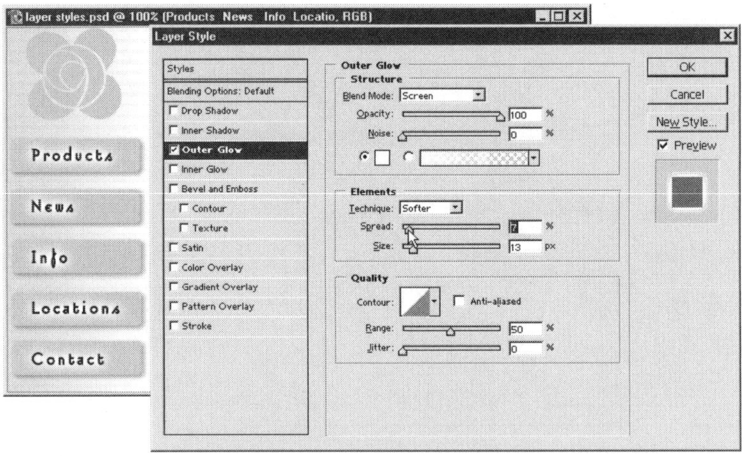

FIGURE 8-6   Outer Glow is an excellent effect for web buttons.

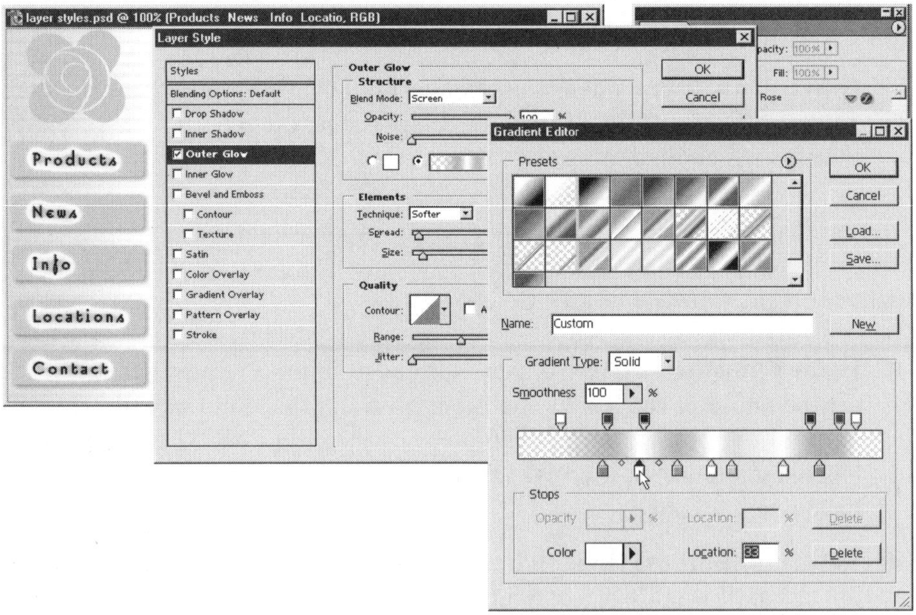

FIGURE 8-7   The Outer Glow color can be changed using the color swatch or by choosing a gradient fill.

FIGURE 8-8   Inner Glow settings including source, choke, and size settings can be set to apply color equally to all sides of the object.

the object on a layer, an Inner Bevel creates a bevel within the object as shown here. Emboss makes an object appear to rise out of the background. This can be especially effective if your object is created using the same color as the background behind it. Pillow Emboss adds a bevel inside and outside the object.

In order to use the Stroke Emboss effect, you'll first need to apply a stroke, then select Stroke Emboss from the Bevel and Emboss menu, as shown in Figure 8-9.

Outer Bevel

Inner Bevel

Emboss

Pillow Emboss

8

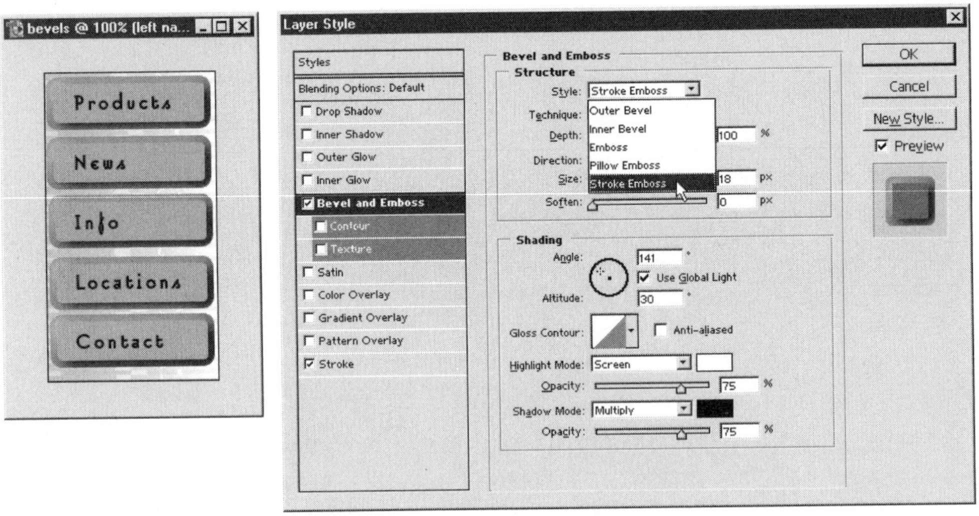

FIGURE 8-9 Create a stroke first, then select stroke emboss from the style list.

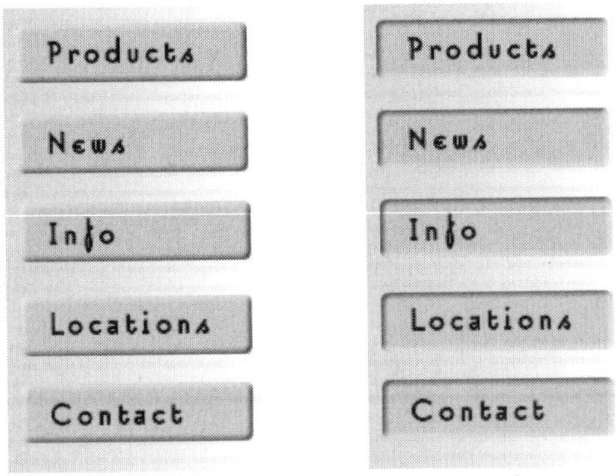

You can control the way the bevels and embossing are applied by selecting the Up or Down radio buttons. If you're creating web sites, creating a button with a bevel applied in the up and the down states can give the illusion of a button being pressed, as shown here, where an inner bevel was applied with a setting of Up, and a setting of Down.

Below the Bevel and Emboss setting on the left you'll see two other choices—Contour and Texture. Select Contour to choose a Contour shape, as shown in Figure 8-10, enabling you to create more elaborate bevels.

Select Texture to chose from a variety of textures. You can also choose Scale and Depth for the texture. The textures come from the current pattern fill set, so if you've created your own custom patterns, as covered in the preceding chapter, they'll appear in the list as shown in Figure 8-11.

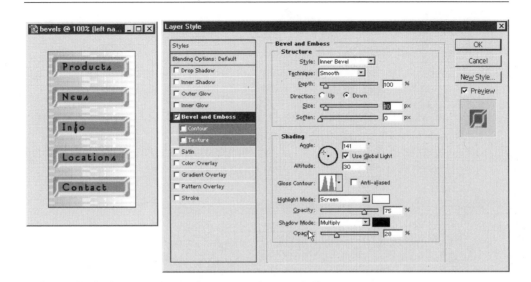

FIGURE 8-10   Set Contour and Texture features in the Bevel and Emboss dialog box.

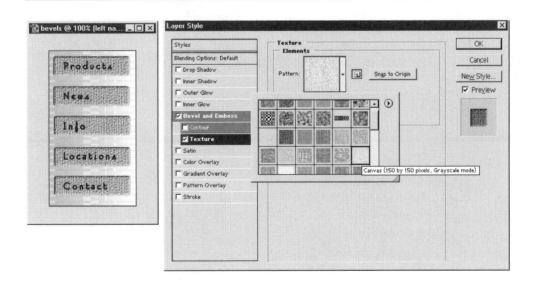

FIGURE 8-11   Setting a texture fill.

■ **Satin** A Satin effect adds a shadow effect to the object on the layer. This can be useful for creating metallic looks. Adjusting the Contour setting yields very different effects.

■ **Color Overlay** You can add a tint or color to your object by selecting Color Overlay. You can also adjust the Blend Mode and Opacity of the color.

■ **Gradient Overlay** This is the easiest way to add a gradient to text while keeping the text editable. Of course, you can add a gradient overlay to any layer with this option. You can select from any gradient, and change the Style, Angle, and Opacity to create the exact effect you want, as shown here.

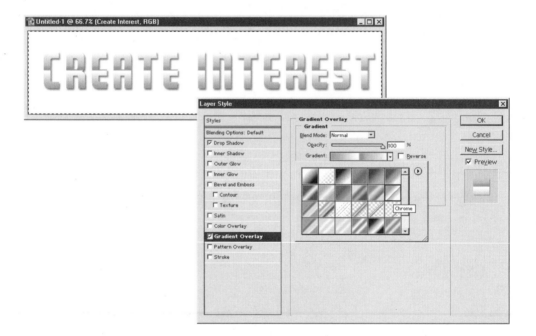

■ **Pattern Overlay** This option creates the same effect as the Texture setting listed under Emboss. You can add a texture from the patterns you have loaded or created when using Edit | Define Pattern, as described in Chapter 6.

■ **Stroke** Add a single color, gradient, or pattern outline to objects on a layer by selecting Stroke. You can change the type of stroke from Color to Gradient or Pattern by selecting the drop-down Fill Type menu, as shown in Figure 8-12.

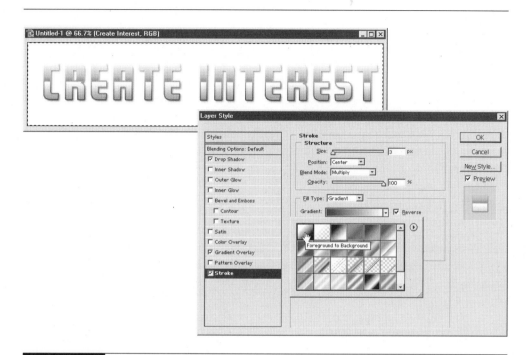

FIGURE 8-12   Change the type of stroke from Color to Gradient or Pattern.

Managing Layer Effects

There is an infinite number of looks that you can create using the Layer Effects command. You can also hide, copy, and delete layer effects after you have applied them. You can collapse and expand layer effects, just as you can layer sets, by clicking on the arrow in the Layers palette as shown here. You can also hide layer effects by toggling the eye icon in the Layers palette.

Hiding Layer Effects

A layer effect might get in your way as you're working—a drop shadow obscuring a layer behind it, or a bevel hiding the edge of an object—so you may want to toggle the visibility of individual effects on and off. This is easy to do in the Layers palette. Simply toggle the Eye icon to the left of the effect name to hide and reveal the layer.

Copying Layer Effects

If you want to copy layer effects from one image to another, or from one layer to another, it's a very simple process. Right-click/CTRL-click on the layer name to reveal a popup menu as shown to the right, or select Layer | Layer Style. Then select Copy Layer Style. Select the layer you want to copy to, and right-click, or click and hold on the new layer, or Select Layer | Layer Style, and choose Paste Layer Style. You can copy individual layer effects from one layer to another by dragging the layer effect to the target layer until you see a line appear beneath the layer, and then dropping the layer.

Deleting Layer Effects

To remove layer effects from a layer, you can click and drag individual layer effects in the Layers palette to the Trashcan icon. You can right-click, or click and hold on the layer label and select Clear Layer Style. Or you can select Layer | Layer Style | Clear Layer Style.

Applying a Layer Style

Layer styles are saved layer effects that you can apply to objects on any layer (except the Background layer). Layer styles are a good way to create a consistent look for objects, such as headings for a document or buttons for a web site. Like brushes, gradients, and patterns, layer styles are stored in sets that can be saved, loaded, and edited.

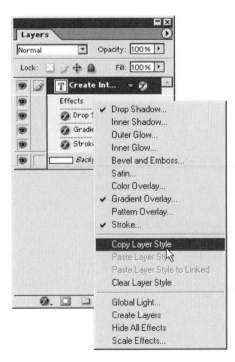

To find the layer styles, select Window | Show Styles. This opens the Styles palette, as shown in Figure 8-13, which you can dock and undock as you can with any palette in Photoshop. To apply a layer style, first choose the layer you want to apply the style to, then select any of the thumbnails shown in the Styles palette.

FIGURE 8-13   You can dock and undock any palette such as this Styles palette.

NOTE   *You can't apply layer styles or layer effects if the Lock All checkbox for the layer is checked on the Layers palette.*

8

Creating a Layer Style

You can create a new layer style by selecting the New Style button while you're editing layer effects in the Layer Effects dialog box, as shown in the following illustration. This adds the current settings as a preset to the Styles palette.

Deleting a Layer Style

If you've decided that you want to remove a layer style from the Styles palette, drag the preview of the layer style to the Trashcan icon at the bottom of the Styles palette.

Saving a Layer Style

To save a new set of styles, click on the popup menu on the Styles palette, as shown here, and select Save Styles. Enter a name for your styles.

Loading Layer Styles

You can load styles from your hard drive by clicking on the popup menu on the Styles palette and choosing Load Styles. Browse your hard drive to find the styles and select them to load them. You'll find more styles you can download from web sites listed in Chapter 14.

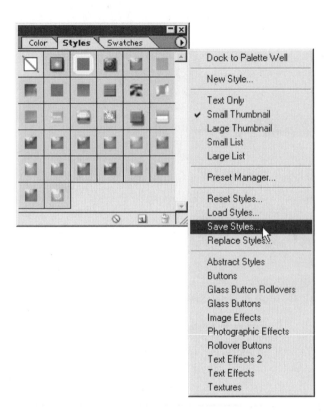

Chapter 9

Creating Special Effects with Filters

How to...

- Add artistic effects
- Go wild with filters
- Create three-dimensional effects
- Create edge effects

Filters enable you to change the appearance of your image with the click of a button. You can use filters to add a soft blur or create a sketchy or pop art look.

In Chapter Five, you learned how to apply corrective filters to clean up and improve scanned photos. In this chapter, you'll discover how to create effects ranging from artistic to wild. You'll also discover how to create exciting edge effects for your images, ranging from soft vignettes to high-tech pixelation.

Adding Artistic Effects

Before you apply a filter, you'll want to decide if you want to apply a filter to an entire layer, or only a portion of a layer. You can use any of the selection tools to choose the area you'd like to apply the filter. If you want a soft transition between the filtered selection and the unfiltered portion of a layer, consider feathering the selection by using Select | Feather, as shown here.

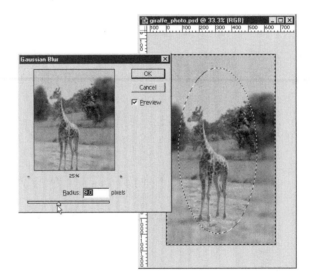

Under the Filter menu, you'll see a wide assortment of filters. Some of these filters use your currently selected foreground and background colors in order to create the filtered effect, as shown in Figure 9-1.

> NOTE
>
> *Your image must be in RGB or grayscale mode before you can apply filters to it. To change the color mode of an indexed image, or an image created in CYMK color, select Image | Mode | RGB.*

Under Filter | Artistic, you'll see a group of filters that you can apply to your image, as seen in Figure 9-2. These effects range from the subtle, such as Film Grain, to abstract, like Cutout, to eerie, like the Neon Glow filter.

The Artistic filters all have preview windows. You can change which part of your image appears in a preview window by clicking and dragging within the preview. There are also zoom in and out buttons located under the previews. All filters also have a series of sliders to enable you to control the way the filters are applied to the image, as shown here.

The original photo

Filter | Sketch | Charcoal applied, with the foreground color set to black and the background color set to white.

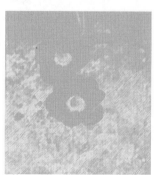
Filter | Sketch | Charcoal applied, with the foreground color set to light gray and the background color set to red.

FIGURE 9-1   The effect a filter has on an image is sometimes influenced by your currently selected foreground and background colors, as shown in these examples.

The original photo

Filter | Artistic | Colored Pencil

Filter | Artistic | Cutout

Filter | Artistic | Dry Brush

Filter | Artistic | Film Grain

Filter | Artistic | Fresco

Filter | Artistic | Neon Glow

Filter | Artistic | Paint Daubs

Filter | Artistic | Palette Knife

Filter | Artistic | Plastic Wrap

Filter | Artistic | Poster Edges

Filter | Artistic | Rough Pastel

Filter | Artistic | Smudge Stick

Filter | Artistic | Sponge

Filter | Artistic | Underpainting

Filter | Artistic | Watercolor

FIGURE 9-2   The Artistic Filters applied to an image.

You can add even more artful effects to your images by selecting one of the Brush Stroke filters as shown in Figure 9-3 and applying it to your image.

You can find further artistic effects grouped under the Sketch setting on the filter menu, as shown in Figure 9-4. These filters provide the same previews and assortments of sliders that the Artistic filters have. These filters are especially effective when used to create edge effects, which are discussed later in this chapter.

In addition to the Artistic, Brush Stroke, and Sketch groups of filters on the Filter menu, you'll find that the Texture group of filters also offers a good way to add an artistic touch to a rather plain illustration, as shown in Figure 9-5.

original photo

Filter | Brush Stroke | Accented Edges

Filter | Brush Stroke | Angled Strokes

Filter | Brush Stroke | Crosshatch

Filter | Brush Stroke | Dark Strokes

Filter | Brush Stroke | Ink Outlines

Filter | Brush Stroke | Spatter

Filter | Brush Stroke | Sprayed Strokes

Filter | Brush Stroke | Sumi-e

9

FIGURE 9-3   Apply Brush Stroke filters to an image for all kinds of results.

Original Photo

Filter | Sketch | Bas Relief

Filter | Sketch | Chalk & Charcoal

Filter | Sketch | Charcoal

Filter | Sketch | Chrome

Filter | Sketch | Conte Crayon

Filter | Sketch | Graphic Pen

Filter | Sketch | Halftone Pattern

Filter | Sketch | Note Paper

Filter | Sketch | Photocopy

Filter | Sketch | Plaster

Filter | Sketch | Reticulation

Filter | Sketch | Stamp

Filter | Sketch | Torn Edges

Filter | Sketch | Water Paper

FIGURE 9-4   The Sketch filters.

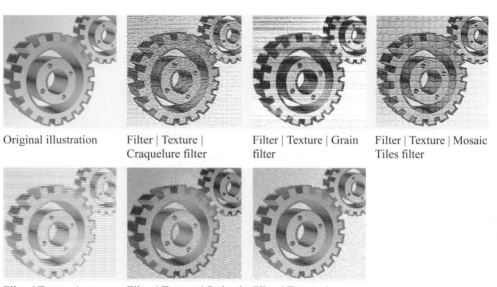

Original illustration   Filter | Texture | Craquelure filter   Filter | Texture | Grain filter   Filter | Texture | Mosaic Tiles filter

Filter | Texture | Patchwork filter   Filter | Texture | Stained Glass filter   Filter | Texture | Texturizer filter

FIGURE 9-5   Add a Texture filter to change the character of your image.

Altering a Filter Effect

You have to experiment with filters to find the exact effect you're looking for. The more you experiment with the Filter menu, the more familiar you'll become with the kinds of effects you can create. You'll find that combining filters can create more sophisticated effects.

Fading a Filter

If you like an effect, but it appears too strong, you can fade the effect after you've applied it. Apply the filter, then select Edit | Fade, as shown here. You can choose how much to fade the Opacity of the filter, and you can also select what Mode the filter

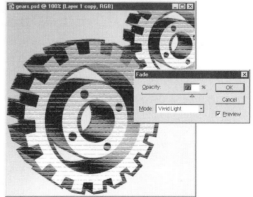

uses. Experimenting with the Mode setting in combination with a filter can provide some extremely interesting results.

Reapplying a Filter

To reapply a filter, you can select Filter and then select the last filter you applied, which is listed at the top of the Filter menu as shown here. You can also use the keystrokes CTRL-F/COMMAND-F. This applies the last filter you used, which is especially effective if you want to apply the same filter, using the same settings, to different layers in order to maintain continuity in an image.

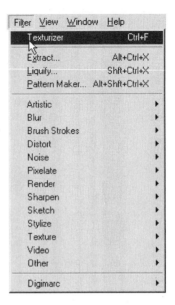

Going Wild with Filters

If you're looking for bold, exciting effects to create interest in your image, you'll want to explore the filters found on the Pixelate groups of filters. These effects range from dizzying to boldly graphic and highly stylized.

You've seen these filters used dozens of times recently in advertisements and in artwork in videos, television, and print, as shown in Figure 9-6. The Crystallize filter gives a fractal-like appearance to images, and the Fragment filter gives a high-tech look to an image. The Mosaic filter breaks an image up into large squares. The Pointillize filter uses the foreground and background colors to create a pointillist style, much like the style of the impressionist painter Seurat.

Creating Three Dimensional Effects

Want to create 3D effects without having to shell out for an expensive 3D program? You can create simple effects using the 3D Transform filter in Photoshop. Along with the 3D Transform filter, the Render group of filters also includes the Clouds and Lighting Effects filters, which can also add depth to your image.

original photo   Filter | Pixelate | Color   Filter | Pixelate | Filter | Pixelate | Facet
                        Halftone   Crystallize

Filter | Pixelate | Filter | Pixelate | Filter | Pixelate |
Mezzotint   Mosaic   Pointillize

FIGURE 9-6   With the Pixelate filters you can create some pretty wild effects.

Create 3-D Figures in Space

To create simple three-dimensional figures in space, follow these steps, which guide you through creating simple shapes and adding a cloud-filled background:

1. Create a new file, 500 pixels wide by 400 pixels tall by selecting File | New.

2. Select the Background Layer, and apply Filter | Render | Clouds to create a truly three-dimensional background effect. The Clouds filter uses your currently selected foreground and background colors to create clouds. For drama, make sure your colors have high contrast, such as dark blue and pale turquoise. For subtlety, use colors that are close in value to each other.

3. Create a new layer, and fill it with white, or whatever color you want your 3-D shapes to be, as shown in Figure 9-7.

4. Go to Filter | Render | 3D transform. You'll see the 3D Transform preview, as shown in Figure 9-7.

5. Click the sphere, cylinder, or sphere tool and drag it to add a shape to the preview window. To adjust the size or position of a single point on a shape, use the Direct Selection Tool, as shown in Figure 9-8. You can use only the Add and Delete anchor point tools with the cylinder shape.

6. To add a three-dimensional lighting effect to the shapes you've created, use the Trackball tool to rotate the shapes. By clicking and dragging from the

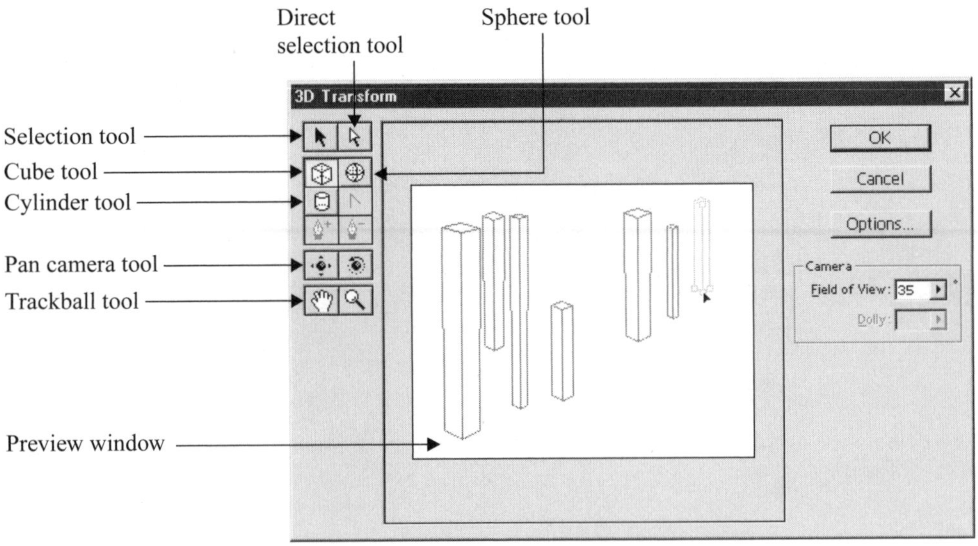

FIGURE 9-7   Using the 3D Transform tool.

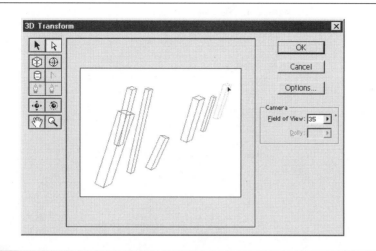

FIGURE 9-8   Direct Selection Tool.

right to the left side of the preview window, you rotate the figures about
180 degrees, which adds shading and depth to the figures, as shown here.

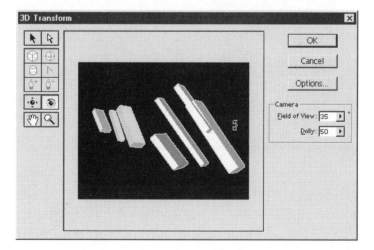

7. To finish the image, click the Options button on the right side of the dialog
box. To create a high-tech, blocky look, select Resolution: Low, and
Anti-aliasing: None. To create smoothly rendered figures, select Resolution:

High, and Anti-aliasing: High. Deselect the Display Background checkbox to remove the background, as shown here.

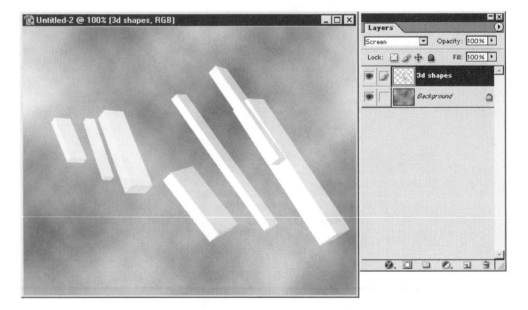

The final effect should look something like the example below.

Using Lighting Effects

By using the Lighting Effects filter in your image, you can increase depth and add drama. The Lighting Effects filter simulates the way light falls. You can control the amount and color of light that you add to your image.

Select Filter | Render | Lighting Effects to open the Lighting Effects dialog box, as shown below. The left side of the dialog box provides a preview of your image. The light is represented in the preview window by an ellipse with handles. In the center of the ellipse is the "hot spot," represented by a small white circle. You can drag the hot spot to reposition the source of the light. You can also drag the handles to change the angle and range of the light, as shown in Figure 9-9.

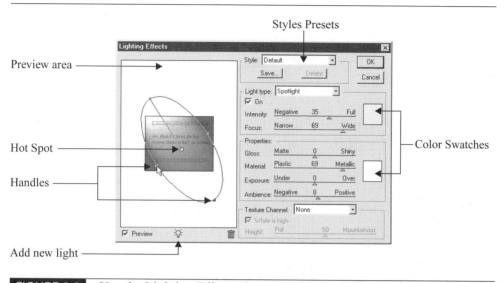

Styles Presets

Preview area

Hot Spot

Handles

Color Swatches

Add new light

FIGURE 9-9   Use the Lighting Effects dialog box to change the angle and the color of light.

To change the color of the light, click the color swatches on the far right of the dialog box. You can explore some interesting lighting effects by clicking the Style drop-down menu at the top of the dialog box.

You'll want to flatten the layers that you want to apply the lighting effects to, as shown here, to create a consistent three-dimensional effect.

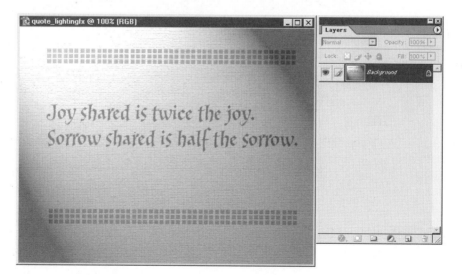

9

Creating Edge Effects

Although there are several third-party filters you can purchase to simulate different edge effects, you can use Photoshop selections and filters to easily create your own effects by following these steps:

1. Open a photograph or other artwork in Photoshop.

2. Create a new layer. Set the Mode to Screen.

3. Fill the new layer with white.

4. Select the part of the photo you want to keep unaffected by the edge effect. You can use any selection tool, including the rectangular or elliptical marquee, or the lasso tool. On the options bar, set the Feather amount to 10 pixels.

5. Fill the selection with black, which reveals your image as shown in Figure 9-10.

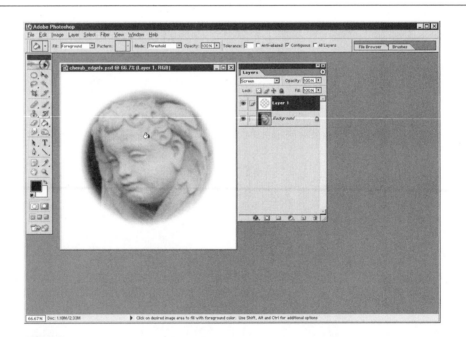

FIGURE 9-10   You can create your own edge effect by filling a new layer with white, select the part of the photo you want to keep unaffected, then fill the selection with black as we did here.

6. Now you can experiment with filters and have fun. Select a filter, such as Pixelate | Color Halftone, as shown here.

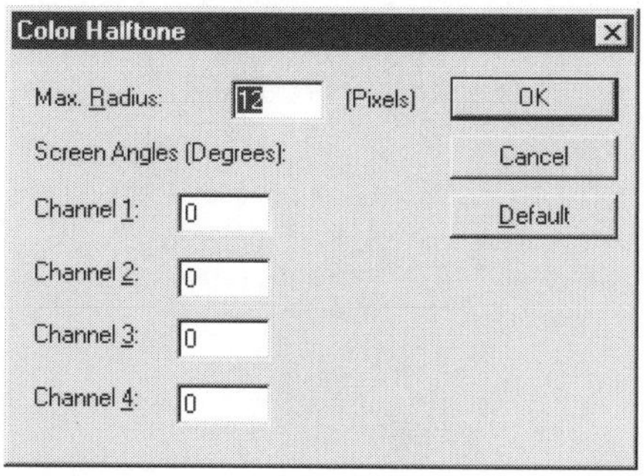

You can see a number of interesting effects that were created using a variety of filters in Figure 9-11.

9

Filter | Artistic | Brush Stroke

Filter | Artistic | Rough Pastels

Filter | Artistic | Smudge Stick

Filter | Brush Strokes | Crosshatch

Filter | Brush Strokes | Spatter

Filter | Brush Strokes | Sprayed Strokes

Filter | Distort | Glass

Filter | Distort | Ocean Ripple

Filter | Pixelate | Color Halftone

Filter | Pixelate | Crystallize

Filter | Pixelate | Mosaic

Filter | Sketch | Water Paper

FIGURE 9-11   You can use filters to create different edge effects in your images.

Chapter 10

Creating Graphics for the Web

How to...

- Understand goals for web graphics
- Create a GIF file
- Create a JPEG file
- Preview web graphics
- Create a transparent GIF
- Create an image map
- Make rollover buttons
- Create a web page background
- Create an animation

Creating graphics for the Web is very different from creating graphics for print. When you create web graphics, your goal is to create images that both look good and download quickly. Images that take a long time to download encourage visitors to your web site to click away, so learning how to optimize your images for the Web is important.

Although standards for web graphics can limit your images in some ways, creating images for the Web can offer opportunities for creativity. You can design interactive rollover graphics that change appearance when the cursor "rolls" over them. You can also create animations that turn a static page into a lively experience.

You will learn how to use ImageReady in this chapter. ImageReady is a companion program that ships with Photoshop and is used to create web graphics. Although its interface mimics that of Photoshop, it provides additional capabilities including animation, rollovers, and optimization of images for the Web.

Understanding Goals for Web Graphics

Whether you're creating a web site for yourself or someone else, the main goal is to provide visitors to the web site with information, and to keep them coming back. Images that take a long time to download encourage visitors to move on.

The type of web site you're creating dictates how impatient visitors will be. Web site visitors viewing a personal web site, or a web site for a museum, will be more tolerant of longer downloads than visitors using a search engine. Contrast the bare bones design of Yahoo (http://www.yahoo.com) or Google (http://www.google.com) with the image-rich web sites of the Louvre museum (http://www.louvre.fr) or the Fine Arts Museums of San Francisco (http://www.famsf.org). Taking into consideration the type of web site you're creating will help you create graphics that fit the needs of the visitor.

As a rule of thumb, you want your images to add up to less than 40K for a medium-weight web site. You can reduce image sizes by reducing the actual pixel width and height of an image, and by using the correct file format and optimization settings when you save the image.

As you work with web graphics, you'll find that the key to productivity is planning. Use layers for separate elements for animations and rollovers. You'll also want to remember to keep the original layered copies of your images in PSD format for editing and changing.

GIF vs. JPEG

There are two file formats for web graphics that are widely supported—GIF and JPEG. There is a third file format that is not yet universally supported—PNG. You'll be optimizing your web graphics either as GIF or JPEG files for the widest audience.

GIF files are indexed, or reduced to 256 colors or fewer. GIF is a good format for line art, simple graphics made up of blocks of color, or images containing very few colors. The size of the image in pixels, the complexity of the image, and the number of colors the image contains all contribute to the file size of a GIF file.

The JPEG file format was created specifically for photographs—JPEG stands for the Joint Photographic Experts Group. JPEG is a good format for photographs or images that contain many colors, or smooth gradients. The size of the image in pixels, and how little complexity the image contains contribute to increase the file size of a JPEG file.

Creating a GIF File

At the end of Chapter 2, you learned about Photoshop's Save for Web feature. However, if you'll be creating more than just a few graphics for the Web and you want to have more control over how your images are saved, you'll want to use ImageReady. ImageReady is a companion program to Photoshop. You can either

launch ImageReady by itself, or you can "jump" from
Photoshop to ImageReady by clicking the icon at the bottom of
the toolbox, as shown on the right. Any images you have open
in Photoshop automatically open in ImageReady when you
click the icon.

When your image opens in ImageReady, you will see
four tabs across the top of the image window. These tabs
provide access to four viewing options, as shown here:

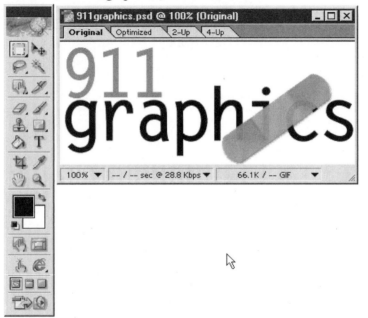

- ■ **Original**   Choose this option to display your image without any color
  reduction and compression.

- ■ **Optimized**   Choose this option to display your image as it would be
  compressed as a GIF or JPEG file.

- ■ **2-Up**   Your original image displays on the left, as shown here, while the
  compressed file displays on the right.

- ■ **4-Up**   View four versions of your image: your original plus three
  compressed versions.

As you click the tabs at the top of the screen, you will note that the 2-Up and
4-Up views also contain the file format for compression, file size, and approximate

download time, as shown here. At the bottom of the image window you'll see the zoom amount, the image size, and download times for the image.

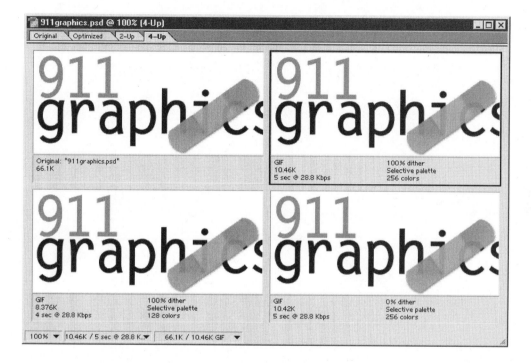

Remembering that your goal is to create a good quality image while maintaining a small file size, you will want to experiment with different GIF settings. Try using the 4-Up view. Select the second preview, and make sure the Optimize palette is open. Select Window | Optimize to open the palette if it is not open.

The Optimize palette offers a number of different settings. Since each image is unique, you should experiment with the settings, selecting a new preview in the 4-Up image window, and comparing the images and file sizes until you find a combination of settings that work well for you.

At the top of the Optimize palette is a drop-down menu for preset settings. You can also create your own presets. Below the Settings you'll find the other options, as shown to the right:

■ **File Format**   You can choose to preview your file in the following formats: GIF, JPEG, PNG-8, and PNG-24. PNG-8 is an 8-bit-depth, or 256 color, PNG file, while PNG-24 is a 24-bit-depth PNG file.

■ **Lossy**   You can choose to compress your image using lossy compression. Drag the slider to create more or less lossy compression. You can reduce the file size of an image quite a bit by using just a small amount of lossy compression.

■ **Color Reduction**   You can select a method for reducing the number of colors in an image.

   ■ **Perceptual**   This option reduces color in your image by using colors that are perceived by the eye to give the best result.

   ■ **Selective**   This option is similar to the Perceptual method, but colors are weighted towards the "web-safe" color palette.

   ■ **Adaptive**   This method uses colors that appear most frequently in an image. An image of the sky, for instance, would be made up of many shades of blue.

   ■ **Web**   This option indexes the color to the "web-safe" color palette of 216 colors. This can create additional dithering and larger file sizes.

   ■ **Custom**   This option uses a fixed color palette that does not update with the image.

■ **Number of Colors**   You can create a color palette with 2, 4, 8, 16, 32, 64, 128, or 256 colors for the image. You can also type a number into this menu if you'd prefer to select a different number than the presets offered. The fewer the colors, the smaller the final image size.

■ **Type of Dither**   The way in which limited colors are presented is called dither. You can select a method of dithering that suits your image, as shown in Figure 10-1.

   ■ **No Dither**   This option presents flat areas of color only. If you have an image made up of line art or text, this is a good choice.

   ■ **Diffusion**   This option adds dots of color in areas of transition from one color to another, such as across a gradient. Diffusion dither is a good choice for images that have shading or gradations of color.

Original image   No dither

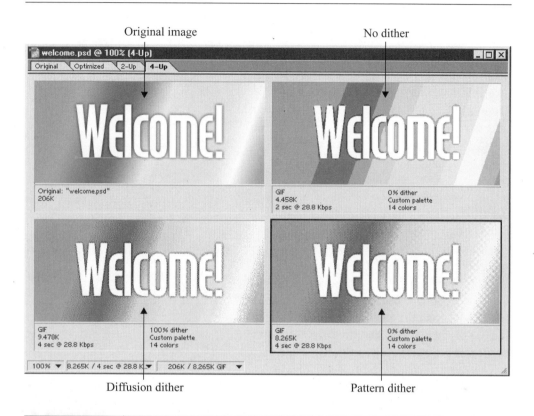

Diffusion dither   Pattern dither

FIGURE 10-1   Compare the original image to the same image using No Dither, Diffusion
Dither, and Pattern Dither.

■ **Pattern**   This option uses a pattern to represent areas of transition.
It's very distinctive and not attractive in most images.

■ **Noise**   The Noise diffusion creates a random pattern of colored pixels,
and is similar to the Diffusion dither method.

■ **Amount of Dither**   You can control the amount of dither in your image
by using this slider. More dither usually creates smoother transitions,
but it also increases file sizes.

When you've found the best settings for your image, you can save. To save a
GIF file in ImageReady, select File | Save Optimized.

Getting Really Small with GIFs

Once you've mastered the basics of saving and compressing images to the GIF format, you can further decrease your image size by altering the color table for a GIF image. Open the Color Table palette. You'll see the colors that make up your image. When you position your cursor over the individual color swatches, the hexcode for that color pops up as shown on the left. Hexcodes are used in HTML to specify colors for text, backgrounds and other elements controlled by HTML.

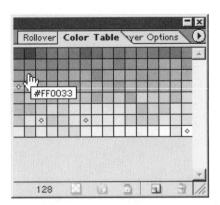

You can maintain precise control over your images by individually deleting colors from the color table. If you have many colors that are very close together, you can click a swatch in the color palette, then drag it to the Delete icon at the bottom of the palette. Remember, the fewer the colors, the smaller the file size. If you want to change a color to its nearest web-safe color, select the color swatch, then click the Cube icon at the bottom of the palette, as shown here. Once you've shifted a color swatch, a small icon displays on top of the swatch to show that it has been shifted.

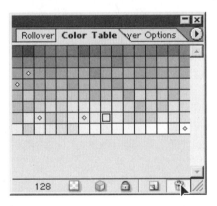

Creating a JPEG File

Saving an image in JPEG format means selecting from fewer options, because JPEGs don't reduce the colors to a set number (256 or fewer for GIFs).

In the Optimize palette, select JPEG as the Filetype, as shown here, then experiment with the following settings to find the right balance of quality and file size.

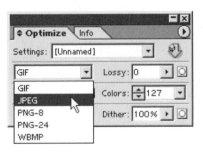

■ **Optimized Checkbox** Check this checkbox to reduce the file size of the JPEG by a small amount.

■ **Image Quality** You can set the quality of the image either by choosing High, Medium, or Low from the drop-down menu, or by setting an amount in the numeric box to the right of the drop-down menu, as shown in Figure 10-2.

■ **Progressive** A progressive JPEG image downloads in progressively higher quality. On a slower modem, the web site viewer looking at a progressive JPEG first sees a very low quality JPEG, followed by a higher quality JPEG.

■ **Blur** Add a small amount of blur to create a smoother image that is also smaller in file size.

When you are happy with the file size and image quality, select File | Save Optimized.

FIGURE 10-2 Setting JPEG image quality levels.

Previewing Web Graphics

Unfortunately, what you see in ImageReady or Photoshop is not always what you see in a web browser. It's always best to check your work in a browser before you upload pages to your web server.

There are several ways to preview an image. You can preview the image in your default web browser by clicking the web browser icon on the ImageReady toolbox, as shown on the left.

This launches your web browser with the image. It's helpful to do this to gauge the relative size of the image, and to see how the colors display.

Because different operating systems display the same colors differently, you will want to be able to preview your image as it would appear for both Windows and Mac users, regardless of your own operating system. You can do this by selecting View | Preview | Standard Windows Color, and View | Preview | Standard Macintosh Color in ImageReady as shown below.

If you're concerned about users with monitors set to 256 colors or fewer—recent statistics put these users at 5-10% of all web users—you can select View | Preview | Browser Dither.

Legibility and Web Graphics

If you'll be using type in graphics, there are a few things you can do to improve the legibility of your type in the low-resolution environment of the Web.

- **Size** You'll want to create type that is readable, and at about 8 points most typefaces start to become unreadable. However, for very small type there are typefaces designed specifically for use in web graphics at small sizes. These typefaces are known as screen, or bitmap, fonts. You can see a sample of these fonts below. You can find these fonts at http://www.atomicmedia.net, http://www.miniml.com, http://www.larabiefonts.com, http://www.myfonts.com, and http://www.kottke.org/plus/fonts.

Bylinear at 6 points	MICROSCOPIC AT 6 POINTS
FAIRLIGHT AT 6 POINTS	Scriptometer at 6 points
Joystik at 6 points	SEVENET AT 6 POINTS
Kroeger at 6 points	WIRED AT 6 POINTS

- **Contrast** The easiest combination of background and type to read is a white or very pale background with black type. You can also use a very dark background with white type, but too much of this, called reversed type, can be very tiring to read. Keep the contrast between the background and type high to maintain legibility. Adding a drop shadow or outer glow layer effect to type can make the type pop out from the background, as shown here.

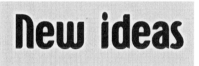

- **Anti-Aliasing** Applying anti-aliasing to type creates smooth edges, increasing legibility. However, at about 10 points or less, anti-aliasing just makes the type fuzzy. When you use the type tool, you can select the type of anti-aliasing in the options bar. For very small type sizes, set the Anti-aliasing to None.

Creating a Transparent GIF

A transparent GIF has areas that are transparent, so that the web page background on which the image sits shows through the GIF. In order to create a transparent GIF, you'll need to know what color your web page background will be. If you create a transparent GIF on a white background, then move it to a colored background, an undesirable halo effect occurs around the image, as shown in Figure 10-3.

TIP *If you'll be using a pattern as a web page background, use the darkest color in the background to fill the background of your image when creating a transparent GIF, especially if you have glows or drop shadows.*

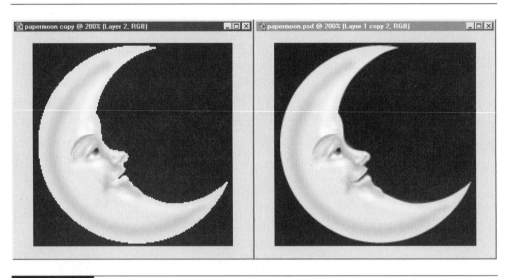

FIGURE 10-3   Undesirable halo effect in transparent GIF.

To create transparency in your image, follow these steps:

1. Flatten the layers in your image by selecting Layer | Flatten Image.

2. Use the eraser tool, background eraser, or magic eraser tools, as described in Chapter 5, to delete the parts of the image that you want to make transparent. Photoshop and ImageReady both display transparency with the checkerboard pattern, as shown in Figure 10-4.

3. In ImageReady, use the Optimize palette to select the settings for the GIF. In Photoshop, use Save for the Web, or select Image | Mode | Indexed, and make sure the transparency checkbox is selected, as shown here.

4. In ImageReady, select File | Save Optimized. In Photoshop, select File | Save, and be sure that the Filetype is set to GIF.

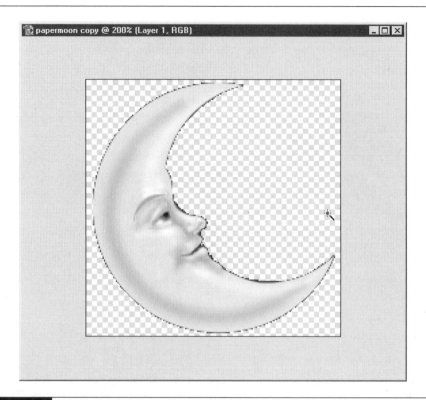

FIGURE 10-4 Selecting a transparent background.

Creating an Image Map

An image map is an image in which you create clickable areas that link to different web pages. One of the most obvious uses of an image map is to create a map of the world, for instance, where each country's outline is linked to a different page of information. Creating an image map is the only way to link a single image to more than one page.

Using the Image Map Tools

With the Image Map tools, you can create rectangular, circular, or polygon shapes. Make sure the Image Map palette is open in ImageReady. Select Window | Image Map if the palette is not open.

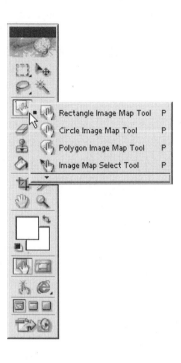

Select one of the Image Map tools, as shown on the left. Click and drag to outline the area you wish to make a clickable link. When you have finished outlining the image map shape, in the URL box, enter the path to the HTML page you want to link to.

ImageReady automatically names the slice, which you can rename to something more descriptive, as shown below.

It's a good idea to type in descriptive text for the ALT tag, which will show up in the web browser when the user moves the cursor over the image, as shown in Figure 10-5.

If you need to move or change the image map, use the image map selection tool. To access this tool, click and hold on the image map tool.

When you have finished creating various links, save the file by selecting File | Save Optimized. Preview the image in a web browser by selecting the preview button in the ImageReady toolbox.

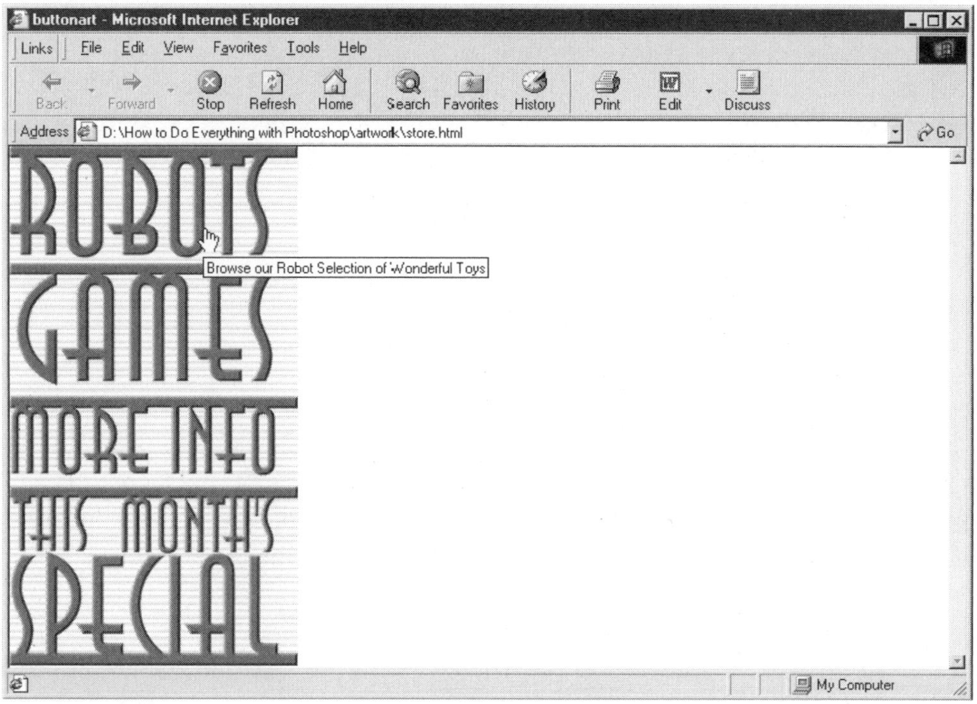

FIGURE 10-5   Descriptive text using the ALT tag as it appears in a browser.

Creating an Image Map from Slices

You can use the slice tool to cut a large graphic into smaller individual graphics.
ImageReady automatically creates the HTML that puts the slices into place when
you select File | Save Optimized. To create an image map from slices, you'll want
to make sure that the Slice palette is open in ImageReady. Select the slice tool from
the ImageReady toolbox, and use it to create a rectangular slice. In the Slice palette,
type the path to the web page.

Making Rollover Buttons

One way to add interactivity to your web site is to create rollover buttons. When a visitor to your web site moves his cursor over a button or clicks a button, the button can change color, shape, bevel, drop shadow, glow, and so on. Rollovers aren't just for buttons—you can use them to highlight an image when it's rolled over.

Creating Simple Rollover Buttons

To create simple rollover buttons, first create all of your buttons in a layered file. If you want to create different colors or add layer effects for each state, create those states on layers as well, as shown in Figure 10-6, which shows the original layered image along with two copies so that you can see what each button state looks like.

You'll be using the Rollovers palette in ImageReady to create the rollovers for the buttons. To begin creating rollovers, open your layered file in ImageReady. Use the slice tool to select the first button. Make sure the layers are displayed so that the normal state of the button is showing. Toggle off any layers that you don't want visible by clicking the Eye icon next to the layers in the Layers palette.

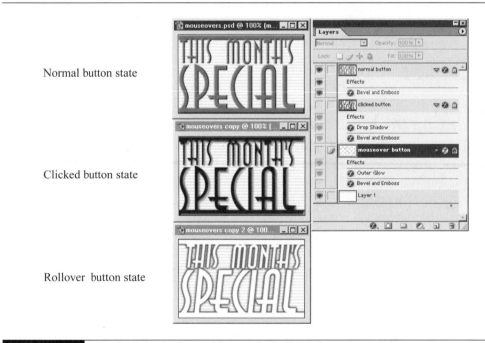

FIGURE 10-6   Designing the layered image for rollover buttons.

In the Rollovers palette, click the Create New State icon at the bottom of the Rollovers palette. This creates the rollover state. Display the layers you want to show in this state by clicking the appropriate layers in the Layers palette, as shown here.

To create a Down state—the way the button will appear when it is being clicked—you'll need to make another state using the Rollovers palette. Click the Create New State icon again, and make any alterations that you want to the button for its Down state.

Select Save | Optimized. Check how your rollovers work in the web browser by clicking the Preview in Default Browser icon in the toolbar.

Creating Secondary Rollovers

You can easily create secondary rollovers, or rollovers where the button displays an image somewhere else on a web page. These are sometimes called non-concatenated rollovers. In this example, you'll see how to create a web page where a product can be previewed by moving the cursor over the navigation buttons.

Create the buttons that will control the rollover first, and create the rollover effect in the same, layered file. This can be done in either Photoshop or ImageReady, but the rollovers are created within ImageReady.

In Figure 10-7, buttons were created for the web page, and previews of the products were also created. These photos will appear on the right side of the web page as the user moves the cursor over the navigation buttons.

To begin, create a slice for a button using the slice tool. In the Slice palette, name the slice and add the URL that the navigation button will link to. In the Rollovers palette, create the rollover state by clicking the Create Rollover State button. Make sure that the correct color image is showing by toggling on the correct layer in the Layers palette. In this example, the eye icon for the giraffe was toggled off and the eye icon for the robot was toggled on. Preview the rollovers in a web browser by selecting the Preview in Default Browser icon. You will first see the web page with the giraffe. When the user moves the cursor over the robots button, the giraffe image is replaced with the robot image, as shown in Figure 10-8.

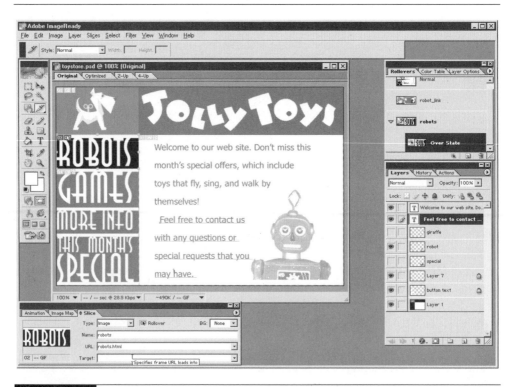

FIGURE 10-7   It's easy to create a web page with secondary rollovers.

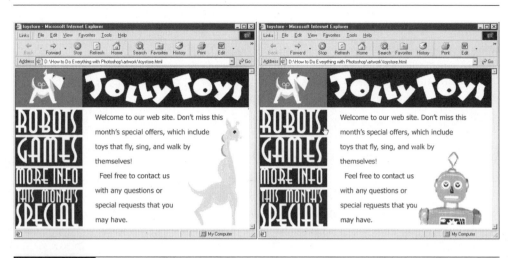

FIGURE 10-8   Rollover previews.

> **NOTE**   *While creating rollovers and secondary rollovers can add interest and interactivity to a web page, each image does add download time.*

Continue to create slices and toggle on and off the appropriate layers in the Layers palette until you are finished. Select File | Save Optimized to save the web page.

Rollover States

As you can see, you can make rollovers simple or dramatic. In addition to Over and Down and Click states, you can also use the Rollovers palette to create Selected, Out, and Up states for the rollovers. The Out state displays when the user's cursor moves off the button. Normally, you use the default appearance of the button for the Out state. The Up state appears when the user releases the mouse button.

You can also used animated GIFs for rollover states, creating more emphasis and interest to your web page.

Creating an Animation

With ImageReady you can create animated GIFs for your web pages. An animated GIF draws attention to an area of a web page. You'll want to use restraint and subtlety with animation, because too much blinking, flashing, and zooming can detract from all the other information.

Create the animation as a layered file, then toggle layers on and off to create different parts of the animation. You can also use a technique in ImageReady called tweening, which creates frames that go in between existing frames to smooth out the visual appearance of the animation.

As with all web graphics, you'll want to watch the size of your image. The bigger the width and height of your animation, and the more frames it has, the larger the resulting file size will be.

Creating a Simple Animation

This is a simple animation technique that is also subtle. Create an image with text. Fill the background layer with one color and create a new layer with a second color. With the Animation palette open in ImageReady, click the Duplicate Frame icon at the bottom of the Animation palette. Toggle the second background layer so that the two frames, frame 1 and frame 2, have different background colors, as shown in Figure 10-9.

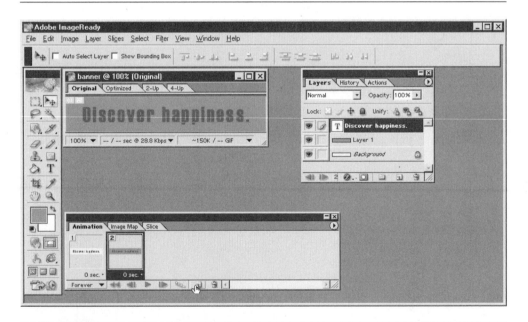

FIGURE 10-9   Add a new frame to the animation by clicking the icon in the Animation palette. You can then change the background color of the second frame by toggling on Layer 1, which is filled with a different color.

Now you have an animation with two frames. To add more subtlety, you can tween, or add frames that make the animation flow more smoothly. Click the Tween icon at the bottom of the animation palette, and use the default setting of 5 frames.

The result will be a seven-frame animation, made up of the two initial frames plus the five tweened frames. The animation changes color. The default timing for animation is 0 seconds, or very fast. To slow the animation down, click 0 second and change it to 0.5 seconds between frames, as shown in Figure 10-10.

Creating a Web Page Background

You can create web page backgrounds with plain color, or you can create web page backgrounds with texture or pattern. If you'll be placing text over textured or patterned backgrounds, you'll want to remember to keep the contrast between the background and text high so that reading is easy. The best way to do this is to create a very light background.

Seamless patterns are important if you'll be creating backgrounds for web pages. If a seam is visible in a background, it's very obvious and detracts from the rest of the page, as shown in Figure 10-11.

10

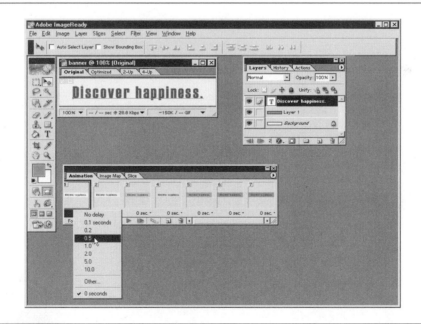

FIGURE 10-10   To slow the animation down, click 0 second and change it to 0.5 seconds between frames.

A seamless background on a web page

A background with obvious seams on a web page

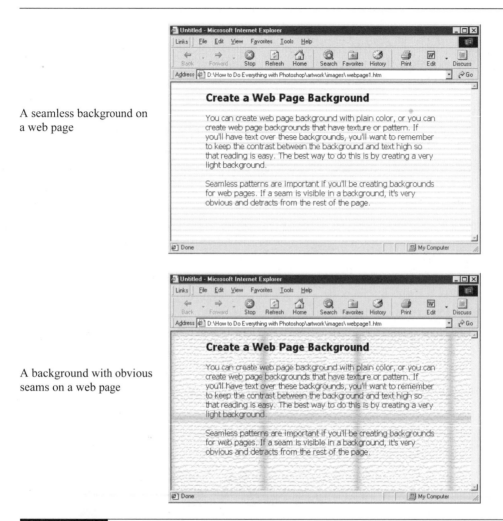

FIGURE 10-11 It's important to design backgrounds where text is legible. Creating seamless backgrounds for web pages is easy in Photoshop.

You can use a built-in tool in Photoshop— called the Pattern Maker—to create your web page backgrounds. You can also use the Offset filter and the paint tools in Photoshop to create seamless patterns.

Seamless patterns are not just for web pages. Many 3-D programs use them as texture maps, to create texture on 3-D forms. You can also save seamless patterns to use as pattern fills, or as textures for custom brushes.

Using the Pattern Maker in Photoshop

Using any photograph, painting, or drawing, you can create a seamless pattern in Photoshop using the Pattern Maker filter.

1. Open the Pattern Maker by selecting Filter | Pattern Maker.

2. Marquee the area you would like to use as a basis for your seamless pattern, as shown here.

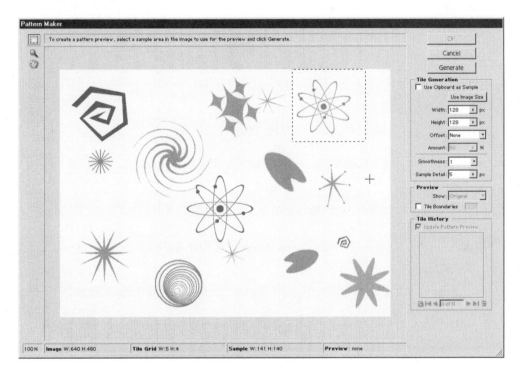

3. Select the Generate button to create a sample seamless pattern. If you don't like it, click the Generate button again to create a new pattern. You can experiment with the Smoothness and Sample Detail numbers to achieve different results, as shown in Figure 10-12.

4. If you want to return to a previous pattern you've generated, use the arrow below the Tile History swatch to browse the patterns you have generated.

5. Note that the image tile default size is 128 pixels by 128 pixels. Save the tile by clicking the Disk icon at the bottom of the Pattern Maker window as

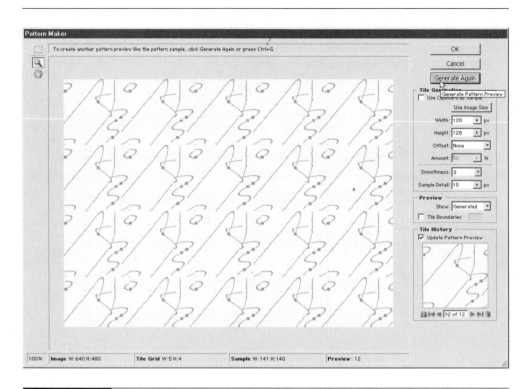

FIGURE 10-12   Click the Generate button again to create a new pattern.

shown below. This saves the file to your pattern list, which is located under Edit | Fill | Pattern, where you can access it to use as a fill. It will also be available as a texture for brush options, and as a texture in layer effects.

6. Open a new file, 128 pixels by 128 pixels, the same size as the tile you've created in the Pattern Maker.

7. Select Edit | Fill, and select Pattern. Select the Contents: Pattern, and click the Custom Pattern swatch to display the Pattern picker. Then select the pattern you've just created using the Pattern Maker as shown on the right.

8. If the pattern has too much contrast to use as a background, you can lighten the image by creating a new layer, filling it with white, and adjusting the opacity as shown below.

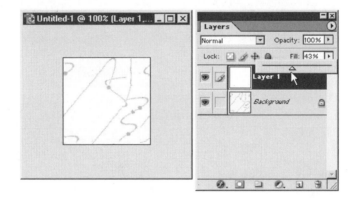

9. Select File | Save for Web, and save the file as a GIF.

Creating a Seamless Background by Hand

Although the Pattern Maker is a handy tool, sometimes you want more control over a background that you're creating. You can create your own custom seamless background patterns for web page backgrounds by using the Offset filter and the retouching tools.

1. Create a new file, 200 by 200 pixels. In this example, the image was filled by selecting Filter | Render | Clouds.

2. Select Filter | Other | Offset, and enter Horizontal and Vertical amounts of 100 pixels as shown here. Select the Undefined Areas to Wrap Around. This moves the "seamed" areas to the center of the image where you can eliminate them. As you see here, the seams are quite obvious.

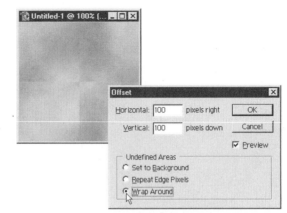

3. Use the Healing brush to select areas that are not seamed by using ALT-click/CTRL-click. Then drag the healing brush over the seams. Repeat until all the seams have been eliminated as shown here.

4. If the image contains too much contrast to use as a background, you can lighten the image by creating a new layer, filling it with white, and adjusting the opacity.

5. Save the file as a GIF or JPEG file by selecting File | Save for Web.

Creating Simple Geometric Backgrounds

You can use any of the painting tools in Photoshop to create geometric backgrounds. It's simple to create a striped background:

1. Open a new file, 20 pixels by 20 pixels.

2. Turn the rulers on the image by selecting View | Rulers. Use the marquee tool to create a selection 10 pixels high. Fill this area with a color, as shown in Figure 10-13. If you want to create smaller stripes, you can use the pencil tool to draw lines instead of filling a selection.

3. Save the file as a GIF by selecting File | Save for Web. You can also save this pattern to your list of custom patterns by selecting Edit | Define Pattern.

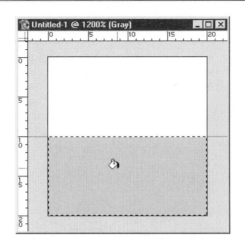

FIGURE 10-13   Fill the 10 pixels high marqueed area with a color.

Experiment with the painting and selection tools to create new patterns. Remember that these tools are also useful for adding texture and interest to images. The striped pattern created in the previous section was set to multiply and then was used over a photograph to create an interlaced pattern, as shown here.

10

Using Seamless Patterns

Once you create seamless patterns, there are lots of ways to use them to create special effects. You can use the patterns with filters, brushes, and layer effects to create more interesting images.

Using Seamless Patterns with Filters

If you save your newly created seamless background in grayscale Photoshop PSD format, you can also use it as the basis for texture for the following filters:

1. Filter | Artistic | Rough Pastels

2. Filter | Artistic | Underpainting

3. Filter | Distort | Displace

4. Filter | Distort | Glass

5. Filter | Render | Lighting Effects

6. Filter | Render | Texture Fill

7. Filter | Sketch | Conté Crayon

8. Filter | Texture | Texturizer

To save a seamless pattern in the correct format to use with filters, change the mode to grayscale by selecting Image | Mode | Grayscale. Then save the file in Photoshop .psd format by selecting File | Save As, and selecting .psd as the file type.

To apply a pattern with a filter, select the filter, then select Texture, and scroll down, as shown here, to select Load Texture. Then browse to find the texture you want to apply to your image.

Using Seamless Patterns With Layer Effects

There are two ways to use seamless patterns with layer effects: you can apply the pattern as an overlay, or you can use the pattern as a texture when you apply a bevel.
To create a layer effect with a pattern overlay:

1. Select the Layer Effects icon at the bottom of the Layers palette, and select Pattern Overlay from the drop-down menu.

2. Click the pattern swatch to open the Pattern picker. Select the pattern you want to apply.

3. Choose a blending mode and tweak the opacity to achieve the results you want, as shown here.

10

To create a texture for a beveled effect:

1. Select the Layer Effects icon at the bottom of the Layers palette, and select Bevel and Emboss from the drop-down menu.

2. Select Texture on the left side of the Layer Effects dialog box.

3. Click the pattern swatch to open the Pattern picker. Select the pattern you want to apply. Change the Scale or Depth settings to get the look you're aiming for.

Using Seamless Patterns with Brushes

You can also use seamless patterns to create custom brushes. To create a brush using a texture you've created, follow these steps:

1. Select the paintbrush tool.

2. Open the Brushes palette, and select a brush preset to begin with.

3. Select texture, as shown here.

4. Click the pattern swatch to open the Pattern picker. Select the pattern you want to apply.

Chapter 11

Using the Shape and Pen Tools

How to...

- Use the shape tools
- Edit shapes
- Create a custom shape
- Use the pen tool

Vector objects offer power and flexibility in the graphic arena. They are editable, smooth graphics that scale flawlessly with your document. If you want to create an image that will be used over and over again at many different sizes—such as a logo— you'll want to create the image using vector tools.

Photoshop offers two main types of vector tools—the shape tools, which include basic shapes such as rectangles and ellipses, and the pen tool. The pen tool enables you to create your own shapes. The shapes you create with the pen tool can be as simple or elaborate as you like.

Using the Shape Tools

Photoshop offers six shape tools that you can use to create shapes. These tools are found by clicking and holding down the rectangle tool in the toolbox, as shown here.

You can also combine multiple shapes to form more elaborate shapes. When you click and drag a shape tool, Photoshop automatically places the shape on its own new layer.

- **Rectangle tool** This tool to creates rectangles or squares. To create a square, hold SHIFT as you drag the rectangle tool.

- **Rounded rectangle tool** This tool creates rectangles or squares with rounded corners. You can adjust the size of the corners in the options bar, under Radius. A larger radius size gives larger rounded corners, as shown here. To create a square, hold SHIFT as you drag the rounded rectangle tool.

- ■ **Ellipse tool**   The ellipse tool creates ellipses and circles. To create a perfect circle, hold SHIFT as you drag the ellipse tool.

- ■ **Polygon tool**   The polygon tool creates shapes with as few as three sides (a triangle) or as many as 100 sides. To adjust the number of sides the polygon has, change the Sides number in the options bar as shown here.

- ■ **Line tool**   The line tool draws lines. You can set the width of the line in the options bar. To constrain the line to a straight vertical or horizontal line, hold SHIFT key as you drag the line tool. To add an arrowhead to the end of the line you're creating, click the Geometry Options arrow on the options bar, as shown in Figure 11-1. Then you can set whether the arrow should appear at the start or the end of the line, and the size of the arrow. The size of the arrow is measured as a percentage of the line width.

- ■ **Custom shape tool**   You can use a custom shape from the set of shapes that comes with Photoshop. When you select the custom shape tool, a drop-down menu of shape presets appears. There is a menu available at the top of the custom shape presets that enables you to load new shapes and adjust how you view shapes, as seen in Figure 11-2. Select a shape, and click and drag the shape tool in your image to add the selected custom shape.

11

FIGURE 11-1   Clicking the Geometry Options adds an arrowhead to the start or end of a line.

Shape Layers

Like type layers, shape layers are slightly different than regular layers in Photoshop. A shape layer is made up of a fill layer linked to a vector mask, as seen here in the Layers palette. The fill layer preview is linked to the vector mask preview in the Layers palette.

　　To change the color of the shape, double-click on the fill layer preview in the

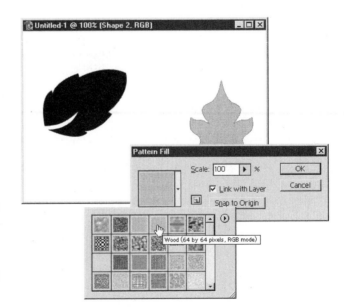

FIGURE 11-2   Custom shape presets.

Layers palette, which opens the Color Picker (Figure 11-3). Select a different color for the fill.

To change the fill of the layer from a flat color to a pattern or texture, select Layer | Change Layer Content | Pattern, and select a pattern. To change the fill of the layer to a gradient, select Layer | Change Layer Content | Gradient, and select a gradient to apply, as shown in Figure 11-4.

You can also add drop shadows, glows, and bevels to shapes as you can to any layer, by selecting the Effects icon at the bottom of the Layers palette.

Changing a Shape Layer to a Regular Layer

There may be times when you want to change a vector layer to a bitmapped, or rasterized, layer. To rasterize a vector layer, right-click/CTRL-click the label for the layer to reveal a context-sensitive menu, as shown here. Select Rasterize Layer

11

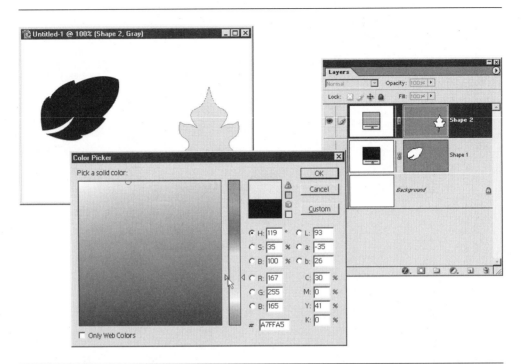

FIGURE 11-3   You can change the fill of a shape at any time. Here, the color picker is being used to change the fill.

from the menu. You can also select Layer | Rasterize | Layer. Remember that once you rasterize a shape layer, you lose the benefits of a wide range of scalability.

Editing Shapes

You can transform a shape as you can any layer, by selecting Edit | Transform, and applying the transformation. Because shapes are vectors, they do not degrade if you scale them up or down.

To edit the outline of a shape, select the vector mask preview in the Layers

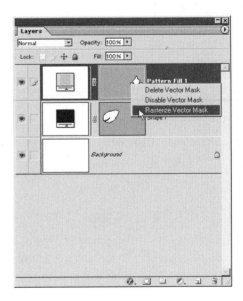

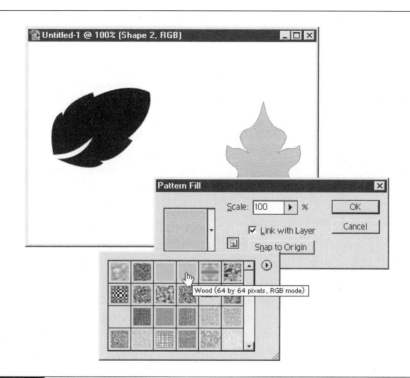

FIGURE 11-4   Change the fill of a shape to a pattern.

11

palette. Then you can use the pen
tools to edit the shape, as shown
here. By clicking and holding the
pen tool in the toolbox, you can
reveal the add anchor point tool.
Click the add anchor point tool on
the edge of the shape, then drag the
point you've added to alter the
shape as shown here. The pen
tools will be described in depth
later in this chapter.

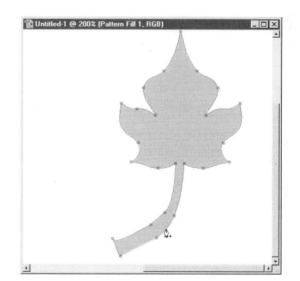

Combining Shapes

As mentioned previously, one way to create more complex shapes beyond the simple geometric shapes that Photoshop provides is to combine shapes. When you're working with shapes, you control how multiple shapes are combined through the options bar, as shown in Figure 11-5.

To create overlapping shapes, create the first shape. Then select the shape tool you'd like to work with and, on the options bar, select the way that you'd like to combine the two shapes.

As shown here, you can quickly create interesting shapes by combining two shapes, and adding an effect. The shapes in Figure 11-6 were created by making a shape with the ellipse tool first, then using the various combine functions from the options bar when adding the arrow.

Creating Shapes as Paths

The default method for creating shapes is to create shape layers. As you've seen, this creates a layer that contains a fill and a vector mask. Some of the benefits of creating shapes as paths rather than as vector layers include:

- Paths can be exported to Adobe Illustrator as vector paths.

- Paths can be stroked with any brush, providing a variety of fills not available using the Stroke command in layer effects.

- Paths can be saved and loaded.

- Paths can be easily converted to selections.

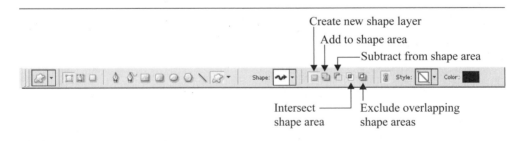

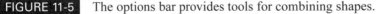
FIGURE 11-5   The options bar provides tools for combining shapes.

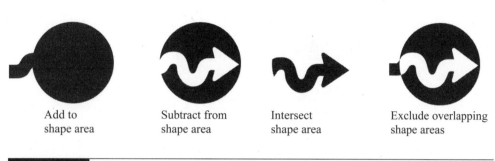

| Add to shape area | Subtract from shape area | Intersect shape area | Exclude overlapping shape areas |

FIGURE 11-6   You can use a variety of different methods to combine shapes.

To create a shape as a path, select the Paths icon from the options bar as shown here. Then create your shape as usual, by clicking and dragging the shape tool.

To edit, fill, or save a path, or to convert a path to a selection, you will want to open the Paths palette. Select Window | Paths if this palette isn't open on your screen already. Select the path in the Paths palette to work with it. There are several icons at the bottom of the Paths palette, as shown in Figure 11-7.

- **Fill path with foreground color**   Click this icon to fill the path with the current foreground color.

- **Stroke path with brush**   Select the brush tool from the toolbox, then select any brush. Set the foreground color to the color you would like to stroke the path with, and click the Stroke path with brush icon, as shown in Figure 11-8.

- **Load path as selection**   Sometimes it's easier to work with a selection rather than a path. Click this icon to convert the path to a selection.

- **Make work path from selection**   You can create a path from any selection. Click this icon to create a path.

11

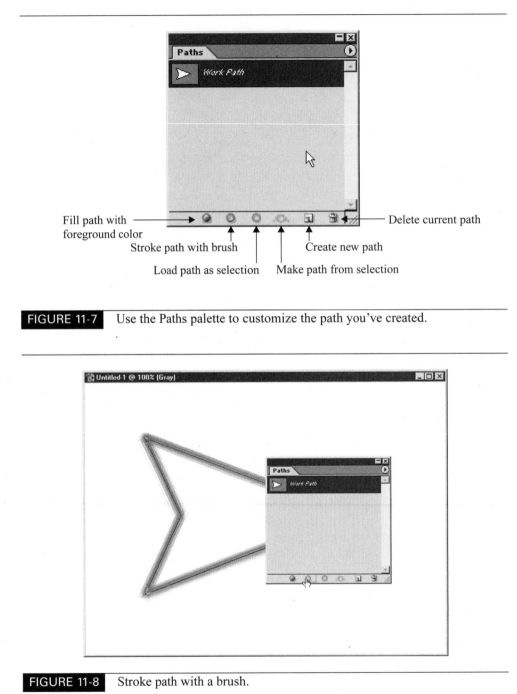

Fill path with foreground color

Stroke path with brush

Load path as selection

Make path from selection

Create new path

Delete current path

FIGURE 11-7 Use the Paths palette to customize the path you've created.

FIGURE 11-8 Stroke path with a brush.

■ **Create new path**   If you want to create a new path using the shape or pen tool, select this option.

■ **Delete current path**   Delete the selected path by clicking this icon.

To save a path, click the drop-down menu at the top of the Paths palette and choose Save Path. To load a saved path into a new image, select Load path from the Paths palette menu.

To export a path for use in Adobe Illustrator, or programs that support the Adobe Illustrator file format, select File | Export | Paths to Illustrator.

Creating Shapes as Bitmaps

If you're working with low-resolution graphics, such as web graphics, and you want to see how every pixel will display in your final image, you may want to work with shapes as bitmaps rather than as shape layers or paths. Select the Fill Pixels option from the options bar, and your shapes will be created as bitmaps in your image, as shown in Figure 11-9. Shapes are not created on a new layer when you use this option.

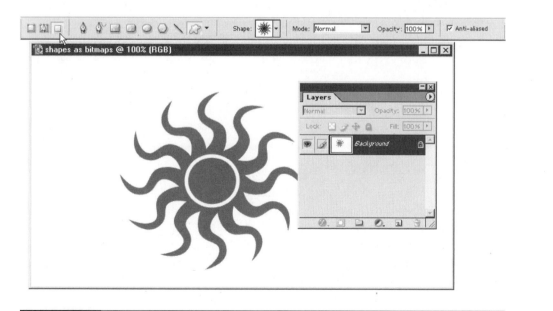

FIGURE 11-9   Using the Fill Pixels option to create shapes makes shapes that are bitmaps rather than vectors. These shapes will not be created on a new layer.

Creating a Custom Shape

One way to make your work easier in Photoshop is to build up a library of frequently used shapes. You can add symbols, logos, or even type to the custom shape set. You'll then be able to drag a custom shape from your own library into any image.

Creating a Custom Shape from Artwork

You can create a shape from almost any kind of artwork, including paths, shape, or type layers. Once you've created a path or shape, change it into a custom shape by selecting Edit | Define Custom Shape, as shown on the right. You'll then be prompted to give your shape a name.

The new shape is then added to your custom shapes list. Be sure to save your shape set by clicking the Custom Shape picker, and selecting the drop-down library. Then select Save Shapes from the menu.

Once you've saved a library of shapes, you can also share this library with other Photoshop users. They will be able to open your library of shapes by selecting Load Shapes from the drop-down menu.

You can also import Adobe Illustrator files and add them to your custom shapes. See Chapter 13 for specifics on how to work with Illustrator and Photoshop together.

NOTE   *You can't create a custom shape from a bitmap. If the only artwork you have is a bitmap and you want to use it as custom artwork, you can create a custom brush by selecting Edit | Define Brush.*

Creating a Custom Shape from Type

Speed up your work in Photoshop by adding extended characters, such as ©, ®, or ™ to your custom shape library. You can also use dingbat typefaces to add pictures to your custom shape library.

Type out the text you wish to convert to a custom shape. Select Layer | Type | Convert to Shape, as shown here.

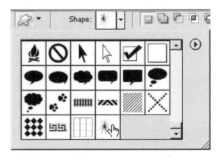

Then choose Edit | Define Custom Shape. The shape will be added to your type library.

Using the Pen Tool

If you've ever tried to use the pen tool on your own, you may have become frustrated, since it doesn't work quite like other painting tools. Learning how to use the pen tool will make creating scalable vector artwork easier.

When you're using the pen tool, you'll find that paying attention to two things will make your work much less frustrating. The first is to select the right tool for creating or editing a path. The second is to watch the cursor change to give you cues about what you're creating.

Click and hold on the pen tool in the toolbox, to see all of the pen tools available, as shown below on the right.

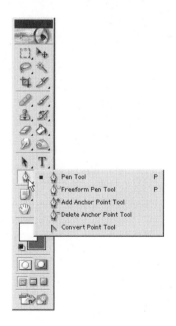

- **Pen tool**   Clicking to add points creates a shape made up of straight lines. Clicking and dragging before you release the mouse creates a curve, as shown here. How far you drag the tool determines how far the curve extends.

- **Freeform pen tool**   If you want to draw a path, as you draw with the pencil or brush tool, you can use the freeform pen. Just click and drag to form the shape you want.

- **Add anchor point tool**   If you want to add a point to an existing path, click on the path with the add anchor point tool.

- **Delete anchor point tool**   To delete extra points from a path, sometimes useful if you've used the freeform pen tool and have areas you wish to smooth out, click the point with the delete anchor point tool.

- **Convert point tool**   If you've created a curve where you want a straight line, or if you've created a straight line where you want a curve, you can change the point by clicking it with the convert point tool, as shown here.

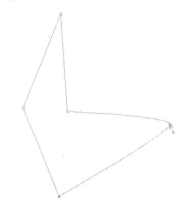

There are two more useful path tools located on the toolbox just above the pen tool. These are the path selection tool and direct selection tool, as shown here.

- **Path selection tool**   You can use the path selection tool to move a path.

- **Direct selection tool**   To access the direct selection tool, click and hold on the path selection tool, and select the direct selection tool. To move a single point, select it with the direct selection tools. To move a number of points, either SHIFT-click to select multiple points, or drag the direct selection tool to marquee the points you want to move, as shown here.

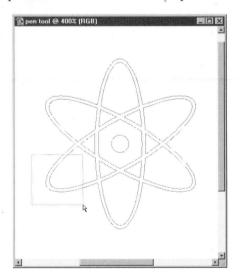

After you draw a path, make sure that the path is closed, unless you're drawing a line. Closing the path completes the shape.

Close a path by making sure that the path ends at the same point that it started, as shown here. The cursor changes to a pen with a circle.

Once you've familiarized yourself with the pen tools, you'll want to pay attention to how the cursor changes as you create and edit paths. As shown in Figure 11-10, the cursor lets you know what you're doing with a path.

The easiest way to become better with the pen tool is to use it. Try opening an image and using the pen tool to trace parts of the image, as shown in Figure 11-11. Since most programs that create vector artwork work in the same way, such as Adobe Illustrator,

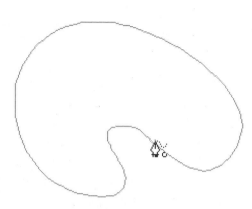

⬧ₓ Start a new path		▶ Adjust a point	
⬧ Continue adding points to path		⌐ Convert a smooth point to a corner point, or a corner point to a smooth point	
⬧₊ Add a new point			
⬧₋ Delete a point			
⬧⁄ Add a new point to an existing path			
⬧ₒ Close a path			
⬧□ Join two paths together			

FIGURE 11-10   The cursors indicate the current state of the pen tool.

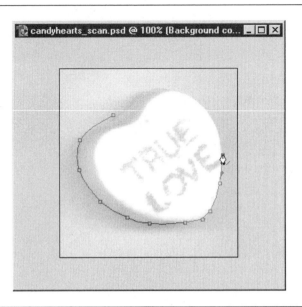

FIGURE 11-11   Using the pen tool to trace parts of the image.

CorelDraw, and Macromedia Freehand, once you master the pen tool in Photoshop you'll have a skill that you can use in other programs as well. Many other Adobe products, such as Adobe LiveMotion and Adobe After Effects, also include a pen tool, as shown in Figure 11-12. Learning the pen tool may be challenging at first, but it's an extremely useful skill for anyone involved in graphic design.

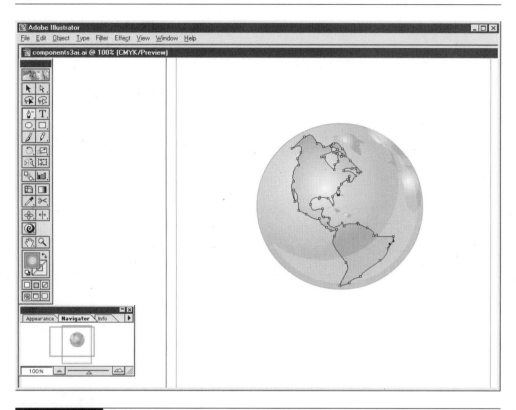

FIGURE 11-12   The pen tool is found in other Adobe products, such as Adobe Illustrator.

11

Chapter 12

Using Productivity Tools

How to...

- Create tool presets
- Use the preset manager
- Create a custom document size
- Use annotations
- Record an action
- Use the batch command
- Create a droplet
- Create a web gallery
- Create a contact sheet

Wouldn't it be wonderful if you could save hours and hours of production time? What if transforming a folder containing hundreds of TIFF format graphics to web-ready GIFs was as easy as pushing a button? What if you didn't have to reset your text or paint tool each time you used it? You can do all these things and much more using presets and actions in Photoshop.

Some timesaving techniques have been discussed in previous chapters. These include creating custom shapes and custom brushes, finding and replacing text, and creating custom styles. This chapter explores some powerful options for speeding up your work in Photoshop. Learning how to use presets and actions will cut down on repetitive tasks in Photoshop, leaving you more time to be creative.

Creating Tool Presets

Doing the same thing over and over again can be boring. Sometimes precise repetition, such as being able to make every logo, web banner, business card, or photograph the same is essential. Taking advantage of tool presets is a great way to cut down on repetition and create accurate results.

Tool presets are tools that save specific settings. If you use the same typeface at the same size frequently, you can save that as a preset and select it every time you need it, without having to reset the font, font color, or size. If you need to crop to a specific size, you can save a preset for a specific size.

Normally when you select a tool, it is still set with the options you selected for it the last time you used it. If you created text using Arial Bold at 36 points, when you start typing with the text tool, it will use Arial Bold at 36 points. The following examples show you how to create useful tool presets for any tool in the toolbox.

Creating a Type Tool Preset

If you use the type tool frequently, you probably have to change typefaces often. To create a type tool that contains the typeface, size, alignment, and color that you want to be able to reuse, follow these steps:

1. Select the type tool from the Photoshop toolbox.

2. Adjust any options you want from the options bar. You can set the font, size, anti-aliasing, and alignment for your custom type preset.

3. Click the drop-down menu for the Tool Preset Picker. Click the arrow to reveal the menu and select New Tool Preset, as shown here.

12

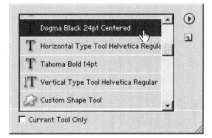

4. Type in a descriptive name for the tool.

5. Your new tool preset appears in the list of tool presets, as shown here.

You have created a new type tool preset that will make it easy and fast to create consistent type. You can create a tool preset for any tool you use in Photoshop. Tool presets cannot be edited once they have been created, but you can delete tool presets and add new tool presets using the menu on the Tool Preset Picker.

Creating a Brush Tool Preset

With so many options for brushes, including texture, size, mode, and scattering, you'll want to save your brushes once you've found the right combination of options:

1. Select the brush tool from the Photoshop toolbox.

2. Open the Brushes palette by selecting Window | Brushes, if the palette isn't already open. Select a brush preset to begin with.

3. Alter any options that you want to customize for your brush. You can also customize the settings on the options bar, such as Mode, Opacity, or Flow.

4. Once you're satisfied with the selections you've made, click on the arrow for the Tool Preset Picker. Click on the arrow to open the menu and select New Tool preset.

5. You'll be prompted to create a name for your custom brush, as shown in Figure 12-1.

6. You'll also see an option to include color with the brush preset. If you select the checkbox, the currently selected foreground color is included with the brush tool preset.

Cropping to a Set Size

If you have a whole batch of photos that you want to crop to a specific size, creating a preset for the rectangular selection tool can make your job go much quicker. You can set a fixed size for the rectangular selection tool, then use Image | Crop

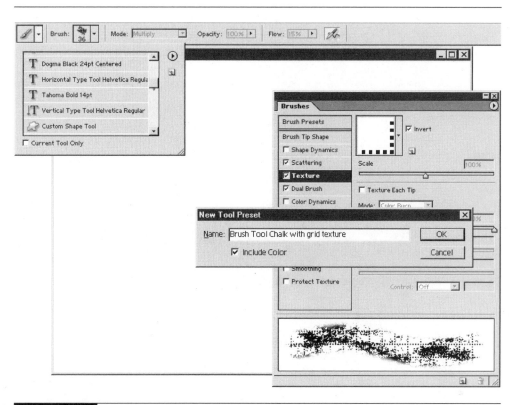

FIGURE 12-1   Naming a custom brush.

12

to complete the task. The crop tool does not offer a fixed size, which is why the rectangular marquee tool is a better choice in this instance.

1. Select the rectangular marquee tool from the toolbox.

2. On the options bar, set the Feather amount to 0. Set the Style to Fixed Size, as shown here.

3. Enter the width and height you want.

4. Click the drop-down menu for the Tool Preset Picker. Click the New Preset icon.

5. Type in a descriptive name for the tool, as shown in Figure 12-2.

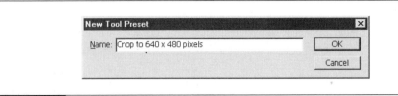

FIGURE 12-2   Creating custom tool presets saves you time by giving you tools with
exactly the right settings at your fingertips.

6. Click the rectangular marquee tool in the image you want to crop. You can
drag the selection in the image until it is positioned exactly where you want
it, as shown here.

7. Select Image | Crop to complete the task.

Saving and Loading Tool Presets

Once you've created tool presets, you'll want to save them. By saving your tool presets, you can share them with other Photoshop users, which is helpful if you're working with others on a project. You can also load presets created by other Photoshop users.

Saving Tool Presets

1. Open the Tool Picker and click the right arrow at the top of the picker window.

2. Select Save Tool Presets, as shown here.

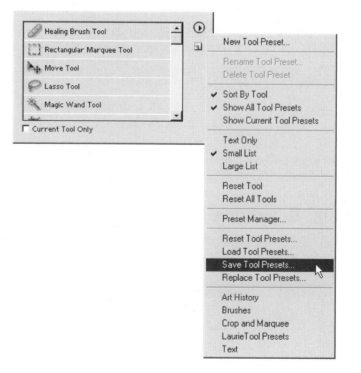

Deleting a Tool

1. Open the Tool Preset Picker, and select the tool preset you want to delete.

2. Click the right arrow at the top of the picker window. Select Delete Tool Preset.

Loading Tool Presets

Photoshop ships with several sets of tool presets you may want to experiment with. These are listed at the bottom of the menu, as shown here. These are the presets that have been saved to your Photoshop | Presets | Tools folder on your hard drive.

Select Tool Presets and, when prompted, select Append, as shown here. Append adds these tool presets to your current list of presets, rather than replacing your tool presets.

To load presets from other users:

1. Open the Tool Preset Picker. Click on the arrow to reveal the menu.

2. Select Load Tool Presets. When prompted, select Append.

Using the Preset Manager

The preset manager enables you to manage all your preset libraries for Photoshop. You can delete, load, rename, and save libraries using the preset manager—all from one location.

Using the preset manager, you can edit your brushes, swatches, gradients, styles, patterns, contours, custom shapes, and tool presets.

Deleting and Renaming Presets

Open the preset manager by selecting Edit | Preset Manager, as shown here. You'll see the previews for a library.

To delete an individual preset, select it and click Delete as shown here.

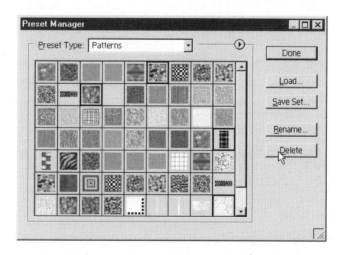

To delete multiple items, SHIFT-click to select the presets, then click Delete, as shown here.

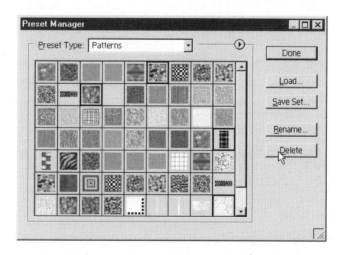

To rename a single preset, select it and click Rename. Enter the new name. To rename multiple presets, SHIFT-click to select the presets you want to rename. Then click Rename and enter the new names.

Changing the View for Presets

You can move individual presets around in the library by dragging them and dropping them, as shown here. This is helpful if you want to keep your most-often-used presets at the top of the list so they are easy to find.

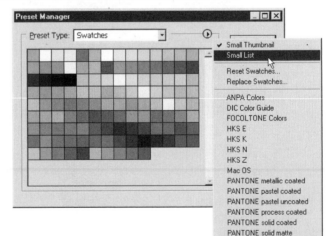

You can also change the way you view a library from the default (small thumbnails) to larger thumbnails or a list by clicking the arrow to open the menu, as shown here. Then select your view preference.

Saving Subsets of Libraries

You can use the preset manager to save a subset of a library. SHIFT-click to select individual presets, then click Save Set. Enter a name for the new library.

To select and save an entire library, use CTRL-A/ COMMAND-A to select all presets in a library. Then click Save Set. Enter a name for the library.

Creating a Custom Document Size

If there's a new document size that you frequently work with, you can create it as a custom setting, so that it appears when you open the File | New dialog.

To create a new document size, you'll want to use a plain text editor, one that doesn't add any formatting to a plain text document. In Windows, open Notepad by selecting Start | Programs | Accessories | Notepad. On the Mac, open Simple Text. Then select File | Open, and browse your hard drive to find the Adobe | Photoshop | Presets folder. Open the file named "New Doc Sizes.txt" as shown here.

```
New Doc Sizes.txt - Notepad                                    _ □ ×
File  Edit  Search  Help
; Version of the file, 1 for Photoshop 7.0

1

; Blank lines and lines starting with ; are ignored

; Document preset sizes are lines formatted as:

; "Preset Name"    Width     Height     Units

; or

; "Preset Name"    Width     Height     Units            Resolution

;      "Preset Name" requires quotes around it

;      Width is the decimal width of the preset, in units

;      Height is the decimal height of the preset, in units

;      Units is the units for the preset and is one of the following:
;              pixels
;              inches
;              cm
;              mm
;              points
;              picas

;      If a Resolution value is not present, the resolution in the
;      dialog will not be changed.

;      Otherwise resolution is one of the following:
```

Enter the name of your custom size in quotations, followed by the measurements, followed by the type of measurement. To create a custom document size titled Laurie, with the dimensions of 450 pixels wide by 300 pixels high, as shown here, type in:

```
"Laurie 2" 450 300 pixels
```

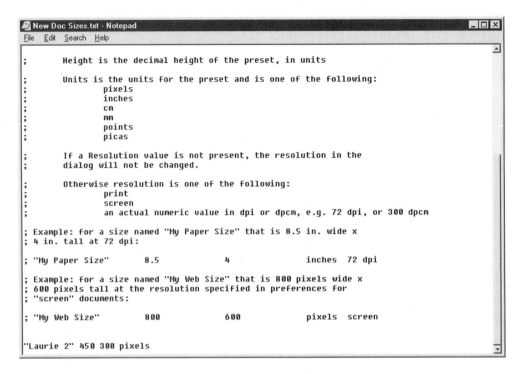

Save the text file. Next, open Photoshop. (If Photoshop was open you'll need to close and relaunch it to see the changes.) Select File | New. Under Preset Sizes, scroll down to find your new preset, as shown here.

You can save more than one new document size. Just be sure to name them descriptively so that you'll remember which one is which.

Using Annotations

It's often useful to save notes about a file that you're working on. You may want to remind yourself about the fonts you've used, ideas you've had for further development, and so on. When you're exchanging files with other people, it's often helpful to add a note so everyone stays informed.

Photoshop has a nifty tool called the notes tool. Use this tool to add a note, or annotation, to your Photoshop file. The annotation shows up as a small icon on your image, as shown here.

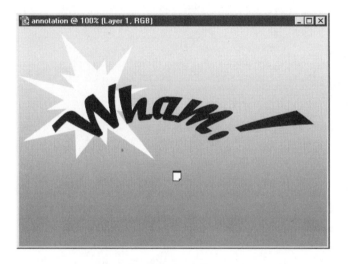

12

NOTE *Text annotations are saved only if you save your file in native Photoshop format (.psd) or Adobe Acrobat PDF file format.*

Double-click the annotation icon to open the note, as shown in Figure 12-3.

Adding a Text Note

As long as you save your image in PSD or Adobe Acrobat PDF format, your text note is saved with the file. It's a great help to be able to save a file to PDF format, since the person looking at the file doesn't need to have Photoshop installed in order to read the file. All you need to read a PDF file is the Acrobat Reader, downloadable free from Adobe.

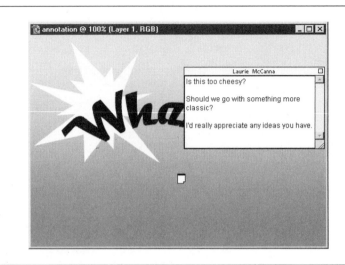

FIGURE 12-3 Using text notes is a great way to keep track of comments between coworkers or clients. You can also use text notes as a reminder to yourself about color, size, fonts, or any other important details.

To add a text note to your image, follow these steps:

1. Select the text note tool from the Photoshop toolbox.

2. Fill in the Author's name, and select font, font size, and note color from the options bar. If you're exchanging notes back and forth with someone else, it's helpful if each person uses a different color for his note, as shown here.

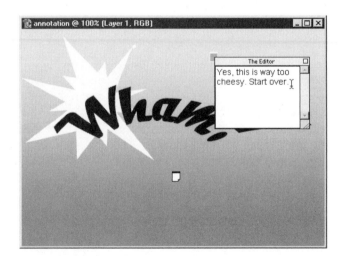

3. Click on your image to place a note, or you can click and drag to create a note size.

4. Type your text inside the note area.

5. To delete a note, right-click/CTRL-click to reveal a context-sensitive menu. Select Delete.

Recording an Action

Actions are macros, or changes made to an image in Photoshop, recorded so that they can be applied to other images. Actions can save a great deal of time and increase your productivity by automating repetitive tasks. Actions are also useful for recreating techniques and creating special effects. Actions can be easily shared between Photoshop users. See Chapter 14 for sources for download actions created by other Photoshop users.

Actions are greatly underused by Photoshop users. Even a simple action that saves you only a step or two can speed up your work and eliminate drudgery if you repeat a particular task several times a day. Although you can create an action that will add shimmery metallic text to an image, include a drop shadow and bevel, then flatten the file and save it as a GIF, simpler actions may be more useful in your day-to-day work.

As with layers, actions can be organized into sets, and they can also be color coded. You can save, edit, and organize actions in the Actions palette, as shown in Figure 12-4.

Creating a Simple Action

To get you started, here's how to create a simple action that will flatten a Photoshop file, something you probably do frequently before saving a file.

1. Open an image. If the image doesn't have more than one layer, create multiple layers by selecting the New Layer icon at the bottom of the Layers palette. You may want to work with a copy of a file so that you don't flatten a file that you need in layered format.

2. Open the Actions palette by selecting Window | Actions.

12

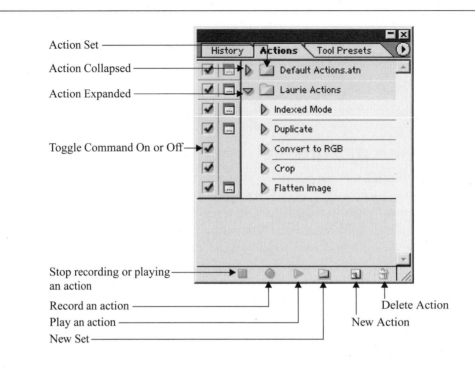

Action Set

Action Collapsed

Action Expanded

Toggle Command On or Off

Stop recording or playing an action

Record an action

Play an action

New Set

Delete Action

New Action

FIGURE 12-4   The Actions palette helps you manage your frequently used actions.

3. Select New Action from the drop-down menu on the Actions palette, or click the New Action icon at the bottom of the Actions palette. A dialog box opens where you can enter a name for your action, as shown below.

4. Enter a name for the action, such as "Flatten Image." Select a color for the action, if you want to. Click Record.

5. Select Layer | Flatten Image.

6. Stop the recording by clicking the Stop icon, as shown in here, located at the bottom of the Actions palette.

Playing, Loading, and Editing Actions

Photoshop comes with a number of actions preinstalled. You may want to use these actions to experiment with, as you learn to play, edit, and load actions. Actions are made up of individual commands, or steps, which can be disabled, deleted, or re-recorded. You can also change how actions are displayed in the Actions palette.

■ **Play an Action** To play a previously recorded action, open an image. Then click the Play icon at the bottom of the Actions palette.

■ **Load Actions** If you've received actions from other Photoshop users, you can load them by clicking the drop-down menu on the Actions palette. Select Load Action and browse to find the actions you want to use. To load actions that come with Photoshop, choose a set at the bottom of the drop-down menu, as shown on the right.

12

■ **Save Actions**   Select the set you want to save in the Actions palette, and select Save Actions from the drop-down menu.

■ **View Actions in Button Mode**   If you've finished editing actions and want a simple view, you can view your actions in button mode, as shown here. Select Button Mode from the drop-down menu. To revert back to the regular view of actions, select Button Mode again.

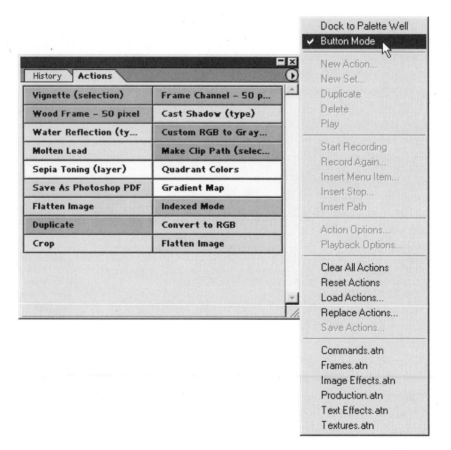

You can't edit Actions if you are in Button Mode.

■ **Change the Order of Actions**
You can drag and drop an action
to another place in the set, as
shown here.

■ **Edit Actions** There are
several ways to temporarily or
permanently change existing
actions. You'll want to view the
action to be edited in expanded
view, by clicking the right-facing
arrow next to the name of the
action in the Actions palette, as
shown here.

■ **Disable a Command** You can temporarily disable a single command
by clicking the checkmark to the left of the command, as shown below.
When you play the action, that particular step will not be applied to
your image.

■ **Delete a Command** Drag the command you want to delete to the icon
at the bottom of the Actions palette.

■ **Re-record a Command** Delete the command you want to re-record.
Then click Record at the bottom of the Actions palette. Click Stop when
you have finished.

Using the Batch Command

You can take any action and apply it to an entire folder of images, or selected files, in a few simple steps. This can save you an enormous amount of time and prevent you from having to repeat tasks. Faced with the daunting task of converting a CD full of TIFFs to GIF format would make most people cringe but, by using the Batch command, you can set up the process, and grab a cup of coffee while Photoshop does the work!

First, you'll want to create the action you want to apply to a series of images. If you want to select certain images to apply the action to, use the File Browser or CTRL-click/COMMAND-click to select the files you want to use. If you want to apply the action to a folder of images, you can omit this step.

1. Select File | Automate | Batch to open the Batch dialog box, as seen here.

2. Select the set and action you wish to use.

3. Choose a source for the files. (Skip this step if you've chosen the files using the File Browser.) Click Choose to find the folder. If you want to apply the action to all the files you currently have open in Photoshop, select Opened Files.

4. Select a destination, or folder in which you want the batch-processed files to be saved. Click Choose to browse to find a file.

5. Click OK to apply the batch command to the images you've specified.

Creating a Droplet

Have you ever wanted to create a simple change to an image, but haven't wanted to open Photoshop, open the file, make the change, and save the file? You can do this using Photoshop to transform an action into a droplet. A droplet is a small program onto which you can drag and drop an image. The program causes Photoshop to automatically launch, and the action to be applied to your image.

To create a droplet, you'll need to record an action first. Then select File | Automate | Droplet. The dialog box, shown here, displays.

Click Choose to select where you'd like to save the droplet. If it's a droplet you'll be using frequently, you may want to save it to your desktop where it's easy to find.

Select the set and action you wish to transform into a droplet. If your action includes saving a file, you'll want to change the Destination from None to Save and Close, or choose Folder.

To use a droplet, simply drag and drop an image onto your droplet, as shown here.

When you drag and drop your image onto the droplet, Photoshop automatically launches and performs the action on your image. You can exchange droplets with other Photoshop users.

Creating a Web Gallery

If you're looking for a quick way to create a gallery of images for the Web, there's a fantastic feature built into Photoshop that can create the thumbnails and web pages. This is a great timesaver if you want to put up several quick samples on the Web for approval from a client, or as the beginning of a web site to show off your work.

You'll want to make sure that all the images that you include in your web photo gallery are in the same folder on your hard drive. Move any images that you don't want to include.

In Photoshop, select File | Automate | Web Photo Gallery. Under Styles, you can browse and preview the different styles of web page layouts you can choose from. Type in your e-mail address if you want to include an e-mail link on the web page. Next, browse to find the folder that contains the images you want to include in your web photo gallery.

You need a folder, different from the folder that contains your original images, to save the web pages and images to. Select this file, as shown in Figure 12-5.

There are several selections under Options. In the Banner field, you can enter a page title, date, and other information. Under Thumbnails, you can select the layout of the thumbnails on the web page. The Custom Colors option enables you to select custom colors for web page backgrounds, links, and text. The Large Images selection enables you to determine the size and layout of the images that the thumbnails will link to.

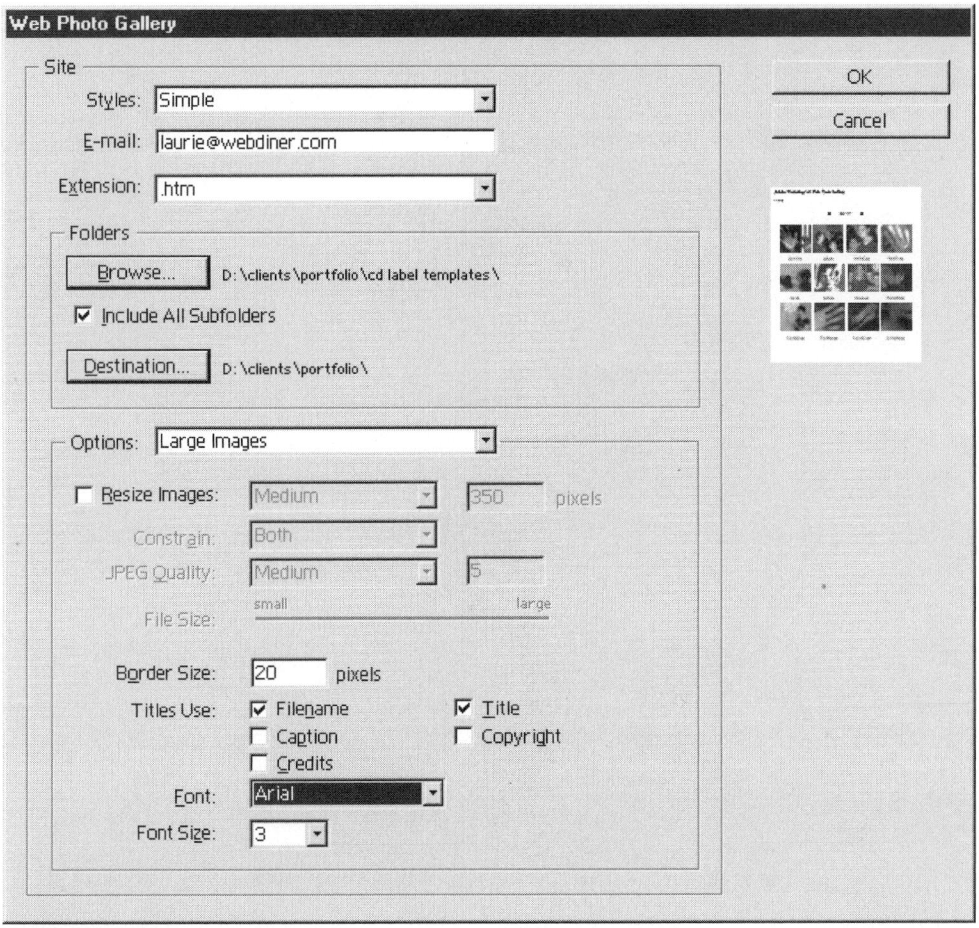

FIGURE 12-5   The Web Photo Gallery will automatically create a set of linking HTML pages that contain images. It's a quick and easy way to show a client various revisions of an image, or a good way to start an online portfolio of your work.

When you have finished making your selection, click OK. The Web Photo Gallery generates all the images and HTML pages necessary. When the process is finished, you'll see the page of thumbnails in a web browser, as shown in Figure 12-6.

Each thumbnail is linked to a larger version of the image. Click on the thumbnail and another web page opens, as shown in Figure 12-7. These gallery pages have navigation arrows at the top that enable you to move from image to image.

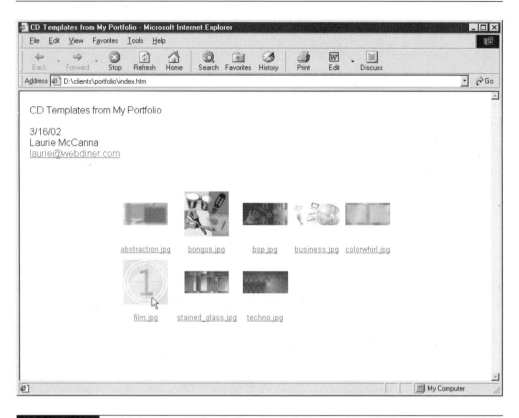

FIGURE 12-6   This is an example of what the main page of a web photo gallery would look like. You can click any of the thumbnails, as shown here, to go to a page that shows a larger version of that image, as shown in Figure 12-7.

Creating a Contact Sheet

Instead of creating a gallery of a collection of images for the Web, sometimes you will want to print multiple images on a single sheet of paper. Photographers often do this, and it is called a contact sheet.

As with the web gallery automation feature, you'll want to put all the images you want to print in a single folder, and make sure to remove the images that you don't want to include in your contact sheet.

1. Select File | Automate | Contact Sheet II. This opens a dialog box that enables you to create the layout for your images on the page.

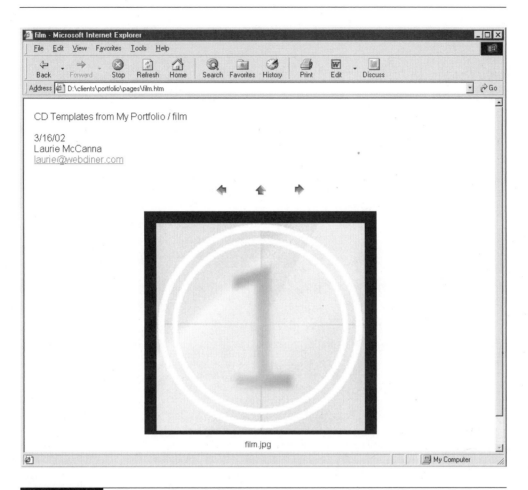

FIGURE 12-7   The page for an individual image created with the Web Photo Gallery feature shows the image at a larger size, along with navigation arrows to move between different gallery pages.

2. Click the Browse button and select the folder you want to use.

3. Next, set the Document settings, including the total Width and Height of the contact sheet, the resolution you want to print out, and the color mode you want to use.

4. In the Thumbnails section, you can select how many rows and columns of images you want to include on a page, as shown in Figure 12-8.

12

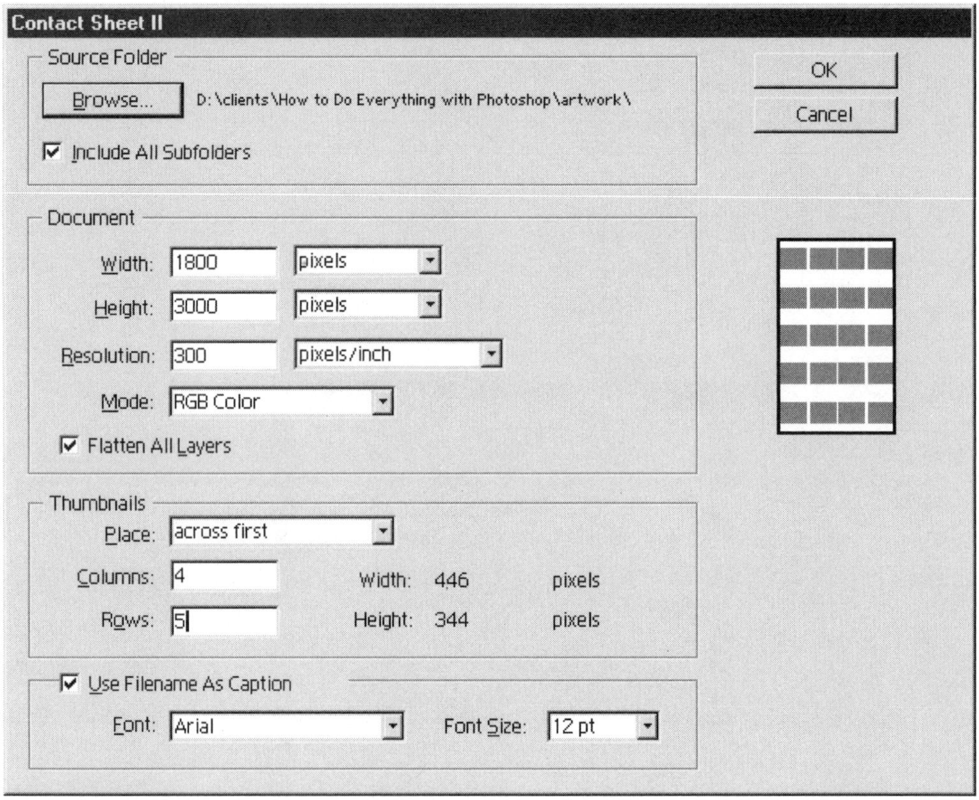

FIGURE 12-8   You can create a contact sheet that contains multiple images, and customize the layout of the contact sheet.

5. Finally, you can choose to use the file name as a caption for each image and set the font and font size for the captions.

6. When you have finished, click OK. Photoshop creates the thumbnails and adds them to a page, or multiple pages if you have many images. The final pages look like the example shown in Figure 12-9.

3dshapes.eps	apple_photo....	Astro.eps	biplane_phot...
brushes.psd	candyhearts_...	candylove.eps	chair.psd
circle_gradien...	exotic_destin...	hi_res_biplan...	hummingbird...
leafshadow.psd	lightening_bo...	lion.psd	model_t_phot...
paint_tube.eps	papermoon.psd	seashells.psd	stag.tif

12

FIGURE 12-9 This is an example of what a contact sheet looks like when you're finished. If you're working on a project with many images, it can be extremely helpful to have a printed reference to keep your project organized.

Chapter 13

Moving Between Applications

How to...

- Work with Adobe Illustrator

- Work with Adobe After Effects

- Work with Adobe LiveMotion

- Work with Macromedia Flash

- Work with Microsoft Word

- Work with Microsoft PowerPoint

You learned how to save files for the Web in Chapter 10, and how to set up your files for print in Chapter 5. In many cases, you'll be using Photoshop to create images that will be used in other software programs. This chapter will help you decide what file format will best suit your needs, and will guide you through techniques that will help you get the best possible results when you work with images in multiple software applications.

Wherever possible, you'll want to save images in a layered Photoshop format, to maximize your ability to edit. You can work with the native Photoshop file format with all Adobe applications.

Working with Adobe Illustrator

Adobe Illustrator is a vector-based drawing program, and its strength lies in its handling of vector objects. Working between Illustrator and Photoshop can provide you with a rich set of tools for creating both bitmap and vector effects. Many Illustrator tools will be familiar to Photoshop users, which makes working between these applications easier.

Working with Linked Files

To work most efficiently between any Adobe applications, you need to understand the notion of linked files. You can add a linked Photoshop file into an Illustrator document. This creates a link between the Illustrator file and the Photoshop file, without actually embedding the Photoshop file within the Illustrator document. The main benefit of linking a file is that when you update the image within Photoshop, the changes are automatically made to the linked file in the Illustrator document.

The drawbacks of using a linked file are minimal. You must include both the Photoshop and the Illustrator file if you'll be sending the file to another person to use, because if the linked file isn't included, the link is broken and the Photoshop file does not appear in the Illustrator document. If you move the location of the linked file, the link is also broken.

Working with Photoshop Files in Illustrator

There are several ways to work with files in Illustrator. If you won't be using Illustrator to make any changes to the Photoshop file, you'll want to place the file. If you want to make additions, or edit paths or shapes created in Photoshop, you'll want to either open the Photoshop file in Illustrator or export paths from Photoshop.

Placed Files

To bring a Photoshop file into Illustrator, in Illustrator, select File | Place. Browse to find the Photoshop file you wish to use, and click the Link checkbox as shown here. The files are now linked, and any changes you make to your Photoshop file within Photoshop are reflected in the Illustrator document.

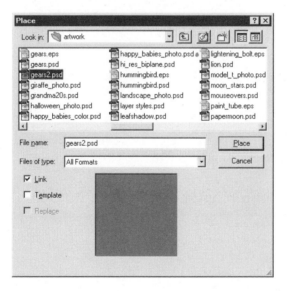

To edit a placed file, you can select the Photoshop image in the Illustrator document and select Edit | Edit Original, as shown in Figure 13-1. This automatically launches Photoshop and opens the Photoshop file so that you can edit the file. Save your Photoshop file and the changes are reflected in the placed Photoshop file in Illustrator.

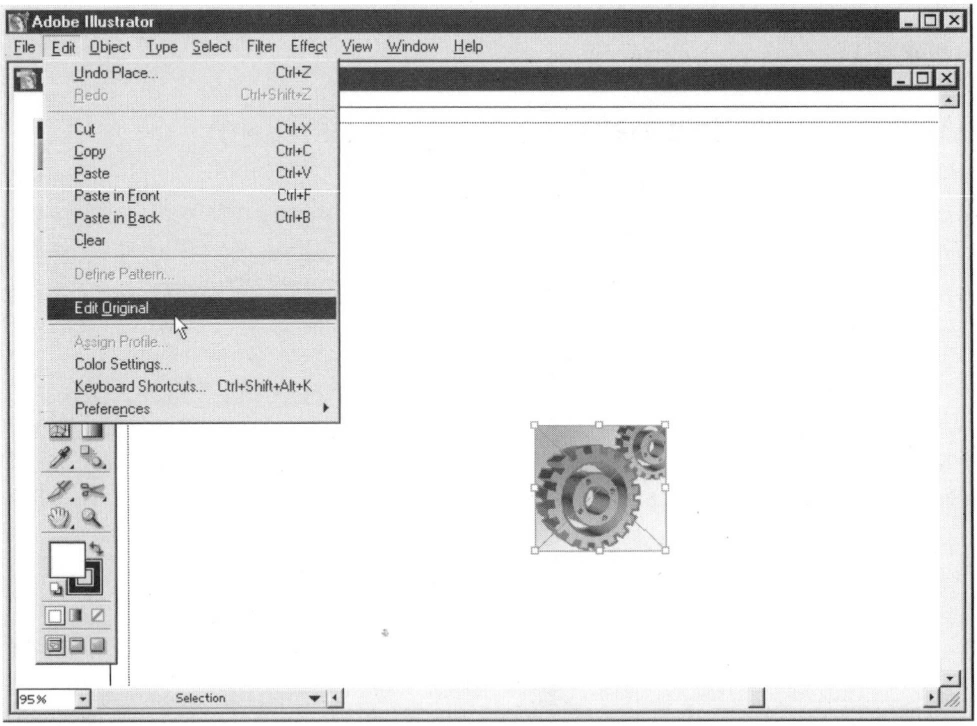

FIGURE 13-1 One way to work with Photoshop and Illustrator is by placing a Photoshop file into Illustrator. Then, by selecting Edit | Edit Original, the image will automatically open in Photoshop for editing.

Opening Photoshop Files in Illustrator

If you want to work with a Photoshop file in Illustrator, select File | Open. When prompted, select Convert Photoshop layers to objects. This creates a layer in Illustrator for each Photoshop layer as per the options shown in Figure 13-2, enabling you to work with layers independently.

When you open a Photoshop file in Illustrator, text is transformed to bitmaps and is no longer be editable. However, shapes are editable with Illustrator tools. You can move, delete, or duplicate layers. You can also use Illustrator tools to add new elements to your image.

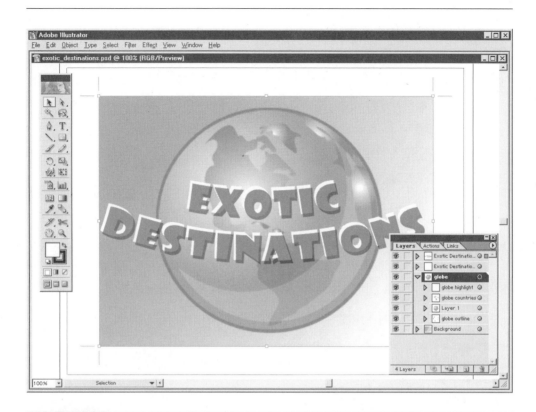

FIGURE 13-2   Photoshop layers will become editable Illustrator layers when you open a
Photoshop image in Adobe Illustrator.

Working with Paths Created in Photoshop

You can export paths created in Photoshop to Illustrator by selecting File | Export |
Paths to Illustrator in Photoshop. To open the path in Illustrator, select File | Open.
Even if you filled the path in Photoshop, it will open in Illustrator with no outline
and no fill. However, you will see crop marks that show the position of the path.
In order to see the path in Illustrator, select View | Outline and you will be able to
see your path, as shown in Figure 13-3.

13

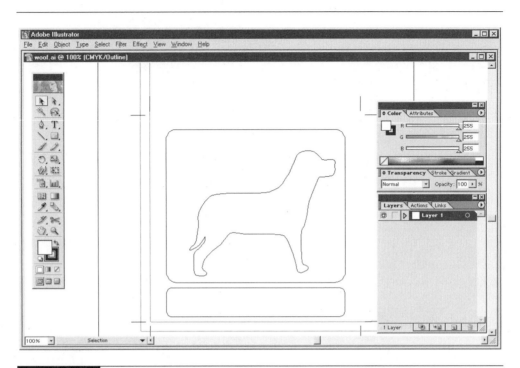

FIGURE 13-3   Your Photoshop path will be easier to view in Adobe Illustrator if you select View | Outline.

Select the path with the selection tool, and add a fill or outline. Then change your view back to normal view by selecting View | Preview, as shown in Figure 13-4.

Working with Illustrator Files in Photoshop

If you want to work in Photoshop with a file you've created in Illustrator, you will need to make a decision—will you want to export your file in bitmap or vector format? If the file is something like a logo that you'll be reusing at many sizes, your best choice is to save in a vector format like EPS or PDF. However, if you will be using the file at one size, you'll want the convenience of saving the file in Photoshop layered file format.

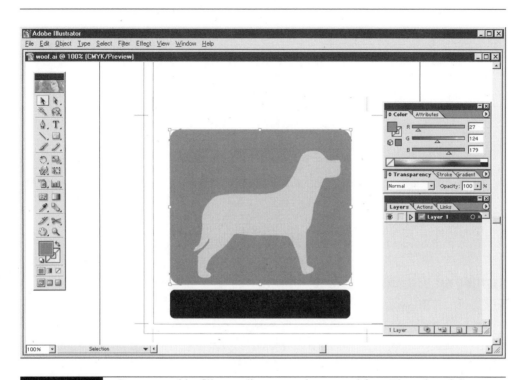

FIGURE 13-4   Once you add a fill or outline to a path exported from Photoshop, it becomes visible in Illustrator.

Exporting Files in Photoshop Format

To export an Illustrator file in native Photoshop format, keeping layers intact, select File | Export. Select PSD as the file type. You'll then be presented with a dialog box, as shown here, that enables you to set your preferences for the exported file.

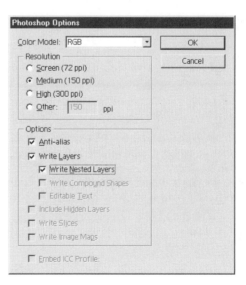

13

- **Color Model**   Select RGB for video or web work, or if you're not certain. Select CMYK for print files.

- **Resolution**   Select the resolution according to the final output of the file format. You can always size an image down without much loss of quality, but remember that if you set the resolution too low you'll need to enlarge the file, which will cause a loss of quality. When in doubt, select a higher resolution and resize the image in Photoshop.

- **Anti-alias**   Select this checkbox for the best quality.

- **Write Layers**   Select this checkbox so that objects are created on their own layers, giving you more flexibility when you edit the file in Photoshop.

- **Write Nested Layers**   Select this checkbox to create nested layers, which will provide additional flexibility when you edit the file.

Exporting Files in Vector Format

To export an Illustrator file in a vector format for use in Photoshop, select File | Save As. Choose either EPS or PDF file format.

To open an EPS or PDF file in Photoshop, select File | Open. You'll be presented with this dialog when opening either EPS or PDF format files.

- **Width and Height**   You can change the default size for the file to whatever you need.

- **Resolution**   You can change the file's resolution.

- **Anti-aliased**   Check the anti-aliased checkbox to ensure the best quality image, especially for lower-resolution images.

- **Constrain Proportions**   If you will be resizing the image you're importing— changing either the width or height—check the Constrain Proportions checkbox. This will ensure that the file resizes proportionately.

Using Illustrator Artwork to Make a Custom Photoshop Shape

You can use Illustrator's powerful vector editing tools to create shapes that you can reuse in Photoshop as custom shapes. This is especially helpful if you'll be creating something that needs to be used over and over again in different sizes, such as a company logo.

1. Create the artwork in Illustrator. You'll want to keep the shapes simple, without any bitmap or transparency effects.

2. In Illustrator, select Edit | Preferences | Files & Clipboard. Make sure the AICB checkbox is checked, as shown here.

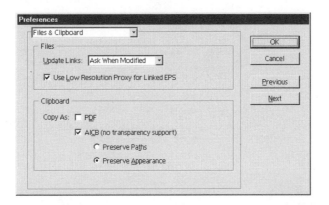

3. Select your artwork in Illustrator and choose Edit | Copy.

4. Open Photoshop, and select File | New. Then Select Edit | Paste. A dialog box appears, as shown here.

5. Select Edit | Define Custom Shape. You'll be able to name your custom shape, as shown here.

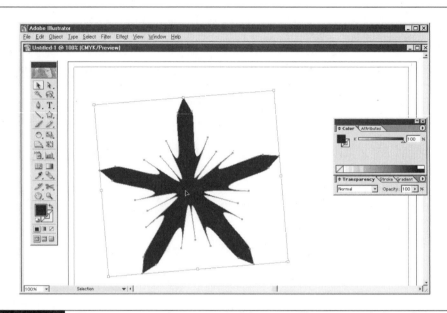

FIGURE 13-5 You can copy and paste artwork between Illustrator and Photoshop.

Your custom shape is included in the custom shape picker, at the bottom of the list, as shown here.

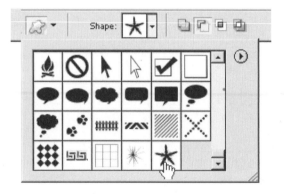

Working with Adobe After Effects

Adobe After Effects is a very powerful video animation program. After Effects and Photoshop work extremely well together to create dynamic animation. You can bring in layered Photoshop files and animate the layers individually.

To create Photoshop files to use in After Effects, remember to put items that you want to animate on individual layers. Name all the layers with distinctive names so they will be easily identifiable within After Effects. Layered Photoshop files do not import with layer effects, so you will want to change layer effects into layers. Select the layer effect, and select Layer | Layer Style | Create Layer.

If you want to create an animated background, make the image large enough so you can create the effect of movement. For instance, if you want to create the impression of waves behind a title, create the image of the waves in Photoshop so that it's large enough to drag across the After Effects composition as shown in Figure 13-6.

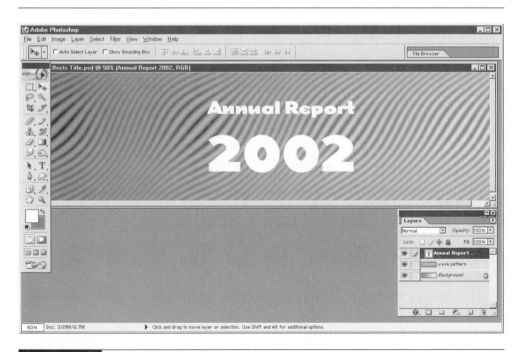

FIGURE 13-6   For maximum flexibility, you can create layered files in Photoshop and animate layers individually in Adobe After Effects.

Importing a Photoshop File as a Composition

You can import a layered file into After Effects by opening a new composition.
Then select File | Import File. Next, choose the Photoshop file you want to import.
Select Composition, then click Open, as shown here.

Your layered Photoshop file is imported into your After Effects composition, as
seen in Figure 13-7. You can animate each layer individually.

Importing Photoshop Files as Footage

If you want to create a series of Photoshop files and animate them in After Effects,
you'll want to create your images in Photoshop, flatten them, and then name them
in sequential order, such as file01.psd, file02.psd, file03.psd, and so on.

To import the files as footage into After Effects, open a new composition in
After Effects. Then select File | Import | Multiple Files, as shown in Figure 13-8.

Once you've imported the sequence of files, click Done. You can then move
the files into the composition and animate each file individually, as shown in
Figure 13-9.

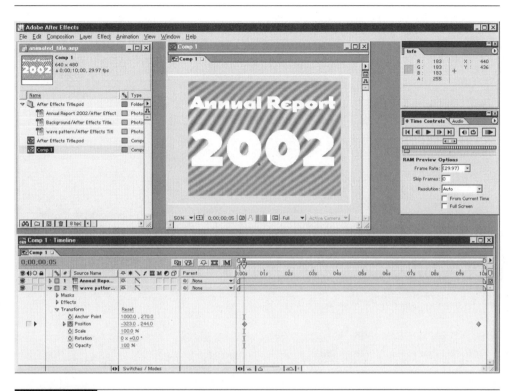

FIGURE 13-7   Your Photoshop file will import with its layers intact.

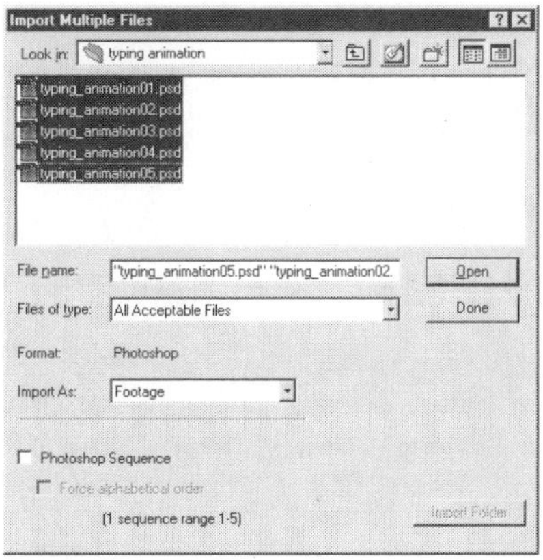

13

FIGURE 13-8   Importing multiple files as footage into After Effects.

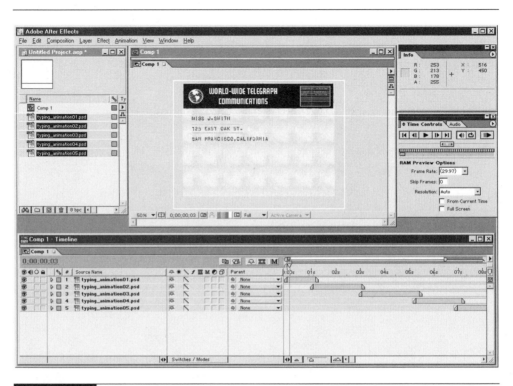

FIGURE 13-9   You can import and animate a sequence of Photoshop files into Adobe
After Effects.

Editing an Imported Photoshop File

To edit a Photoshop file that you've imported into After Effects, select the file in the
Project, Composition, or Timeline window. Then select Edit | Edit Original, and the
file automatically opens within Photoshop for editing.

Working with Adobe LiveMotion

Adobe LiveMotion is a software program that enables you to create Flash format
animations for the Web. Flash files can be played within a web browser and
can contain interactive elements. You can import Photoshop files and animate
layers individually.

Place objects that will be animated individually on separate layers, and name
layers so they are easy to identify in LiveMotion.

Importing a Photoshop File into LiveMotion

To bring a layered Photoshop file into Adobe LiveMotion, open a new composition, then select File | Place, and select the file you would like to animate in LiveMotion. The Photoshop file is imported as a single item, as shown in Figure 13-10. In order to work with individual layers, select Objects | Convert Into | Objects.

Working with Macromedia Flash

Flash creates animations for the Web. The best file format to use when exporting files from Photoshop to Flash is the PNG file format. PNG, or Portable Network Graphics file format, supports transparency so you can export your file with a selection that creates transparency when imported into Flash.

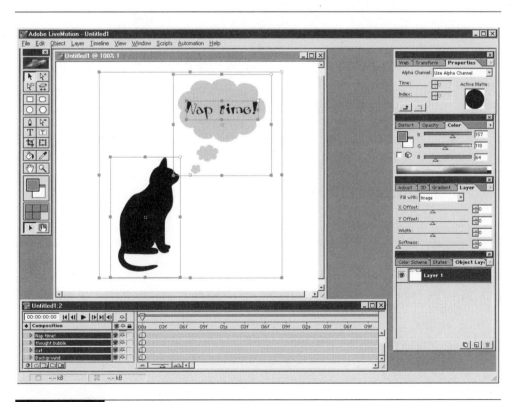

FIGURE 13-10   Converting an imported Photoshop file into objects in Adobe LiveMotion allows you to animate each object separately.

In Photoshop, create your file. To indicate a transparent area, use any of the selection tools to create a selection that includes all parts of the image you wish to remain transparent, as shown here.

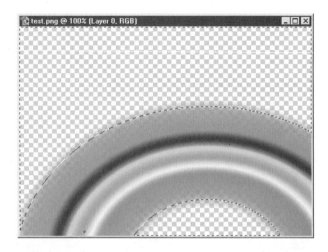

Next, save the selection. Choose Select | Save Selection, and name the selection. Flatten the file by selecting Layer | Flatten Image. Then choose File | Save As, and choose PNG as the file format.

To import the file into Flash, select File | Import, and browse to find the PNG file you've created. You can see that the transparency has been included when you add a background behind the transparent PNG, as shown here.

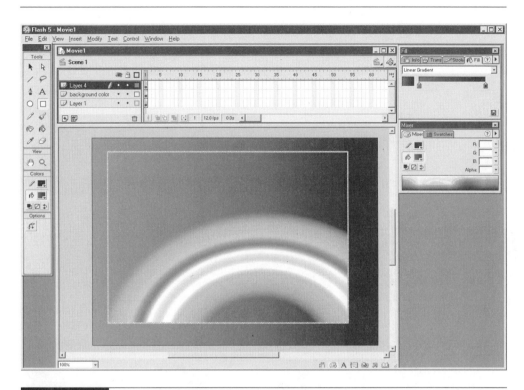

FIGURE 13-11   Importing a PNG file with transparency gives you more control and freedom than working with other file formats when working with Macromedia Flash.

Working with Microsoft Word

Microsoft Word is the most popular word processing program used in businesses today. Getting graphics to look good both on screen and in print is the challenge with Word documents. Although Word supports a variety of different file formats, for best output and onscreen viewing, you'll want to save your images in TIFF format.

As you can see in this example, the resolution that you save your image with in Photoshop is important to how the image imports into Word.

Saving Graphics for Microsoft Word

To save graphics for Microsoft Word, start with a resolution of between 150 to 300 pixels per inch. This ensures the best output when the document is printed. Flatten

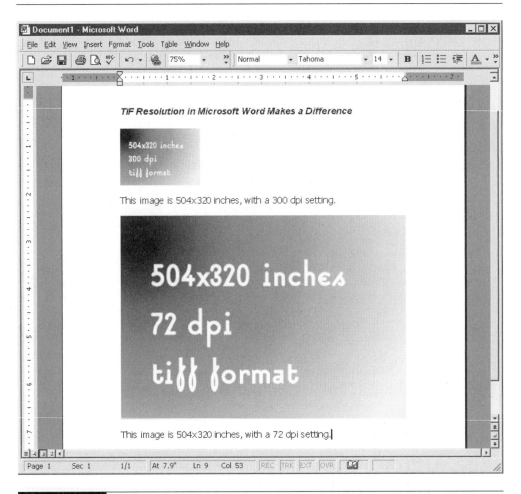

FIGURE 13-12   When importing images created in Photoshop into Microsoft Word, the resolution (dpi) determines how large or small the image appears.

the file when you are finished working with it by selecting Layers | Flatten. Select File | Save As to save the file, and choose TIFF as the file format. Under Image Compression, select None. For maximum compatibility, select IBM PC byte order.

Although TIFF graphics give the best possible output, if file size is a concern, try saving graphics as PNG files to reduce the file size. After flattening your file by selecting Layer | Flatten Image, select File | Save As and select PNG as the file format.

Importing Graphics into Microsoft Word

In Microsoft Word, place your cursor where you want to insert the graphic. Then select Insert | Graphic | From File, and browse to find the file you'd like to import.

Working with Microsoft PowerPoint

Microsoft PowerPoint is a business presentation tool, used for presenting information with text, images, charts, and graphs. Photoshop graphics can be used in PowerPoint for backgrounds, illustrations, or animations. PowerPoint presentations are made up of individual slides. Because PowerPoint presentations are generally viewed only on screen, you'll want to orient your graphics horizontally, to fit the aspect of a computer monitor or television screen, as shown in Figure 13-13.

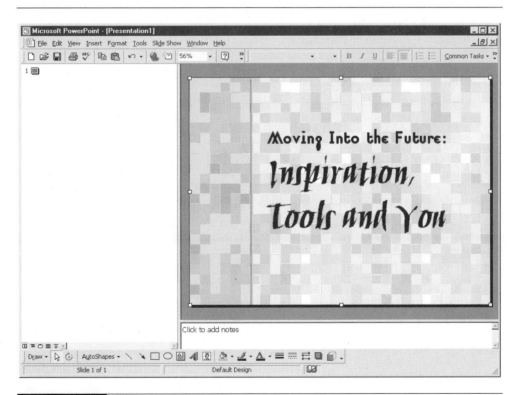

FIGURE 13-13   You will want to create your images to fit the format of a computer screen when working with Microsoft PowerPoint.

Creating a Full Screen Graphic for PowerPoint

Because PowerPoint graphics are displayed on computer monitors, you'll want to design your graphics for a common monitor display size, such as 800×600 pixels, or 1200×1000 pixels. The resolution of the image doesn't matter as much as it does for graphics used in Microsoft Word.

The best format for static PowerPoint graphics is PNG, which results in small file sizes and high-quality graphics. To save your image in PNG format, flatten your Photoshop file by selecting Layer | Flatten Image, then choose File | Save As and select PNG as the file format.

Transparent Graphics and Animated Graphics

If you want to add an animated graphic, or a graphic that allows a background to show through, you'll want to save your image in GIF format. Although PowerPoint does well with PNG graphics for solid images, GIF images are much better for transparent graphics. Save your animations or transparent GIF as described in Chapter 5.

Adding Graphics to PowerPoint

Open a new presentation in PowerPoint, then select Insert | Picture | From File and browse to find the graphic you would like to add to the presentation.

Exporting Slides from PowerPoint

There may be occasions when you want to start with a slide from a PowerPoint presentation and improve it in Photoshop. To export from PowerPoint, select File | Save As, and select PNG as the file format as shown in Figure 13-14. You can then choose whether to save all the slides from a presentation, or just the current slide.

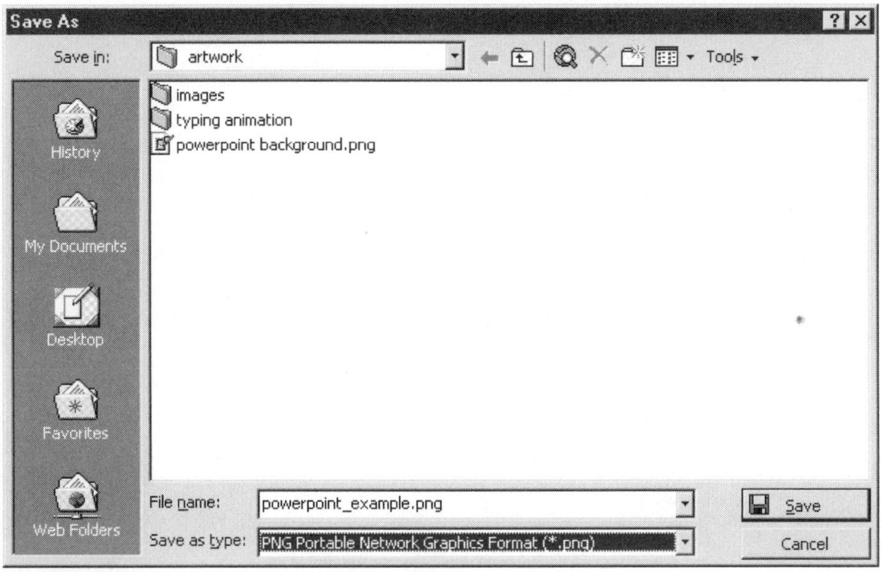

FIGURE 13-14 Exporting from PowerPoint.

Chapter 14

Resources for Photoshop

How to...

■ Learn more about Photoshop

■ Download goodies for Photoshop

■ Connect with Photoshop users

■ Try out commercial plug-ins

■ Browse copyright information

Because Photoshop is such a popular program, there are lots of tutorials, downloads, and help available for Photoshop users on the Internet. In this chapter you'll find places where you can learn to create special effects, download brushes, layer styles, and actions, and connect with other users to share techniques. Remember that the Web is a flexible medium and that URLs change frequently.

Learning More about Photoshop

There's always something new to learn about Photoshop, no matter how long you've used the program. These resources can guide you through learning more techniques to expand your repertoire of tricks. These links can also help you find solutions, such as identifying a particular font you want to use.

Laurie McCanna's Web Site

http://www.mccannas.com

This is the author's web site, and offers more Photoshop tutorials. You can also download brushes and clipart.

Computer Arts Tutorials

http://www.computerarts.co.uk/tutorials/

Computer Arts is a graphic design magazine from the UK. They offer software reviews and tutorials for Photoshop and many other graphic programs, as shown in Figure 14-1.

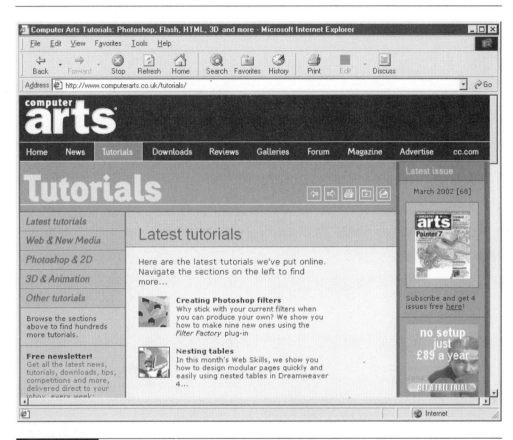

FIGURE 14-1 Computer Arts magazine offers software reviews and extensive Photoshop tutorials.

Designs by Mark Photoshop Tips

http://www.designsbymark.com/pstips/

Photoshop tips are arranged by topic, and are available for download in Adobe Acrobat format.

Identifont

http://www.identifont.com/

If you ever need to identify a font, this is the tool to use. You answer a series of questions, and Identifont identifies the font, as shown in Figure 14-2.

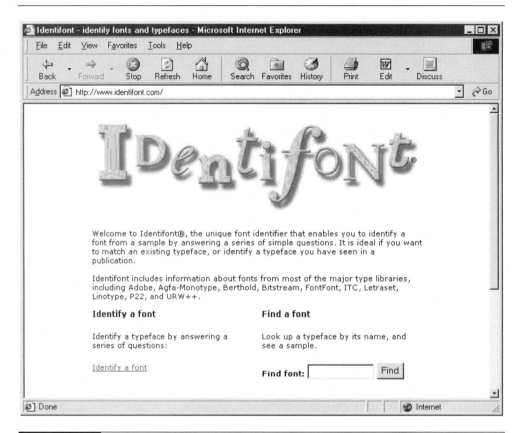

FIGURE 14-2   Easily identify almost any font using the Identifont web site.

Jay Arraich's Photoshop Tips

http://www.arraich.com/ps_intro.htm

This site contains a number of useful tutorials that walk you through the basics of Photoshop.

Metallic Tutorials

http://www.metallicgraphics.com

Find out how to make objects look like rusty metal, chains, or wire. This site offers links to hundreds of tutorials that help you create gold, silver, and chrome effects.

Production Graphics with Wendy Peck

http://webreference.com/graphics/

Discover tutorials, quick tips, and helpful hints for achieving many different effects with Photoshop.

Team Photoshop Tutorials

http://www.teamphotoshop.com

Browse tutorials, downloadable actions, and an active Photoshop forum where you can ask questions.

Download Goodies for Photoshop

Browse these links to find great downloads for Photoshop, including brushes, styles, and actions.

About.com Photoshop Downloads

http://graphicssoft.about.com/cs/photoshopdownloads/

Here you'll find free downloads of brushes, custom shapes, presets, utilities, templates, add-ons, palettes—plus other resources for Adobe Photoshop.

Acid Fonts

http://www.acidfonts.com/

Download a variety of text and dingbat fonts in both Mac and PC formats.

Action Xchange

http://xchange.studio.adobe.com

Browse through thousands of downloadable actions to create effects ranging from time-saving shortcuts to exciting text effects. Figure 14-3 shows the front page of the Adobe Xchange web site.

Adobe Expert Center

http://studio.adobe.com/expertcenter/main.html

After a one-time sign up process, you can enter the Adobe Expert Center. Rest assured that you don't need your PHD in Photoshop to benefit from the premium content offered here, including downloadable buttons, backgrounds, and actions. You can also view tutorials in video format.

14

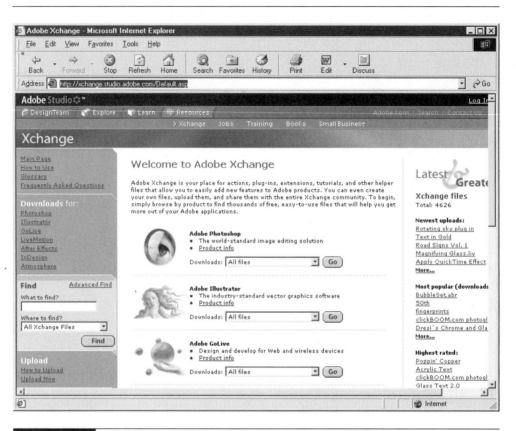

FIGURE 14-3 The Adobe Xchange offers many downloads for Photoshop users including actions and brushes.

Cybia Freeware

http://www.cybia.co.uk/

Download freeware brushes, actions, presets, and filters for Photoshop, as shown in Figure 14-4.

Deep Space Web

http://www.deepspaceweb.com

Message boards, news about graphic design topics, tutorials, and downloadable brushes are all offered on this web site.

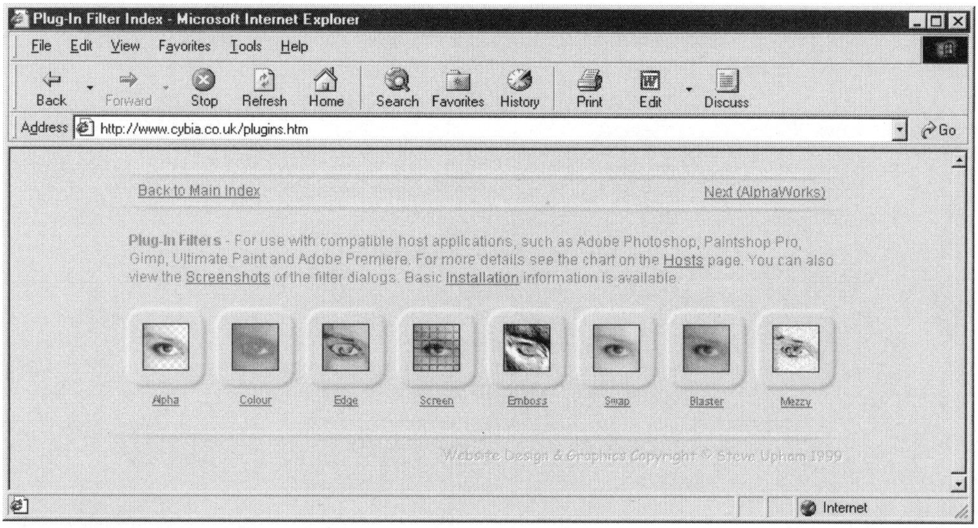

FIGURE 14-4 Download filters you can use to add exciting effects to your images.

Dingbat Pages

http://www.dingbatpages.com/

Download fonts made of symbols at this web site. The fonts are thoughtfully arranged into groups including arrows, beings, business, creatures, esoteric, and more, as shown in Figure 14-5. These fonts are offered in PC format only.

FontFace

http://www.fontface.com

Get a new freeware or shareware font daily, and search the archive of fonts featured on the site in the past. This web site offers fonts in both Mac and PC format as shown in Figure 14-6.

FontFreak

http://www.fontfreak.com

FontFreak offers shareware and freeware fonts in both Mac and PC format for download. Browse through a large collection of fonts, as shown in Figure 14-7.

14

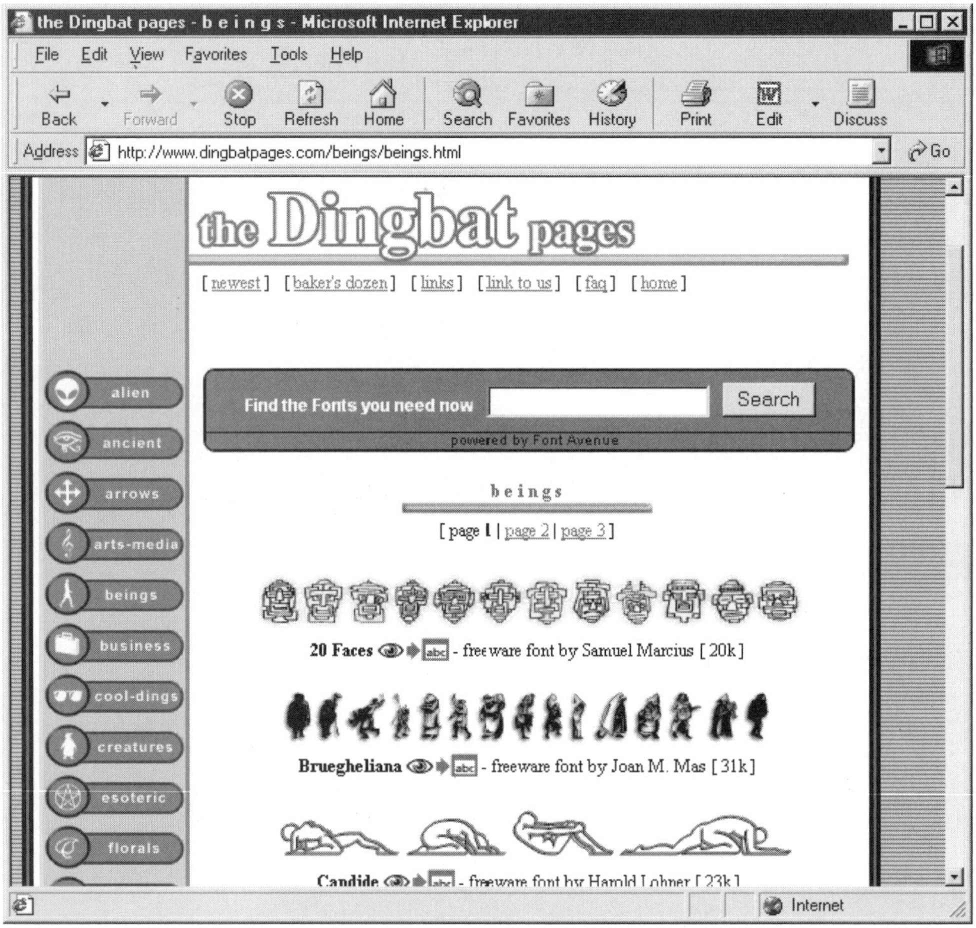

FIGURE 14-5   Symbol fonts offer a huge variety of images that you can add to your artwork. Visit the Dingbat Pages to browse through a huge selection of symbol fonts.

Photoshop Roadmap

http://www.photoshoproadmap.com/photoshop-downloads.html

This is a guide to other web sites that offer downloads for Photoshop, including an interesting variety of brushes, shapes, and layer styles.

FIGURE 14-6   Visit the FontFace web site for interesting and unusual fonts.

The Scriptorium

http://www.fontcraft.com

The Scriptorium offers shareware fonts based on historical type forms. You'll find fonts from ranging from ancient, Celtic, gothic, and art nouveau to the Wild West.

V-Brush

http://veredgf.fredfarm.com/vbrush/main.html

This site offers hundreds of brushes that you can download after a brief sign-up. These brushes are amazing—ranging from high tech looks to bits of old handwriting and illustrations. This site also offers a big list of links to other sites that offer Photoshop brushes for download.

FIGURE 14-7   FontFreak is another web site offering free and shareware fonts for downloading.

Connect with Photoshop Users

Adobe's User-to-User Forums

http://www.adobe.com/support/forums/main.html

Browse through other users' questions and answers about Photoshop as shown in Figure 14-8. These forums are also searchable, which is very helpful if you're looking for information on a specific Photoshop topic.

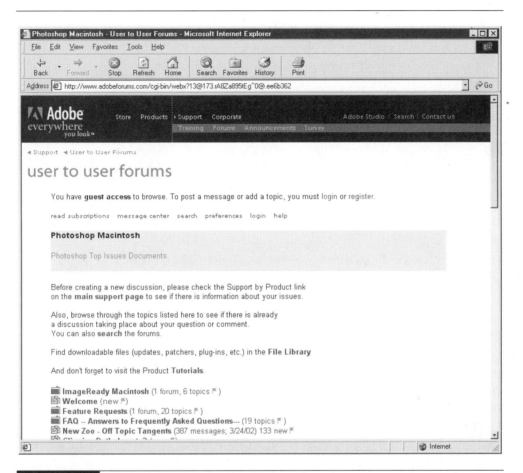

| FIGURE 14-8 | If you run into a Photoshop frustration, chances are you're not alone. Visity the busy Adobe User to User forums to search for answers and exchange information with other Photoshop users. |

comp.graphics.apps.photoshop and alt.graphics.photoshop

You'll need a newsreader, like Microsoft Outlook Express or Netscape Messenger, to read these Usenet Newsgroups that connect Photoshop users. Once you have your newsreader set up, you'll want to subscribe to comp.graphics.apps.photoshop or alt.graphics.photoshop. If you'd prefer to read these newsgroups through a web browser, you can use http://groups.google.com.

14

Photoshop Beginner's Group

http://groups.yahoo.com/group/photoshop-beginners
This group is aimed at beginners. Browse the web site to find step-by-step help in archived e-mail messages.

Photoshop Discussion List by E-mail

http://www.listmoms.net/lists/photoshop/
This very active discussion list is delivered to your mailbox daily. If you're looking for technical help, tips, or Photoshop information, this list is a great help.

Graphic Café Mailing List

http://www.listmoms.net/lists/graphics-cafe/
You can subscribe to this list or browse the archives via this web site. The topics range from what's the best hardware set up, to graphics, to general graphic design questions.

Search for Photoshop Answers

http://groups.google.com/
By entering search terms at Google Groups, you can search the Usenet discussion group archives. Using specific search terms, like "photoshop gif transparency" or "photoshop epson printer" yield the best results' as shown in Figure 14-9.

Try Out Commercial Plug-ins

One of Photoshop's most exciting features is its extensibility. You can add commercial and freeware plug-ins that help you create special effects, tweak your printer or scanner performance, or make production tasks easier. The following plug-in manufacturers offer trial downloads of their products that work with Photoshop.

Adromeda Software

http://www.andromeda.com
Download demo plug-ins from Andromeda's web site for a wide variety of filters, ranging from 3-D effects to photographic filters to textural and lighting effects.

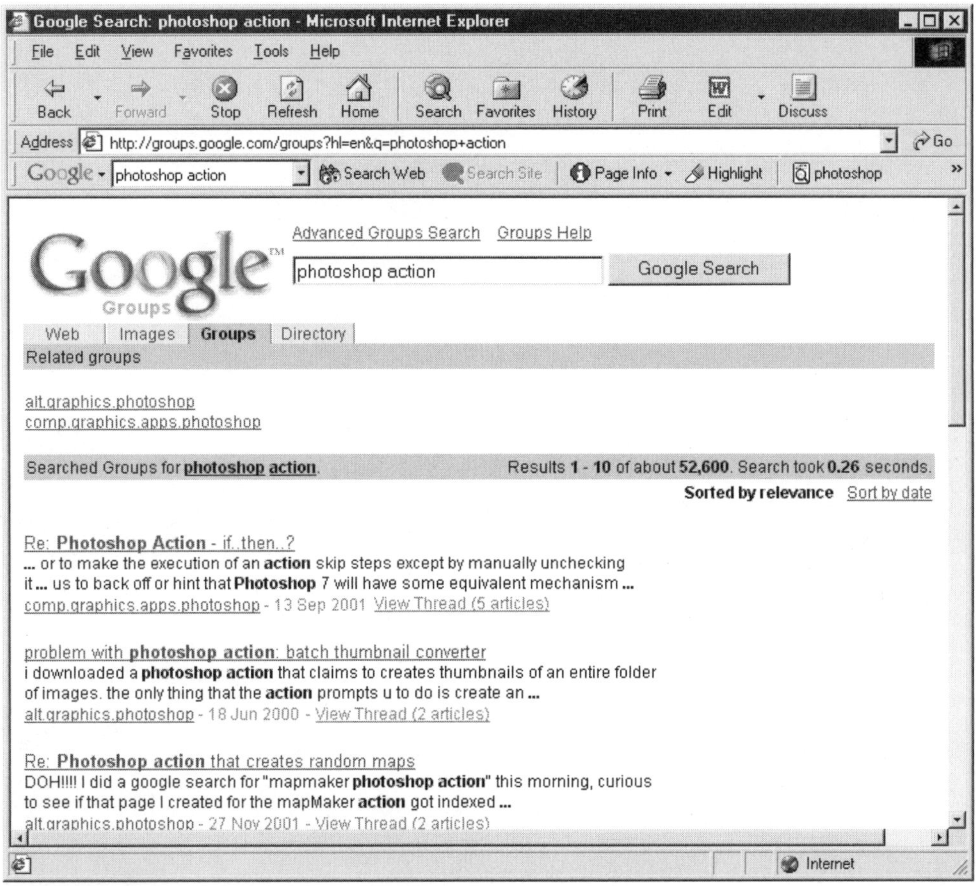

FIGURE 14-9   If you run into a technical problem while using Photoshop, such as using a scanner or printer, try searching Google's Usenet archives for help.

Alien Skin Software

http://www.alienskin.com

Alien Skin makes the Eye Candy 4000, Xenofex, and Splat! groups of plug-ins that enable you to add effects like little fluffy clouds, lightening, frames made of leopard skin or little aliens, and other wild and exciting effects for your images, as shown in Figure 14-10. You can download demos of their plug-ins from their web site.

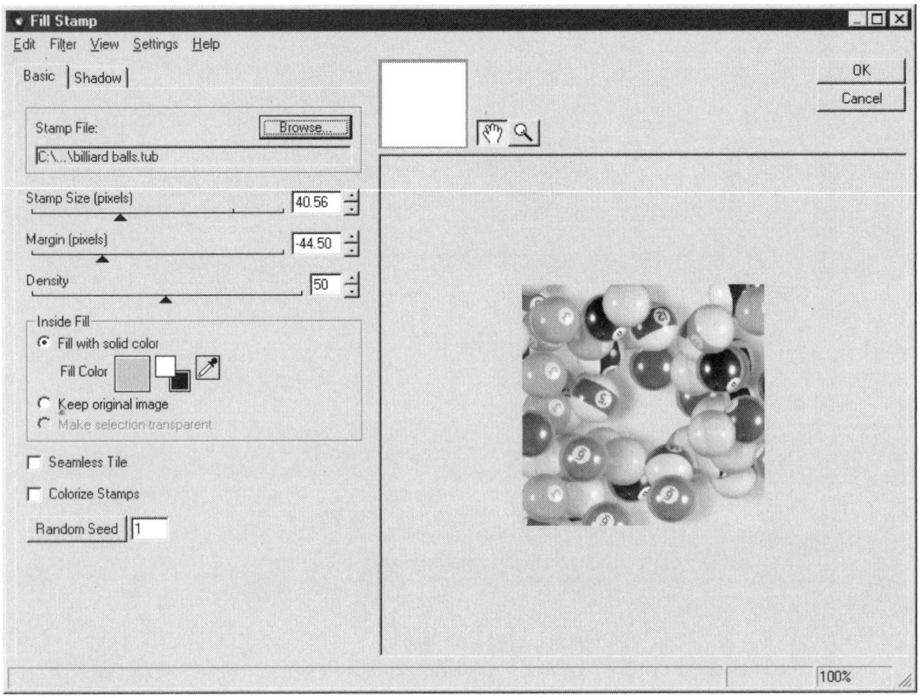

FIGURE 14-10   Plug-ins can be a lot of fun, as shown here with Alien Skin's Splat! filter.

AutoFX Software

http://www.autofx.com

Visit this web site to download demo versions of AutoFX plug-ins. AutoFX sells a number of plug-ins and collections of plug-ins that can add special effects to your images. The DreamSuite collection of plug-ins allows you to create the look of sepia toned images, Polaroid photographs, and much more. The DreamSuite gel series, a separate plug-in, shown in Figure 14-11, allows you to add transluscent and metallic effects.

Extensis Software

http://www.extensis.com

Extensis sells a package of edge effects titled PhotoFrame, which includes over 1000 frames for photos. Extensis also offers a set of plug-ins called PhotoTools that can help you create complex shadows, animations, and complex bevels and

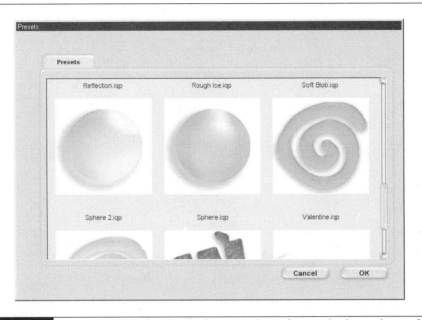

FIGURE 14-11   Auto FX Gel plug-in displays a variety of preset looks to choose from.

buttons, as shown in Figure 14-12. Extensis also offers Mask Pro, a tool for creating complex selections. You can download demos from their web site so that you can try out their software before you purchase it.

Flaming Pear Software

http://www.flamingpear.com

Flaming Pear software offers demo downloads of their plug-ins that create planets, moody photos, and extravagant textures and bevels. Super BladePro is a favorite among Photoshop users who want to create textured or metallic effects for buttons or text. You can download trial versions of all of their products.

Nik Software

http://www.tech-nik.com/

Nik Multimedia offers demo downloads of their plug-ins that can help sharpen and colorize photos. Nik Multimedia also offers nik Type Efex, a group of plug-ins for creating wild type effects, and nik Efex, a set of plug-ins that create 3-D, puzzle, and framing effects.

14

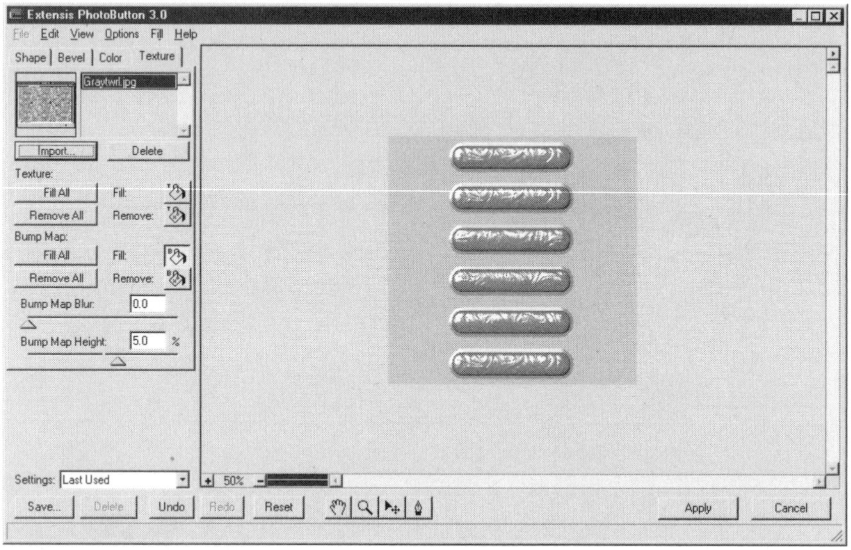

FIGURE 14-12   With Extensis PhotoButton plug-in you can create complex sets of buttons with a few mouse clicks.

Panopticum Software

http://www.panopticum.com

Download demo versions of plug-ins that offer fire, glass, lens, and engraved effects to your image.

Procreate Software

http://www.procreate.com

Procreate software offers a set of plug-ins called KPT effects. These effects include lightening, fractals, and a gradient laboratory.

Sapphire Innovations Software

http://www.sapphire-innovations.com/

Sapphire Innovations sells sets of brushes, patterns, shapes, styles, gradients and plug-ins. A visit to this site is a graphic reminder of how creative and interesting using Photoshop can be. You can download trial versions of Sapphire Innovations softwarefrom their web site, shown in Figure 14-13.

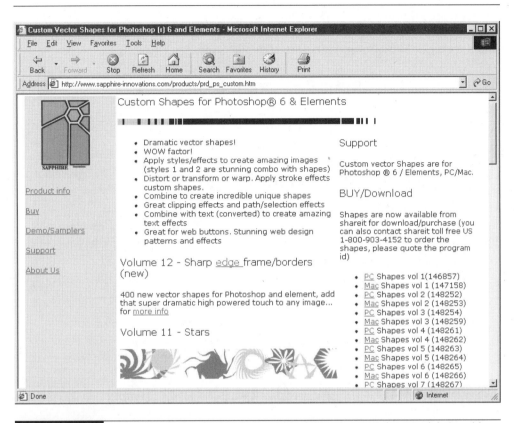

FIGURE 14-13 If you're looking for additional brushes or custom shapes, visit Sapphire Innovation's site, where they offer Photoshop tools for purchase.

Vertigo 3d Software

http://www.vertigo3d.com

Vertigo has a plug-in to Photoshop that is called Hot Text. With Hot Text, you can create three-dimensional text. Download a demo to try out this plug-in.

Browse Copyright Information

Every graphic designer should understand copyright. Copyright protects your own work and it also protects the work of other artists, writers, musicians, and others who produce creative work. Because information is transmitted so easily over the

Internet, copyright infringement has escalated over the past few years. There are many myths about copyright, but browsing through the following web sites should help you understand how creative work is protected.

Ten Big Myths about Copyright Explained

http://www.faqs.org/faqs/law/copyright/myths/part1/

This primer on some of the most common misconceptions about copyright will help you understand what copyright is and isn't.

U.S. Copyright Office – Copyright Basics

http://www.loc.gov/copyright/circs/circ1.html

This is a list of basic copyright concepts for the United States shown in Figure 14-14, including visual works and sound. Every country has its own copyright laws.

Adobe Article on Copyright Questions

http://www.adobe.com/web/features/copyright/main.html

This list of frequently asked questions, written by Poppy Evans, addresses questions about imagery, copyright laws, and how to copyright your own work.

Copyright FAQ (Frequently Asked Questions)

http://faqs.org/faqs/law/copyright/faq/

This list of Frequently Asked Questions provides answers for the most common questions about copyright.

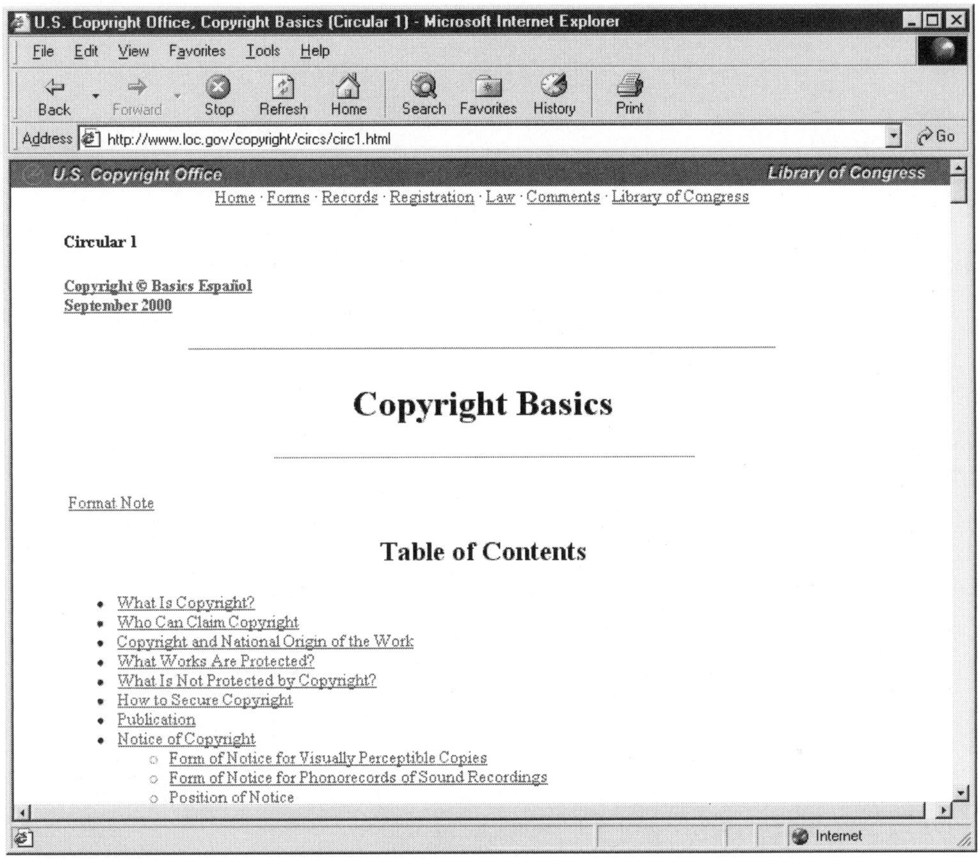

FIGURE 14-14   Every graphic artist should have a basic understanding of copyright and how it protects his work.

Chapter 15

Solving Common Photoshop Problems

How to...

■ Solve performance problems

■ Get unstuck

■ Do "quick tricks"

Have you ever become so frustrated that you're ready to scream? Hopefully this section will include answers to common problems you might encounter, so you can enjoy Photoshop without running into problems. Don't forget that there's a robust, searchable Help feature at Help | Photoshop Help. Before you give up, try the following tips to enhance your Photoshop work.

Solve Performance Problems

Photoshop is a memory monster. It wants as much free hard disk space and RAM as it can get. This is understandable, since Photoshop performs mathematical calculations on every pixel in your image every time you apply a filter or alter your entire image by resizing, transforming, or applying any number of other changes. The general rule of thumb is that Photoshop wants five times as much memory (RAM) as the image size you're working on. If you're working on a 60MB (megabytes) image with 256MB of RAM, you'll see sluggish behavior. The bigger the files you work on, the more memory you need to work with Photoshop.

Although Adobe says that Photoshop needs a minimum of 128MB of RAM as a minimum, 256MB is more of a realistic minimum requirement. If you work on images for print, you should have 512MB of RAM or more.

If you're running Photoshop with 256MB of RAM or less, consider not running other programs at the same time if you start to run into slower than normal performance.

Free Scratch Disk Space

In addition to RAM, Photoshop uses free disk space on your hard drive as temporary memory while processing images. Through normal use, as you install applications, delete, copy, and move files on your computer, information ends up scattered across your hard drive. This is called disk fragmentation. What Photoshop wants and needs are big chunks of free disk space, uncluttered by information. To free up space on your hard drive and make Photoshop happy, use a utility to defragment your hard drive, or hard drives.

Before running a defragmentation utility, it's best to close down any programs you have running. On Windows, select Start | Programs | Accessories | Disk Defragmenter. Click the Show Details button on the Disk Defragmenter to get a good visual sense of what a fragmented drive looks like, as shown in Figure 15-1.

The Macintosh operating system, does not contain a disk defragmentation tool. However, there are several third-party utilities for the Mac that will defrag your hard drive, including Norton Utilities, and Alsoft DiskWarrior.

Free Up Disk Space

As noted above, Photoshop wants plenty of free hard disk space. It's a good idea to check to see how much free disk space you have to make sure you're not running short.

To see how much free disk space a drive has in Windows, go to My Computer, right-click on the drive you want to check, and select Properties from the drop-down menu. As shown here, you will see a screen that gives a visual representation of how much free space is remaining on that hard drive.

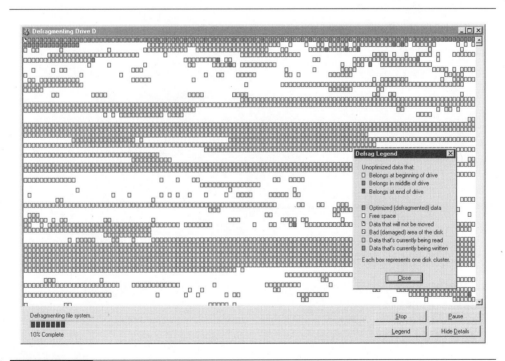

15

FIGURE 15-1   Running Window's Disk Defragmentor utility helps to create larger areas of defragmented space on your hard drive for Photoshop to use as swap space.

To find out how much free disk space you have on a Mac, select Apple Menu | Apple System Profiler from the Apple menu. Select the Devices and Volumes tab.

Once you've taken a look at the amount of free disk space remaining on your hard drive, you may find that you want to make more room on your drive by deleting files, or moving files to another drive, a Zip disk, or CD ROM.

Set the Scratch Disk Settings

Once you've cleaned up your hard drive and it's happily humming away, you'll want to make sure that Photoshop is using the correct hard drive for image caching. You need to worry about this only if you have more than one hard drive.

- To adjust the scratch disk setting, choose Edit | Preferences | Plugins & Scratch Disks, as shown in Figure 15-2.

- Under First Scratch Disks, make sure that the drive with the most free space available is selected.

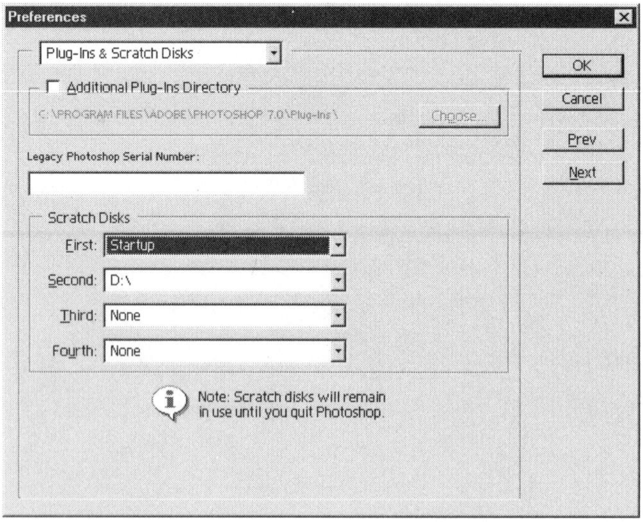

FIGURE 15-2   Setting preferences for your scratch disk can give Photoshop the extra disk space it needs for temporary memory.

Update Drivers for Hardware

If you're having display problems, or your scanner isn't working as it should, it's a good idea to check for new drivers for your hardware. Although every hardware manufacturer and software manufacturer tries to make products that are compatible with other software and hardware, sometimes it takes a while for everyone to work out solutions. It's a good idea to check for new drivers for your printer, scanner, and video card every six months or so. Every manufacturer should have a web site where you can download updated drivers for your hardware.

Launch Photoshop Faster

If you want Photoshop to launch more quickly, you can speed it up by uninstalling fonts or by removing plug-ins you don't use. Every time Photoshop launches, it loads the various fonts and plug-ins you have installed, which can bog down the program.

Uninstall Fonts

In Windows, go to your Windows | Fonts folder and delete or move any fonts you don't use.

On the Mac, for OS 9 and earlier, remove fonts from the System folder. For OS X, you will also want to check in the Library | Fonts folder and the Users | Username | Library | Fonts folder.

Remove Plug-ins and Filters

It's easy to get hooked on adding plug-ins to Photoshop, but if you find that you don't use all of your third party plug-ins, you may want to uninstall them. Photoshop also ships with a filter called the Digimarc filter, which checks for a copyright watermark embedded in images created with Digimarc software. To prevent this preinstalled filter from loading, go to your Photoshop | Plug-Ins | Digimarc folder, and rename the folder to ~Digimarc. (The tilde symbol (~) is located to the left of the 1 key on the top row of your keyboard.)

Remove Extra Brushes, Styles, Gradients, Contours, and Presets

If you really want to run a lean version of Photoshop, you'll want to use the Preset Manager to remove extra presets. Select Edit | Preset Manager, and browse through your presets to eliminate any extra presets that you don't use. Make sure to save any custom presets you've created first, by selecting all of the presets you wish to save, then selecting Save Set, as shown in Figure 15-3. You can then return to the originally installed set of presets by selecting Reset Presets.

15

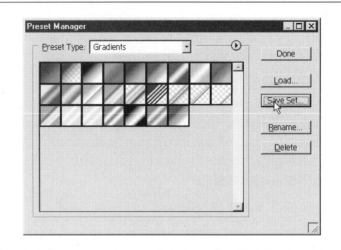

FIGURE 15-3   Be sure to save any custom presets you have before resetting presets to defaults.

Purge Your Memory

If you've copied a large image to the clipboard, the image will take up memory until you either copy something smaller or purge your clipboard. Since that copied image is taking up memory, you may notice that processes like applying a filter slow down.

To purge your memory, select Edit | Purge | Clipboard. You'll see there are other choices too. You can choose to purge your Undos, History, and All, as shown on the left.

Trim Your Image to Free Memory

If you've pasted in a large image, but are using only a small portion of it, you can choose to trim the larger image to match the size of the image you're working on. This reduces the file size and also frees up memory.

Select the layer you'd like to trim in the Layers palette. Select Image | Trim. If you'd like to see what you're deleting before you use the trim command, select Image | Reveal All.

Check for Photoshop Updates

Every few months, you should check to see if there have been updates for the latest version of Photoshop. You can do this by clicking the Photoshop image at the top of the Photoshop toolbar, as shown on the left. Patches and updates can sometimes solve conflicts with hardware or software.

Get Unstuck

If you find yourself unable to do something you thought should be simple, here are some quick solutions to common problems in Photoshop. Don't feel disheartened if you run into a problem doing something simple. Many Photoshop problems have to do with file formats.

Can't Open a TIFF File

■   I saved a file as a TIFF, but my coworker can't open it in another program.

Photoshop 7 introduced a new twist to the TIFF file format—one that enables you to save a TIFF with layers intact. Although Photoshop 6 can read this format, many other programs can't. Also, some of the compression schemes, such as ZIP or RLE, that you can use to compress a TIFF, can also cause problems with other programs.

To save a foolproof TIFF that should be readable by most programs, follow these steps:

1. Flatten your file by selecting Layer | Flatten.

2. Select File | Save As and select TIFF.

15

3. When prompted, set the image compression to None. If you've forgotten to flatten your file before saving, you can check the radio button at the bottom of the dialog box to Discard Layers and Save as Copy as shown here.

TIFF Options

Image Compression
- ⦿ NONE
- ○ LZW
- ○ ZIP
- ○ JPEG

Quality: [   ] Maximum ▾

small file   large file

Byte Order
- ⦿ IBM PC
- ○ Macintosh

☐ Save Image Pyramid
☐ Save Transparency

Layer Compression
- ○ RLE (faster saves, bigger files)
- ○ ZIP (slower saves, smaller files)
- ⦿ Discard Layers and Save a Copy

OK
Cancel

Quick Gif Transparency

■ What's the quickest way to save a transparent GIF from Photoshop?

Sometimes you just need a quick and easy answer. Here's the fastest way to get from a layered Photoshop file to a transparent GIF.

1. Select File | Save for Web from the menu.

2. A big dialog box opens up. Set the file type to GIF.

3. Use the eyedropper tool on the upper left side to select the color you want to be transparent, as shown in Figure 15-4.

Click the transparency button and the image becomes transparent, as shown in Figure 15-5. If there are stray pixels, use the eyedropper to select them and click the transparency button again.

Can't Move Something on a Layer

■ I can't move an object. I've tried everything and can't figure out what I'm doing wrong!

Make sure you have selected the layer that the object you want to move is on. Remember that the layer is selected when the Paintbrush icon appears next to the

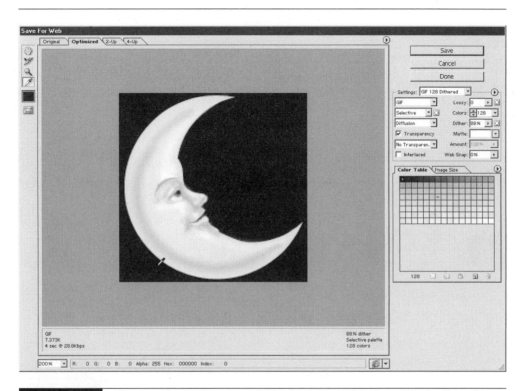

FIGURE 15-4   Create gif transparency quickly from Photoshop by using the Save for Web feature from the File menu.

layer preview in the Layers palette. It's easy to think you're on the right layer when you're not. You can toggle on and off layers to show and hide their contents if you're confused about what layer the object you wish to move is on. It's easy to become confused if you have an image with many layers. Once you've made sure you have the correct layer selected, make sure that the pixels on the layer aren't locked. If there is a Lock icon on the layer, click the Lock icon(s) to unlock it. Remember that it's a good idea to give layers descriptive names so it's easier to select the layer you want.

Once you're sure you're on the right layer, you can use the move tool to drag the object in the image window to where you want to position it.

If you're not sure what layer the object you want to move is on, there's a nifty shortcut to help you out.

1. Select the Move tool from the Photoshop toolbox.

15

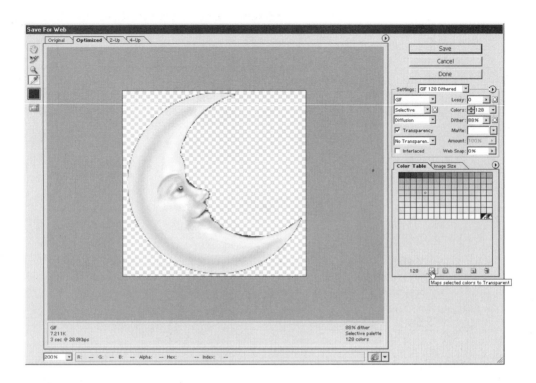

FIGURE 15-5   Preview the transparency you've created in the Save for Web feature.

2. Right-click/CTRL-click on the object you want to select. A context-sensitive menu appears that lists all the layers that contain an object where you've clicked, as shown in Figure 15-6. Select the layer name from the menu.

3. Make sure the layer isn't locked, and move the object.

Brushes Aren't Working as Expected

■ I'm trying to retouch a photo, but the brushes don't seem to be working the way I expect. It's not just the paint brushes, but also the dodge and burn tools.

If you're seeing this problem, after you've selected the brush you want to use, open the Brushes palette. Turn off any of the behaviors, such as Scattering, Shape

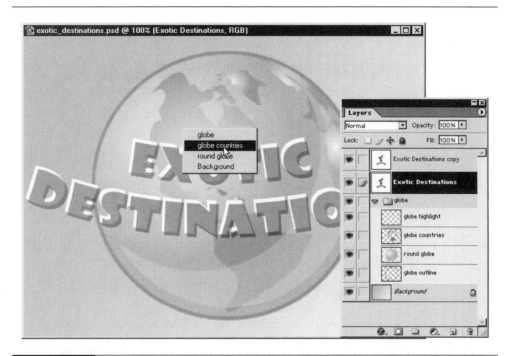

FIGURE 15-6 By right-clicking/ctrl-clicking in the image window, a popup menu with all the layers under your mouse pointer will appear. Then you can select the layer you want to work on from the list of layers, as shown here.

Dynamics, or Dual Brush as shown on the right. These brush behaviors may be interfering with your work if you're simply trying to use the brush without any special effects.

Trouble with Transforming

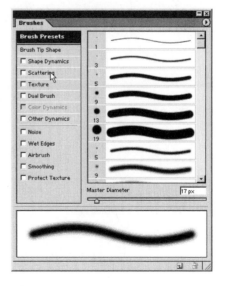

- When I try to rotate or resize a layer that takes up the whole image, I can't see the handles to transform the layer.

15

If the transform handles are at the edge of the image, they can be hard to see and to click on, as shown here.

If you zoom out, as shown here, the handles are easy to see and click on so that you can finish your transformation.

Can't Turn off Slices

■ I made a mistake and used the slice tool. Now I can't get rid of the slices and it's driving me crazy.

Select View | Clear Slices. You'll still have the original slice showing, as displayed here. Click and hold on the Slice tool to reveal the Slice Select Tool. On the Options bar, as shown here, click the Hide Auto Slices button.

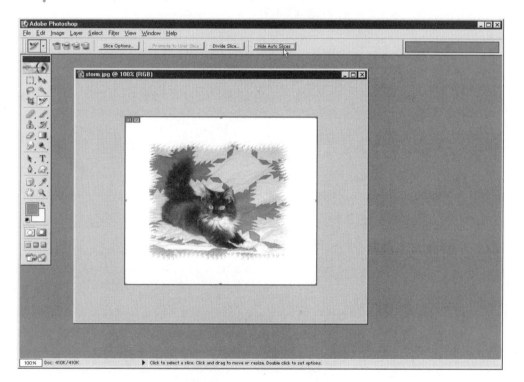

Cursors Not Displaying Correctly

■ Where did the cursors that showed the tool images go?

If your standard cursors suddenly change to precise cursors, check to see if your CAPS LOCK key is on.

15

Can't Get out of Full Screen Mode

■   Help! I selected full-screen mode, which hides all the palettes and menus
    and now I can't figure out how to get back to my menus!

Click the F key, which cycles between full screen display, full screen with menu
bar, and standard screen modes.

Photoshop is Behaving Oddly

■   My palettes aren't showing up, icons are missing, and some of the menu
    items are gone.

These are symptoms of a corrupted Preferences file in Photoshop. Other symptoms
can be that the program won't launch, colors display oddly, or you can't get tools
to function the way that they should. Your best bet is to reinstall Photoshop. Your
customized settings will be lost, such as palette locations and Preference selections .

Printing to Fit a Page

■   I keep getting a message that the image I'm trying to print is too big for the
    page. How can I easily get my image to fit on a page?

Select File | Print with Preview. From there, you can resize your image by
dragging corner handles for the image or click the Scale to Fit Media checkbox, as
shown here.

Quick Tricks

Here are a few tips for working within Photoshop that may make your life easier, and make your work in Photoshop go a little faster.

Snap Your Palettes

To get a palette to snap to the edge of the nearest window border or other palette, hold down SHIFT as you drag the palette.

Change Image Border Colors

You can change the color of the border around images in Photoshop. Select a color, and SHIFT-click with the paintbucket tool on the border of the image, as shown here.

15

Open an Image Quickly

Are you in a hurry? If you double-click on the background of Photoshop, anywhere outside of an image or palette, the File | Open dialog box opens.

Copy a Hexcode

If you're using the eyedropper tool, you can find out the hexcode number of any color in an image easily. Right-click/ CTRL-click over the color you want to sample in the image and choose Copy Color as HTML from the menu, as shown here. You can then paste the hexcode color into your HTML editor.

Easter Eggs Just for Fun

Easter eggs are extra goodies that engineers add into a software program for the sheer fun factor. They can range from animations to jokes. Photoshop has a few you may want to explore.

In case you need a little affirmation, open the Help | About Screen. After a few seconds, the names of the people responsible for Photoshop begin to appear. At the very bottom of the screen you'll see a surprising credit.

To see a different opening splash screen for Photoshop, open Photoshop. Then press CTRL/COMMAND as you select Help | About Photoshop. After the screen credits finish, ALT-click/OPTION-click in the white space above the credits and you'll see witticisms added by the engineers.

To meet Merlin, go to the Layers palette. ALT-click / OPTION-click while you open the palette menu, then click Palette Options, as shown here, to see Merlin.

Index

INTERNATIONAL CONTACT INFORMATION

AUSTRALIA
McGraw-Hill Book Company Australia Pty. Ltd.
TEL +61-2-9417-9899
FAX +61-2-9417-5687
http://www.mcgraw-hill.com.au
books-it_sydney@mcgraw-hill.com

CANADA
McGraw-Hill Ryerson Ltd.
TEL +905-430-5000
FAX +905-430-5020
http://www.mcgrawhill.ca

**GREECE, MIDDLE EAST,
NORTHERN AFRICA**
McGraw-Hill Hellas
TEL +30-1-656-0990-3-4
FAX +30-1-654-5525

MEXICO (Also serving Latin America)
McGraw-Hill Interamericana Editores S.A. de C.V.
TEL +525-117-1583
FAX +525-117-1589
http://www.mcgraw-hill.com.mx
fernando_castellanos@mcgraw-hill.com

SINGAPORE (Serving Asia)
McGraw-Hill Book Company
TEL +65-863-1580
FAX +65-862-3354
http://www.mcgraw-hill.com.sg
mghasia@mcgraw-hill.com

SOUTH AFRICA
McGraw-Hill South Africa
TEL +27-11-622-7512
FAX +27-11-622-9045
robyn_swanepoel@mcgraw-hill.com

**UNITED KINGDOM & EUROPE
(Excluding Southern Europe)**
McGraw-Hill Education Europe
TEL +44-1-628-502500
FAX +44-1-628-770224
http://www.mcgraw-hill.co.uk
computing_neurope@mcgraw-hill.com

ALL OTHER INQUIRIES Contact:
Osborne/McGraw-Hill
TEL +1-510-549-6600
FAX +1-510-883-7600
http://www.osborne.com
omg_international@mcgraw-hill.com